START-UP FACTORY

"A delightful book, which has managed to make a complex, and often confusing, story easily understandable."
- **Bill Fischer, Senior Lecturer at MIT Sloan School of Management; Author of Reinventing Giants**

"This is the best management book I've read in our current era. This is the one I recommend my sons read. But that is not why you should read it. You should read it because it describes human values, philosophies and practices that will open new expanded possibilities to you. It is a book about enabling our human potential and creative freedom to change life around us — which we all know is important today. Uniquely, it is a book about doing this yourself, and about doing it across business ecosystems of global scale. It is a book to give your friends, to read in your book club."
- **James F. Moore, Author of The Death of Competition**

"This is a must-read for every business to get inspired, learn and develop your organisation's future way of working by common principles of user-centricity, decentralisation, and focus on humans!"
- **Jochen Goeser, Expertise Owner People & Culture at Bosch Power Tools; Member of Corporate Rebels Academy Community**

"A remarkable real-life story of transformation, entrepreneurship, and belief in the power of people. Philosophically elegant, Haier's Rendanheyi model unleashes the entrepreneurial desire of each employee and harnesses this energy to create a flourishing business of micro-enterprises operating as close as possible to the customer. To an outsider, this eco-system seems mind-boggling, complex and difficult to understand — Start-up Factory is just the antidote. This book provides a direct window into how Haier operates; well thought-out, clear, direct, and full of humorous moments that we have come to expect from Corporate Rebels. It's a fun read, and a book you will be thinking about long after you finish the last page. For anyone who believes bureaucracy is something that is unavoidable in a large company, this is for you!"
- **Meghan Kirkland, Talent & Org Design Specialist; Member of Corporate Rebels Academy Community**

"I have visited Haier HQ many times, spent time talking with its managers and leaders worldwide, and been to a number of its production sites, but still I have always struggled to make sense of the scale and scope of Haier's innovations in management. Start-up Factory provides the answers. It brings together many different experiments, processes and systems at Haier to make sense of what this remarkable company actually does. It is as inspirational as it is practical. Managers should read it and then re-think everything they and their organisations do."
- **Stuart Crainer, Cofounder at Thinkers50; Member of Corporate Rebels Academy Community**

"The exciting and revolutionary Rendanheyi management model has enabled China's Haier Group to rid the company of the stranglehold of bureaucracy, empower the creativity of employees, and bring better service to their customers. Start-up Factory is a well-researched, accessible, and detailed book that effectively captures both the spirit and method of Rendanheyi, and will surely inspire corporate leaders to give serious thought to following Haier's pioneering lead."
- **Danah Zohar, Visiting Professor at Chinese Academy of Art School; Author of Zero Distance**

"This book is a shining example of what students studying management should absorb and what management in traditional companies should adopt. It is an inspiring read for young entrepreneurs, who must learn from the ground-breaking journey of Haier. The in-depth study and analysis of the organisation has broken down its complex functioning in an easily comprehensible way. The best part about the book is that it beautifully describes the relation of human values and philosophies with management function. It humanises the practicality of management and emphasises organisational evolution."
- **Nand Kishore Chaudhary, Founder, Chairman and Managing Director at Jaipur Rugs; Member of Corporate Rebels Academy Community**

"It's easy to become lost in the complexities of Haier's business model innovations but this book demystifies and humanises it all. Corporate Rebels have created a treasure trove of stories from Haier employees and the legendary philosopher-CEO Zhang Ruimin, as well as a guided tour through the remarkable evolution of this company and its influence on the business world."
- **Lisa Gill, Author of Moose Heads on the Table; Member of Corporate Rebels Academy Community**

"Must-read for CEOs: it's not about you! It's all about the customers and employees!"
- **Willie Lagraauw, Founder at Will-b Different; Member of Corporate Rebels Academy Community**

"Every now and again a book comes along to rock the old adage that there's nothing new under the sun. For any forward-thinking, entrepreneurial company that needs that final nudge towards the future of work, this is a highly engaging yet practical must-read. Forty years after 'the Semco way', we are now gifted 'the Haier way' — a monumental achievement, and a final nail in the coffin of industrial-age thinking. My favourite takeaways: 'external adaptation with internal perseverance', 'always be close to customer', and 'everyone here is an entrepreneur'."
- **Ed Capaldi, Strategic Advisor & Transformation Coach; Member of Corporate Rebels Academy Community**

"Finally, the book we have all been waiting for! Dive into the fascinating case of Haier and learn how a small, failing factory in China was able to transform into a global ecosystem leader with worldwide entrepreneurs innovating at scale. An exceptionally well-written, detailed breakdown of how you can make this happen."
- **Scott Newton, Managing Partner at Thinking Dimensions; Member of Corporate Rebels Academy Community**

"We have often been presented with books or case studies describing a CEO's gait in achieving organisational success. This is still a dominating source of inspiration and gives an idea of how a company leader should, more or less, be a 'hero' for the organisation. But you will get and learn different things from this book. Leaders still have a crucial role, but they are not alone; all employees can really be heroes for their company. The question is: What is the role of top leadership in making their organisation a home for these heroes? You will find the answer here!"

- **Pande Kadek Yuda Bakti, Chief Strategic Officer at PT. Fajar Benua Indopack; Member of Corporate Rebels Academy Community**

"Success is to move with the times. The story of Haier is a fascinating tale of a highly competitive organisation that uses emergent leadership to allow employees to bring more of themselves to work. At Haier, they say success is to move with the times. This book describes how that can be done using Rendanheyi philosophy and the latest technology to be very close to customers."

- **Arne Åhlander, Founder at Aqqurite AB; Member of Corporate Rebels Academy Community**

"After reading so many vague snippets about Haier this is a fascinating deep dive into the inner workings of the organisation. Corporate Rebels have brought clarity to the mystery surrounding the Haier model and the company's culture and philosophies."

- **Dani Bacon, Founder at Distinction Business Consulting; Member of Corporate Rebels Academy Community**

"A truly inspiring read, one which has turned a complex story of a pioneering company into an understandable and practical guide on how to eradicate bureaucracy, unleash human creativity and generate more value to customers. Just what all current and aspiring leaders should read so they can re-think what they do and how their organisations generate value."

- **Gerry Grattan, Cofounder at Impactara Ltd; Member of Corporate Rebels Academy Community**

"Start-up Factory by Joost Minnaar, Pim de Morree, and Bram van der Lecq puts you, the reader, in the passenger seat on their exploration of an ever-evolving, yet always new, take on work and on life. The book focuses on Haier, a Chinese company that was a failing refrigerator manufacturer in the 1980s; today Haier is a multinational home consumer appliance and electronics manufacturer whose success is based on the home-grown and Rendanheyi business model. The authors break down the principles and practices that make up Rendanheyi and Haier's evolution to this unique way of working in a way that is both illuminating and surprising, presenting their story as a travelog to another planet or civilisation. Much of what you'll learn is not in any way typical of business practices here on Earth — prepare to take on a revolutionary way of working that values and trusts people over all else. Start-up Factory is a remarkable lens into the hearts and minds of revolutionary business thinkers creating, nurturing, and evolving workplaces that thrive — because the people who work there thrive."

- Dotti Cummings, Enterprise Coach, New Ways of Working Advocate; Member of Corporate Rebels Academy Community

"Start-up Factory is not only an easy to read guide to the ground-breaking Rendanheyi model of Haier. It also entails the latest management innovations of ecosystem thinking. The authors created an impressive compilation of deep dives into the practical details of the model, exemplifying success stories and personal insights embedded in the philosophical thinking of its inventor Zhang Ruimin. A real must read for those who are interested in maintaining and creating start-up spirit in larger organizations in order to thrive in the era of IoT ecosystems."

- Andre Stuer, Managing Partner hs:results consulting; Member of Corporate Rebels Academy Community

AUTHORS:
Joost Minnaar
Pim de Morree
Bram van der Lecq

EDITORS:
John Mann
Hal Williams

ILLUSTRATOR:
Javier Juvera

EDITORIAL DESIGN:
Keno Cordero

ISBN: 9789083190396
Copyright© Corporate Rebels Nederland B.V. & HMI 2022

START-UP FACTORY

Haier's RenDanHeYi model and
the end of management as we know it

Joost Minnaar & Pim de Morree
with Bram Van Der Lecq

Contents

Foreword by Bill Fischer	I
Preface	V
Prologue	1
Earth	7
Water	26
Air	58
Fire	116
Space	157
DIY Rendanheyi	196
Epilogue	203
Acknowledgements	204
Appendices	207
Bibliography	236
About the Authors	237

Foreword
by Bill Fischer

Believe it or not, there are still places on this planet where, if you use the word "innovation", your audience hears "technology". This confining, but instinctive, linking of things, products and devices with innovation is not uncommon, and, as the Haier saga illustrates, there are more, and grander, definitions.

One way of summarising the evolution of Haier is to reference the changing focus of its innovative efforts; from products and better quality (1984); to improved service and swifter responses (1998); to intimacy with customers, and knowing more about them (2005); to being truly outside-in with zero-distance to the marketplace, and replacing knowing with learning (2015). Now, increasingly ecosystem-driven, it truly makes the world "Haier's R&D department".

Each of these apparently simple changes in innovation focus represents an enormous transformation in the way that Haier works, and the role of its employees. To accomplish so much in just 40 years is testament to the way change has been continuously embraced; it's a vital part of Haier's story.

What makes all this possible is that, as the authors observe, "Haier is on a constant quest to find undiscovered riches and seams of value." But what does that mean, and what might we learn from this? For a start, we should recognise that Haier is not a "normal" organisation. Almost everything about it, from its affinity for change to its ever-shifting structure and the culture that powers such efforts, to the distributed autonomy that marks its microenterprises, is different to a traditional organisation. What Haier's Rendanheyi philosophy presents us with is nothing less than a new management model.

In 1997, management guru Peter Drucker, predicted that "a distinct and quite different management style and management structure" would emerge from China. There is good reason to believe that Rendanheyi — more a philosophy that maximises human value than an approach or technique — could well be considered a world first.

Rendanheyi is built on three guiding principles:

Creating a great customer experience, echoing Drucker's own definition of the goal of a business as being "to create and keep a customer".

Recognising that the entrepreneurial energy of employees, so often overlooked in complex, modern organisations, is exactly the force needed to create those exceptional customer experiences — and fulfil talent potential and reinforce the dignity of employees.

Establishing the equitable sharing of created value among the three principal actors: the value enjoyed by the customer, the value received by the organisation and its stakeholders because of increased marginal revenues, and an obligation to share these marginal returns with the people who created the value: the employee-entrepreneurs.

The story of Haier's evolution is also that of its author: Zhang Ruimin. He has gone through a striking personal and professional metamorphosis, from a functionary for the Qingdao municipal government to overseeing the Qingdao Refrigerator Company — then an almost bankrupt collective — and accepting the role of director general when no one else would step-up to the plate. Ruimin, now chairman of the world's largest home appliances group, is globally recognised as one of the most astute designers of organisation for the future. His understandings form the basis of much of Haier's success:

- The importance of knowing what you are trying to accomplish.

- Aiming everything at maximising human value; there is no ambiguity here, everyone understands where they are going — and after 40 years of moving in this direction, it is surrounded by little controversy.

- The value of a small set of guiding principles to provide every member of the Haier community with a compass. In the words of the Corporate Rebels, "No need to worry about every little detail, or who is responsible for what, because the principles provide sufficient guidance."

- A culture of experimentation to find the path, with trial and error, learning, and iteration marking the cadence of progress.

- Defining the role of the leader as "seeker" — searching for new ideas to inspire the conversational mix throughout the work community, not pretending to be the ultimate decision-maker.

- A willingness to share power in the pursuit of building an organisation that is attentive to customers' needs, and swift in response. Almost as a by-product, an organisation that has fewer managers and more leaders is created.

- An eagerness to seek-out external partners to access knowledge domains that are unfamiliar — and then to share power with them.

- The capacity to go beyond ambitious dreams and pay attention to the granular details that ultimately determine the success of grand schemes.

Haier is heading with confidence into a future that will be markedly different from anything that the industry has yet seen. The advent of the smart home, and the hyper-connectivity that characterises the Internet of Things, are changing Haier's customer journey from a spasmodic search for solutions into a continuous conversation about experiences.

Few organisations are prepared for such profound change in customer engagement, and fewer still have chosen to explore radically different ways of organising to make that engagement succeed.

Haier is moving full speed ahead, amid transformations to demonstrate that large, mature, successful organisations still have a future. Ironically, the company is doing this by making each part of this mammoth organisation smaller, and more autonomous. Economies of scale are giving way to economies of learning, and, as the Corporate Rebels point out: "Haier has porous boundaries … best traced with a dotted line. With big spaces between the dots."

One of the most charming features of this delightful book, which has managed to make a complex, and often confusing, story easily understandable, are the frequent reports from an intergalactic starship heading into the unknown, perhaps in a search for intelligent life. Unlike all too many contemporary complex organisations, which are intellectually barren, planet Haier abounds with intelligent life, and the lessons beamed back from this remarkable journey will hopefully inspire many to go forth on their own journeys of exploration, change, and liberation from the bonds of legacy managerial thinking which have trapped so many in the past. May these insights, and the readers who adopt them, go forth and prosper.

Bill Fischer

Preface

We've been travelling the world in search of organisations that do things differently. We look for management pioneers who dare to break with traditional ways of organising and create workplaces that are purpose-driven, built on trust — and human-focused.

We search for organisations that make work more fun, and inspire us. Our travels have taken us across five continents; we've visited more than 100 progressive organisations and spoken to many pioneers.

The book you're holding describes the story of the most pioneering company we have so far encountered: Haier.

The Chinese company has managed to transform itself from a poorly managed refrigerator manufacturer to a world-leading appliance giant that has — as side gigs — entered industries such as healthcare, logistics and finance. Simply because their method has given them a competitive edge.

We've researched "the Haier way" for years, visiting locations around the world. We had open access to the company and were able to have

VI | *Start-up Factory*

in-depth, no-holds-barred discussions and interviews with CEO Zhang Ruimin, Haier's entrepreneurial staff, management experts, and many academics.

Getting your head around a company that has been around for almost four decades and yet is as nimble as any start-up is like finding your way around a fast-developing metropolis — and just as intriguing. You don't notice the change as it happens around you, but if you leave and return, certain things will register.

Our visits to Haier in China were cumulatively destabilising. There were familiar sights, but — always — changes, too. Memories were dredged-up and blended with fresh experiences. New images and assumptions formed. These moments were catalysts for realisations. And questions...

How much, for example, does Haier change daily? Is the change, at whatever rate, because of the company's rapid evolution, or the expanding awareness of the observers?

China isn't just another country, and Haier isn't just another company.

Zhang, a humble and amiable 70-year-old, explained his management vision and outlined his belief that bureaucracy was doomed to fail. We can only agree — wholeheartedly — with that belief. Our conversations with Zhang were always inspiring and energetic, and became even more lively after Zhang posed a question to us: "Do you think I'm a rebel as well?"

Yes. Yes, we do.

Like all the other rebels, Zhang has a mission to build better workplaces. Our role, as we see it, is to explain and share the stories behind progressive management models — and Haier has a story that is worth the telling.

Prologue

REBEL LOG, ENTRY ONE: Approaching Haier. These far reaches of the business universe are ruled by forces which will take some time to understand. Consider the paradox of shiny home appliances, forged in modern factories, ordered by app, and delivered — when necessary, in mountainous areas, say — by porters bearing a bamboo platform. There are tales of other, still more outlandish practices. Time alone will tell if they are true. Engaging landing gear and standing-by.

Rebel One, out.

"Soon, we shall be listed and transform from a 'unicorn' to a company on the stock market," explains Hu Qingming, "but we started off as a small, traditional in-house logistics department of Haier. Now, 20 years later, we have transformed into a platform that focuses on specific user scenarios. We have some 2,000 employees and hundreds of thousands of people who help us get our deliveries to the customer."

Hu, a casually dressed 40-year-old who started working at Haier in 2003, is a member of RRS Logistics, a Haier "platform" founded in 2010 to allow people, who are so inclined, to start their own delivery or installation business — without leaving the corporation. Hu is just one who took up the offer. "Most of the process is arranged via an Uber-like app, and right now we have about 6,000 service providers, 100,000 delivery vehicles and over 200,000 delivery and installation workers. Together they cover all districts, even the rural areas. This could mean they have to carry a refrigerator on their backs to reach a house at the top of a mountain." It works like this: Customers place an order. The products are transferred from the warehouse to a hub; from there, "delivery nodes" take care of things. It sounds simple, but the scale of the operation, in Haier's case, is incredible. RRS partners with and facilitates logistics for the Shunguang Social commerce platform, which hosts more than 800,000 external store owners.

The coastal city of Qingdao is home to over 10 million people and is probably best known for its famous beer brand Tsingtao, the world's longest sea-bridge and hosting the sailing competitions during the 2008 Olympic Summer Games. It's a buzzing metropolis to say the least. It's also the place where Haier has its origins and where Hu Qingming told us everything there is to know about RRS Logistics in one of the many meeting rooms, in one of the many offices at the Haier campus. "Back in 2000, all the products we delivered were made by Haier. Last year it was down to 40 percent, and this year only 30 percent of our deliveries are those of Haier products."

Wait, what? Besides the odd juxtaposition of the old and new — using a bamboo carrying platform to deliver a modern fridge — something else catches the eye. RRS is a department that has turned itself into a business — delivering twice as much competitor product as that created in-house. It doesn't make sense.

Exciting tales of new business models, experimentation, and things that at first glance make no sense are no longer foreign concepts to us. This is a fractal universe, and navigating it is like driving through thick mist in some remote part of the world. Visibility is limited, Google Maps is unavailable. You may end up in cul-de-sacs and blind alleys; the need to backtrack is frequent. But you will progress if you learn to experience the terrain as you explore it.

"There is no such thing as a successful company, only one that successfully moves with the times." Haier's chief executive Zhang Ruimin captures the company's essence as we take a sip of our tea. It explains why continual change has become a core principle of the company culture.

Two other key principles can be identified: "Zero distance to the user" and "Everyone is an entrepreneur." The user is all-important to Haier. In our conversations Zhang often quotes one of his major sources of inspiration, Peter F Drucker, according to whom there's only one valid definition of business purpose, and that is to create a customer. Ever since Haier established itself this has been borne in mind. The reason that Drucker is a great source of inspiration becomes clearer when you consider how he has been described: "the man who invented management" and "the father of modern management". Rest assured they weren't talking about traditional corporate management. Drucker opposed bureaucracy and championed creativity [1].

Here is the reasoning: a product is nothing without a buyer. The more value that is created for customers, the more money they will spend. To learn what really adds value to their lives, it is important to be as close to them as possible — and to react swiftly to feedback, demands or criticism. Customers are the driving force; their changing needs set the course. Zhang believes that people are a company's most valuable asset, and two types are involved in creating value: entrepreneurs (internal) and customers (external). The focus has always been on reducing the distance between those who create the solutions and those who evaluate them. At Haier, anyone can become an entrepreneur, with access to the resources they need. Take RRS Logistics, it has been on an evolutionary journey since it first saw the light of day. It has spread its wings and is ready to distance itself still further from the parent company.

Haier has consistently been guided by this philosophy. Changes in context — such as the invention of the internet — have forced it to rethink its way of working. As better ways of interacting with customers arose, the company adapted, honouring the principles first, and facilitating any changes afterwards.

Even with 80,000 employees, this is a company perfectly able to adapt to sudden contextual changes. Whether they reflect customer needs, competition, or a global pandemic, Haier's model allows it to respond more swiftly and efficiently than any of the other giants out there. The company's story is an extraordinary one: from a tired corporation struggling to survive 35 years ago to one of the most successful appliance manufacturers in the world today.

Let's not get carried away in the Haier mythology too early on; the armour is impressive, but there may be questions to consider. People are pulled into the fold, given freedom to create and act autonomously, rewarded for moments of genius and constant striving. An interesting point, though, is this: What happens to the innovators when the innovations themselves do not work? There is no soft bosom for them to sink into; this is no charity providing "forever" jobs. Continued failure to meet the Haier standard can have harsh, and final, consequences.

We started out with healthy scepticism and some tough questions, but Haier has disarmed frontal assaults with modesty, honesty and (less frequently) deflection. And despite the concerns raised by the readers of our blogs, there seems to be a lack of evidence for the accretion of prejudice or suspicion, or the development of an anti-Haier, evil-twin model.

It's possible that the fierce internal competition and pressure to perform might form challenges of their own to the Haier structure. The company itself does not appear to be concerned about this, although we in the West may not be as comfortable with the unusual internal pressures created, or as able to contain, control and even use them to positive advantage. For those workers with big dreams and the requisite entrepreneurial drive, Haier's system can be a greenhouse of opportunity and a hothouse of innovation. The point we are making is that this can become a double-edged sword.

Success may prove to be its own challenge; Haier is moving swiftly into a new direction: becoming a technology firm. This might mean that Haier has the potential to monopolise the home appliance industry, as Amazon has done for retail. Is this something we — the wider world community — are ready for? Even for those who accept this slide to grandeur, governments are slowly acting to cap and hobble those organisations that become too successful. The Economist, in its 2020 end-of-year rundown, comments that China is "at the frontier of regulation".

The magazine refers to China's world-beating approach to e-commerce: "Western firms like to think that they are at the cutting edge. In fact, the future of e-commerce is being staked out in China. Its market is far bigger and more creative than those in the West, with tech firms blending e-commerce, social media and razzmatazz to become online shopping emporia for 850m digital consumers."

A Devil's Advocate — and there are many to be found — might balk at Haier's grand claims. Haier calls everyone an "undiscovered entrepreneur". But surely not everyone is cut out for the role. Some just want a regular job, with regular pay. They don't want to take risks, and they don't see the opportunities. And it seems that redundancies are needed in this model. Is that the optimal path to take? People with entrepreneurial skills and ambitions can thrive. But what about the people lacking entrepreneurial skills or ambition? Are they simply removed from the company?

Pay levels vary, depending on profit-sharing metrics. How does one deal with the initial period of innovation when there are, as yet, no customers? Is it fair to let employees take such risks? This is a performance-driven culture. Hard work and long hours are the norm; is Haier just burning its people out and replacing them with fresh, more ambitious individuals? Could (should?) such a model work in a Western firm? Or is Haier just a product of its time, culture, and size?

Having had the opportunity to meet in China with Haier entrepreneurs, we have come to appreciate how employees' lives have been transformed amidst the development of a powerful team spirit. Similarly, we find that degrees of scepticism reduce substantially once our friends and colleagues discover what's going on over there. And we come to understand that, yes, the Haier model can adapt to other cultures.

We find, in Haier, a radically decentralised company where people run their own little (and not so little) enterprises, where there is healthy internal competition and the most porous organisational borders imaginable. To our mind, Haier is now at the vanguard of modern management thinking.

The management model now in place at Haier is known as Rendanheyi. This expression captures the principle that employees are rewarded for the value they directly create for the user. The contemporary business and management challenges faced by modern enterprises triggered the birth and evolution of the model. Haier's early development under Zhang's leadership — the pre-Rendanheyi period — was followed by three stages of Rendanheyi, introduced in 2005, 2012, and 2019. The model is currently spiralling out of Haier bounds and being replicated in other companies, across cultures, countries, and industries.

The Economist concludes by noting that, "for a century, the world's consumer businesses have looked to America to spot new trends, from scannable barcodes on Wrigley's gum in the 1970s to keeping up with the Kardashians' consumption habits in the 2010s. Now they should be looking to the East".

So, let's explore the most pressing business and management challenges companies face in an era of digitalisation and hyperconnectivity — which triggered the birth of Rendanheyi in the first place.

EARTH

'We want to change two things. First, the company — from walled-garden to tropical rainforest, a self-evolving business ecosystem. Second, we want to change the traditional lifestyle from a product-based approach to one that is ecosystem-based.'

Zhang Ruimin, 2019

> REBEL LOG: Business, they say, is an art as well as a science — something which is not lost on the man at the centre of our exploration of the Haier universe. CEO Zhang Ruimin values the lasting mythology of his firm — and finds fine words to express that awareness...
>
> **Rebel One, out.**

The Management Innovation of Rendanheyi

On December 26, 2019, Haier Group held an event to commemorate its 35th anniversary. In his keynote speech, CEO Zhang Ruimin quoted a Luís de Camões poem, Os Lusíadas: "Aqui, onde a terra se acaba e o mar começa ..."

"Here, where the land ends and the sea begins..." It could almost be a tribute to Haier's continuous, self-iterative history of entrepreneurship and innovation. It reflects the courage Haier showed in bidding farewell to the past, welcoming the future, and entering a new era.

"The 35-year-old Haier is not old-fashioned or depressed," Ruimin said in his speech. "It is youthful and energetic. It is climbing to a new age, the Internet of Things era, led by Rendanheyi. The model is hitting this new peak.

"We are changing the world with the Internet of Things (IoT). This is required by the times. We want to change two things. First, the company — from walled-garden to tropical rainforest, a self-evolving business ecosystem. Second, we want to change the traditional lifestyle into one geared to the IoT era, from a product-based approach to one that is ecosystem-based."

Management thinking is a product of the times. There is no universal truth or law of management. As a craft, management must keep pace with the times. Activities must address, and solve, current problems and challenges. In an age of rapid development, Zhang Ruimin's perspective is this: "If you can keep up, it will be the best time. If you can't, it will be the worst."

But what does it take to survive in a highly uncertain world? What kind of challenges is the current enterprise facing, and what do they bring to the management sphere?

Revolution in the Air
The Industrial Revolution was a journey from an agricultural society to a mechanised one in just over 150 years. It brought massive changes in technology, changes which have over the centuries increased uncertainty in the business world and challenged business models. Change, the old constant, is still at work. And according to Zhang, the most fundamental influence in today's technological revolution is represented by the IoT.

Kevin Ashton first proposed the concept in 1999: a world-class IT revolution that impacts business society beyond computers and the Internet. The Internet builds virtual platforms to establish connections between people, appliances, and services. When we browse the web, we need merely click the mouse to make the leap and be connected to infinite information.

Impressive. But the IoT is something quite different.
Here, every person, every object, becomes a node in an ecosystem. Everything becomes connected, and the islands of isolated information disappear. The IoT is a universe of objects — some 30 billion at the time of writing and rising fast — that "talk" to one another. Devices gather and analyse information in support of a specified task, or to help an individual to learn from a process. The possibilities are almost limitless: anything from a smart refrigerator that sends a message to remind you about those tomatoes you bought five days ago, to a washing machine that signals your mobile phone when the spin cycle has finished. It is about gathering information on the demands of the market, and those of users. The IoT has the potential to improve lives.

Zhang points out that a new era is emerging and being defined. "The power of the first industrial revolution was the steam engine," he said, "the second was driven by the internal combustion engine and electricity. The third has been powered by the internet. The driver of the fourth is the IoT.

"It is the next major economic activity after the mobile internet. IoT is creating a market space that the previous internet generations cannot match. Not just an interconnection at the hardware level, but something companies can use: hardware as a portal to continuous interaction with users.

"The IoT has 'user sensors' rather than 'product sensors'. Companies can continuously dig for, and reveal, personal needs. They can know just who their users are, and what they want."

The IoT era began with the adoption of voice control and the appearance of virtual assistants such as Alexa and Siri. The IoT is leading us to a more connected world, and at a fair clip. This future will bring greater efficiency and save time and money. There is now the potential to disrupt the way in which information, capital, and other resources flow. IoT can disrupt entire industries, and is likely to have a profound impact on business and management models, and on behaviours and lifestyles.

This knowledge of users and their requirements is vital in an uncertain business environment, with increasingly fierce cross-industry competition, exponential start-up growth, and the Sharing Economy.

Cross-Industry Competition
Another 21st Century phenomenon... The rise of digital technologies means multiple borders can simply dissolve. The banking industry may not fear competition from traditional financial institutions, but it will be concerned about initiatives such as Apple Pay, PayPal, Alipay, and cryptocurrencies. Traditional camera-makers such as Nikon and Canon compete not only with each other, but also with smartphone producers such as Apple and Samsung. Traditional media — newspapers, radio, and television — must now battle it out with platforms such as Facebook, and Twitter. The emergence of WhatsApp,

Telegram and WeChat have changed the competitive landscape of traditional communications.

Exponential Growth of Start-ups

Cross-industry competition has been intensified by another contemporary phenomenon: rapidly scaling start-ups. Their exponential growth has changed everything. Tech giants such as Uber, Netflix, Airbnb, Google, Amazon, Spotify, Alibaba, Didi and Tencent have come to dominate industries at break-neck speed by "software-ising" traditional products and services — and dramatically bringing down costs and prices.

These companies also managed to reach millions of potential customers via that one, vital mouse-click. Tencent's WeChat drew 400 million users in less than three years, outpacing and replacing other social media software almost overnight. The Chinese ride-hailing firm Didi was founded in 2012 — and now has more than 500 million users, and tens of millions of drivers.

Whereas traditional brands such as Coca-Cola needed years of marketing to forge their place in the world, digital-born start-ups can achieve notable brand status in months — sometimes weeks. But the rise and fall of WeWork, for example, indicates the double-edged nature of this sword. The leading brands of the 21st Century are being created more rapidly than ever before — and they can fall and fail just as quickly.

The Sharing Economy

A focus on business models that rely on the collaborative sharing of products and services, rather than their individual use, has allowed start-ups to catch another swelling wave of the digital era: the sharing economy.

Sharing models enable products to be used more intensively and efficiently, and promote a view where the importance of exclusive ownership over resources is shifting to the correct use of resources. The importance of owning resources has changed, as has the strategic view on resource dependability.

Digitalisation can lower market-entry barriers for nimble competitors. It's part of a larger phenomenon that brings easier access for all newcomers. Established companies once enjoyed the advantage of owning assets that competitors could not easily replicate because of insufficient capital and high R&D costs. Uber dominates the taxi industry without owning any cars, Airbnb is highly competitive in the accommodation and hotel industries without owning any property. There are many such examples.

Open Innovation

Borders have weakened in our interconnected world. Companies once organised as closed bastions must now open up to outside partners to satisfy diverse, personalised, and evolving customer needs.

Innovation is no longer limited to boffins and inventors in the research department. Go-ahead companies understand that they must innovate transparently and engage with stakeholders — and sometimes even competitors — to satisfy customers. Attracting and engaging with stakeholders is a major contemporary challenge that many traditional organisations still need to crack. We'll consider shortly how Haier rises to this challenge.

> ### *Employee Engagement*
>
> *Another challenge is that of creating an inclusive workplace. Gallup reports that globally, only 15 percent of employees feel engaged at work — and this might be the biggest contemporary challenge of all.[2] "Engaged" in this context means being "highly involved in and enthusiastic about their work and the workplace". They are psychological "owners". They drive performance and innovation and move the organisation forward. But remember: 67 percent are not fully engaged. Their needs are not being met, they're putting time — but not energy or passion — into their work. The remaining 18 percent are actively disengaged and may even sabotage the workplace because of resentment and discontent. People thrive, and organisations flourish, in an exciting and inspiring workplace. In*

our earlier book, *Corporate Rebels: Make Work More Fun*, we looked at pioneering companies that enjoy profitability, productivity, and customer satisfaction. They have lower staff turnover, less absenteeism, fewer accidents, and fewer product and service defects. Creating and sustaining a vibrant work environment should be a priority for all organisations.

Digital Transformations

The digital revolution has impacted and challenged companies internally and externally. With the coming of the internet, the scope, dimensions, scale, speed, and effects of digitalisation fundamentally changed, resulting in more pressure on processes converting from analogue to those processed, stored, and transmitted via digital devices and networks.

For Haier, digital transformation has presented opportunities and challenges. Digitalisation enables production based on phenomena such as the "Industrial IoT" — interconnected devices networking with computers' industrial applications. "Industry 4.0" refers to devices that analyse and diagnose issues without human intervention. Machine-to-machine communication is a direct "conversation" between devices.

Highly useful — but digital transformation is no walk in the park. McKinsey reports that fewer than 30 percent of attempts find success. [3]

Despite the large number of failures, refusing to get involved can be disastrous. Past performance is no guarantee of future success. Detroit — America's "Motor City" — was once home to the Big Three: Ford, General Motors, and Chrysler. It was the heart of one of the most successful industries in the US. Detroit is now better known for its alarming decline in fortunes: few job opportunities and shocking rates of poverty. The Big Three did not move with the times. The increasing popularity of practical, inexpensive, and reliable Japanese and European models forced Chrysler and GM to file for bankruptcy in the late 2000s.

The world is now witnessing the swift and relentless rise of the digital newcomer Tesla, a true disruptor. Time will tell if it eventually kills off the fossil-fuelled laggards hanging onto the past.

These struggles in the motoring sector are illustrative of a cruel fact: companies that do not move with the times cease to be competitive. If they don't upgrade their processes, they can't compete with emerging players rooted in the digital era.

Digitalisation can help companies gather and act upon real-time insights into processes such as manufacturing, production, logistics, and sales and marketing. It can capture information about user needs and market demand via novel channels, including social media. It can help to reduce inventories with solutions such as on-demand manufacturing and drop-shipping. It can also allow for radical decentralisation and improve efficiency by reducing management layers and bureaucracy. These things Haier has proved with its own digital transformation.

Too Big for Comfort
A failure to address these challenges will have consequences, warns Zhang. He speaks of the "large company disease": as companies grow, they tend to lose efficiency. They become less innovative, less responsive to external stimuli. They lose their customer-centricity, find that they have fewer people close to the buyer, and risk becoming overstaffed and bloated.

Bureaucratic companies tend to become increasingly rigid as they scale. They struggle to balance employee numbers with workload and find the sweet spot that adds value for customers. The management of internal activities becomes a focus. Employment drives fail to create any added value for the end-user. These lumbering enterprises continue to provide products and services — but efficiency, flexibility and speed of operations decline. And their innovative power and their corporate character take a dive.

Throughout the ongoing growth of Haier, Zhang Ruimin has fought against this. The company has constantly been transforming its organisational model and management style. The rise of IoT brought Haier a new set of challenges related to increased competition and business uncertainty. But Zhang's reactions and responses have turned this Chinese giant into the world's biggest start-up.

The Start-up Factory
Zhang Ruimin split the company into thousands of small new independent units under the banner of Rendanheyi. This model steers away from a traditional silo organisation of functional departments, developing novel structures that unite. External partners cluster into larger ecosystems to collaborate on the development of products and services. This has enabled the crossing of industry borders, open innovation, and the development of new business models. It has allowed the creation of almost 4,000 internal start-ups with access to all necessary resources, and given them the ability to scale rapidly — and spin off from Haier when desired. These businesses are not only in the white goods space, either. Haier is no one-trick pony; it is active in industries as diverse as real estate, logistics, medical care, fitness, agriculture, and clothing.

The Rendanheyi model was not created in a vacuum. It stands, like so many things, on the shoulders of giants.

• • •

> REBEL LOG: *Networks, collaborations and co-operation: Haier didn't reach its current status by ploughing a unilateral furrow. Zhang Ruimin acknowledges that, and by taking his hand off the management tiller and allowing outsiders to enter the ecosystem, has created something truly unusual, and intimately connected...*
>
> **Rebel One, out.**

The rise of the IoT may one day deliver total interconnection to the world. Zhang Ruimin believes that management innovation should always reflect the realities dictated by technological revolutions. "Management thinking is a product of the times," he told us. "There are no universal truths and laws in management comparable to those found in the natural sciences. As a craft, management must keep pace with changing times. Management activities must address the challenges. That's why there are no 'successful' enterprises, only ones that move on. Only by adapting to change and keeping pace with the times can they survive."

Ruimin and Haier developed the Rendanheyi model as a response to the technological revolution and the IoT. It was built on the foundations of over 100 years of management innovation following the publication of Frederick Winslow Taylor's Principles of Scientific Management. Many notables have left their mark: think Henry Ford and the Ford Motor Company, and Taiichi Ohno and Toyota Motor Corporation.

Looking through the lens of manufacturing, one could divide this century of management innovation into three eras: Ford (1930-1970), Toyota (1970-2010), and Haier (2010-?). In each of these eras, major scientific and technological developments have demanded fresh management ideas and models. Let's explore them one-by-one.

The Ford Era (1930-1970)

This one has its roots in the United States of the early 1900s and strong connections to Taylor's scientific management theory. He made one of the first attempts to apply science and engineering to the pursuit of greater organisational efficiency. He argued that flaws in a work process could be resolved in an empirical manner through improved management methods. And he thought the best way to increase labour productivity was to optimise the ways in which the work was done.

Taylor argued that instead of allowing employees the freedom to use the "rule of thumb" to complete a task, one should determine the "one best way". Reducing the time outlay was the key to increased productivity. He advocated time studies to break a project down into discrete tasks, even using a stopwatch to measure elements, and then reorder those elements into an optimal sequence.

The "one best way" should see the separation of workload between managers and front-line employees. Managers should do the thinking, plan, and train. Front-line employees are there to do the actual work by putting their training into practice. Employees are assigned certain jobs, without the freedom to choose. Managers decide which employees are capable of which specific job, and train them to peak efficiency. In their view, employee performance could be monitored, and their efficiency assessed to guarantee productivity.

Sound familiar?
Taylor's philosophy rapidly became the cornerstone of Western management thinking, and its influence can still be seen today. It is alive and well in the production processes of many companies, and contributed to process analysis, process mapping, standardisation of best practices, and the documentation of processes and mass production.

In the 1920s and '30s, mechanical engineer Henry Ford pioneered mass production by perfecting moving assembly line production technology at the Ford Motor company in Detroit. It is not clear whether Ford was directly influenced by Taylor, but he successfully combined his assembly line technology with Taylor's scientific management philosophy. Ford introduced conveyor belts, which meant that employees no longer had to leave their posts to lug parts from one place to another. They could spend their time on dedicated tasks.

Ford also pioneered the use of interchangeable parts, which allowed a continuous workflow and dramatically decreased production times. The time taken to assemble a Ford Model T dropped from 12 hours to just 93 minutes. It allowed Ford to increase its profit margin and reduce the cost to consumers.

Taylor felt that Ford had stripped away any opportunity for workplace pride and created a labour force of unskilled workers who were mere cogs in a machine. The Ford doctrine nonetheless became the dominant management philosophy in large Western manufacturing firms in the early decades of the 20th Century. It opened the gates for management innovations such as commercial R&D laboratories, HR departments, professional management training, statistical process control, business incubators, management by objectives, T-groups, capital budgeting, matrix organisation, portfolio analysis, strategic planning, project management, and strategic business units.

The Toyota Era (1970-2010)
In the late 1970s, companies in the West began to face stiff competition from Japan's production of high-quality, affordable goods. Firms started looking to the East for inspiration on how to better organise and manage their operations. Most notable was the way the founder of Toyota Motor Corporation, Sakichi Toyoda, his son, Kiichiro Toyoda, and engineer Taiichi Ohno arranged their business.

They developed their own methods while looking for an alternative to the American style of mass production. These people were searching for a system that would adjust to Japan's poor post-war economic conditions and work culture. Two main principles emerged for what became known as the "Toyota Way": continuous improvement, and respect for people.

The first aspect is often associated with kaizen, the Sino-Japanese word for "improvement". Kaizen refers to a business philosophy in which every person, from front-line employee to CEO, is involved in continuously improving all functions, activities, and processes. This is often associated with the reduction of waste — cutting back on anything that does not advance the process or increase value. This meant redundancies, and a hunt for the root cause of problems.

It is argued that the right process produces the right results. A process should manufacture what is needed, when it is needed, in the quantity that is needed. This philosophy was inspired not by Ford or the American automotive industry, but by American supermarkets.

Customers take goods off the shelf; the store restocks to fill the space. In Ohno's view, a car factory should operate in a similar fashion. Toyota pioneered a way of working that — by improving standardised programmes and processes — would minimise waste and reduce inventory.

The "respect for people" element can be seen in Toyota's emphasis on building mutual trust and encouraging teamwork. While still relying on a hierarchy, front-line employees were no longer expected to work alone. Toyota created small groups, with a team leader rather than a foreman. Each team was assigned a set of assembly steps, and collaboratively figured out how best to perform them. Once the teams were running smoothly and accustomed to the process, Toyota periodically organised knowledge-sharing workshops, where team members proposed improvements to work procedures and operations. These teams were often customer-orientated, and flexible enough to meet the individual needs of a wide range of buyers.

Toyota successfully challenged some of the ground rules of Ford's operation. The earlier era focused on mass-production, process optimisation and individualism; Toyota began to adopt concepts that allowed for continuous improvement: a zero-defect mentality, high quality, and collectivism, giving a group priority over the individuals in it. Toyota began sharing its findings with its suppliers in the 1990s and created the next leap in management thinking as it relates to manufacturing. The door was opened for influential management innovation concepts such as servant leadership, Total Quality Management, Just-in-time, Lean, and Six Sigma.

The Haier Era (2010 -?)
Ford and Toyota were at the heart of manufacturing management thinking throughout the 20th Century, reflecting the dominant Western and Eastern philosophies.

With the rise of the Internet, traditional thinking was seriously challenged. In the 21st Century, emergent technologies such as mobile internet, IoT, and big data have had an increasing impact on how manufacturing companies are organised. As a response to the challenges of these times, Haier pioneered its Rendanheyi model on the foundations laid by Ford and Toyota. It combined the best of both worlds and ushered-in what could be considered the Haier Era.

Zhang Ruimin sees that Western and Eastern cultures have individual strengths. "Differences of perspective are evident in traditional Eastern medicine and its Western counterpart," he told us. "Western medicine is quantitative; the Eastern way is holistic. We have paid great attention to combining Eastern and Western cultures, and we try to distil the most valuable characteristics of both."

Haier distinguishes itself from the Ford and Toyota eras in at least three ways: radical decentralisation, internal market dynamics, and the building of micro-communities.

Radical Decentralisation
The Ford and Toyota eras relied on hierarchy. Toyota had a strong focus on mutual respect and teamwork, but the firm was still organised in multiple layers of superiors and subordinates.

Rendanheyi broke away from this. It radically decentralises the organisation by dispensing with most of the formal hierarchy, removing all middle managers, and providing employees with a high degree of autonomy. Haier replaced its former structure with Rendanheyi — a network of teams. They can be seen as independent start-ups, operating under the Haier brand (or others in the Haier Group, such as Casarte, GEA, Sanyo, and Fisher & Paykel).

Each start-up should be as close to its customers as possible; Haier calls this "zero distance". The concept allows the company to move its focus from mass production to mass customisation: made-to-order, or on-demand manufacturing. Haier delivers products and services that address specific customer needs, desires, or pain-points. Marketing and manufacturing efforts combine flexibility and the provision of tailored products and services with the low cost and high efficiency associated with mass production.

The radical decentralisation strategy of Haier has "platform-ised" the company in a manner that provides its start-ups with resources, brings them to maturity, and spins them out of the Haier universe when they are ready to stand on their own. The company consists of around 4,000 internal start-ups. Three of these are now independent listed companies, and five have reached unicorn status; 37 are considered "gazelles" — high-growth companies that are increasing revenues by at least 20 percent annually, for four or more years.

Incubating start-ups is no small feat, and nor is surviving the "Death Valley Curve": the span of time from the start of operations to the generation of revenue. It can be difficult to raise additional financing as the business model has not yet been proven, and there is a heightened risk of failure in this period.

And yet, the rate of successful start-up incubation at Haier is 49 percent — against a global average of just 10. We have come to think of Haier as the world's biggest start-up "factory".

Internal Market Dynamics

Employees during the Ford and Toyota eras were mostly guided and monitored by superiors. Employee reward mechanisms were dictated by fixed labour contracts. Profits accruing from employee activities were mostly passed on to company shareholders, and seldom shared with those who created the value.

Rendanheyi breaks with these conventions. To efficiently co-ordinate thousands of autonomous start-ups and properly motivate employees, Haier introduced internal market mechanisms and blockchain-enabled contracts (to ensure automatic execution). It also encourages employee initiative and entrepreneurial thinking. It still monitors performance, but the emphasis is on making employees responsible for their choices. Haier is convinced that only by giving its employees more autonomy and responsibility, and by allowing self-governance, can the collective remain manageable.

The many employees we spoke to confirmed that they have high levels of autonomy and responsibility. There are, however, lines — set by top leadership — that cannot be crossed. These are considered by employees to be fair and clear. Those who stick to the rules and make the most of their opportunities and decisions can be successful. Employees seem satisfied with their autonomy. Haier regards these freedoms as necessary to motivate people — and employees who make the right decisions and are successful in the market can expect high rewards.

Start-ups are rewarded by the market for the value they create, with profit-sharing mechanisms to steer the firm away from the trap of merely maximising shareholder value. Rewards are distributed to everyone who adds value to the customer, which Haier terms as "maximising human value". When Haier start-ups are successful, all the people involved reap the benefits — individually. Some have been remarkably successful, and certain employees in Haier's internal start-ups that went through the IPO process have become millionaires.

But this internal market mechanism cuts both ways. If employees make poor decisions and are not successful, they face the consequences. Haier people are motivated, and allowed, to make most of their choices — but the market, not the organisation, will decide.

Zhang says that the maximisation of human value is at the core of Rendanheyi — and argues that it should be the core of all business models. Business, he believes, is about people. "They create value, and people are different. So, different people will produce different results. This is the human factor. The factory, its equipment, and even capital, cannot create value. Only people can create value. That is why people are key to any business activity. If you put people aside, the balance sheet will be of little use."

Micro-Community Building
In the Ford and Toyota eras, most companies were closed systems with clear organisational borders that distinguished what was going on within from what happened outside. It was obvious who was part of the company and who was not. But with the rise of technologies such as the Internet of Things, which make total interconnection possible, physical boundaries gradually begin to disappear.

Rendanheyi anticipated this trend by opening-up the organisation: anyone who can create value for the customer may join. Zhang wants Haier to be without boundaries as he believes that all businesses should be open and interactive. Haier values its internal start-ups and external partners equally. Rendanheyi breaks with the other philosophies in this. Manufacturing success will be decided by companies' ability to swiftly locate, and make efficient use of, all necessary resources through connections with stakeholders. Whether these stakeholders are within or without the firm is not important, hence one of Zhang Ruimin's famous declarations: "The world is Haier's R&D department."

Haier start-ups are encouraged to collaborate with internal colleagues and external partners through these porous borders. They create micro-communities that bring value for customers. Where relationships with external partners in the Ford and Toyota periods were guided by competitive thinking — working mainly with suppliers who offer the lowest prices, for example — the relationships within Haier micro-communities are guided by more collaborative thinking.

Under the Rendanheyi model, all parties making up the micro-community interact, sign a collective contract, and share benefits based on the value jointly created. Haier tries to create micro-communities and an environment, or ecosystem, where all stakeholders are integrated. More value for the customer — and a share of the benefits. Haier Group revenues are generated internally and externally with those who have joined the ecosystem.

• • •

Taken individually, these mechanisms are not that novel. Similar practices have been pioneered for quite some time. We have seen similar radical decentralisation at scale practices: Dutch healthcare specialist Buurtzorg, the Swedish bank Handelsbanken, and the Russian supermarket chain VkusVill. We have witnessed similar internal market mechanisms at the Swedish consulting firm Centigo, and micro-community-building practices at the Spanish NER group (for more examples, see Corporate Rebels, Make Work More Fun).

What is novel is Haier's effort to combine these three characteristics and put them into practice in a manufacturing setting, at a completely new scale — sometimes involving thousands of people. Zhang integrated traditional Chinese culture with Western and Eastern management thinking to create these innovative concepts. Over the years, Haier has come to be thought of as one of the most pioneering firms, and one that has attracted the attention of the commentators of the business management world.

To understand the larger Haier story, including the historical context of Rendanheyi development, let's start at the beginning, or thereabouts. What is now the world's leading appliance manufacturer was once churning out sub-standard fridges and trying to keep employees from urinating on the factory floor.

WATER

'Haier should be like the sea. Only the sea has the breadth to accommodate hundreds of large rivers and small streams. It takes cascading muddy waters and purifies them in its vast blueness...'

Zhang Ruimin, 1994*

* From essay: Haier is the sea (Full essay in Appendix 1)

REBEL LOG, FIRST ENTRY SINCE TOUCHDOWN: Discovering a new world. Evolution is a constant, wherever we are. Our Rebel voyages have shown us how circumstances, resilience, variety and challenge can transform an ecosystem. But what happens when a company takes conscious charge of its own evolution, grabbing itself by the scruff and plunging into a new incarnation...? Exiting the Corporate Rebel bubble and entering uncharted territory. Wish us luck.

Rebel One, out

The Birth of Rendanheyi (1986-2012)

The Haier brand was introduced in the early 1990s, but its legacy can be traced back with certainty to the early 1980s. Back then the company was called the Qingdao Refrigerator Company and was in the eastern Shandong Province on China's Yellow Sea coast.

The factory was in debt and production had slowed to a trickle: just 80 machines a month. The refrigerators produced were of poor quality and frequently broke down. Management was weak, CEOs joined and left again quickly, and there was no coherent business development strategy. They were on the verge of bankruptcy, and something had to change. Fast.

Precious little attention was paid to strategy or tactics in the centralised economy of the time. Factories adhered to production quotas, providing often sub-standard goods to customers largely indifferent to quality of manufacture. Markets were controlled by ministries, and often based on geographical proximity.

Fast-forward to the present day. Haier has a presence in 186 countries, a 13.3 percent global market share in major appliances and 44 percent in smart appliances. Through its seven brands — Haier, Casarte, Leader, Aqua, Fisher & Paykel, GE Appliances, and CANDY — Haier serves markets in Asia Pacific, Europe, the Americas, the Middle East, and Africa.

On the stock exchanges of Shanghai and Frankfurt Haier is present via its principal subsidiary: Haier Smart Home Co Ltd. In 2019, that subsidiary reported an operating revenue of RMB 200.8 billion ($31 billion), with a net profit of RMB 5.8 billion ($0.9 billion). In the same year, revenue from overseas operations represented 47 percent of total revenue [4].

Just to give a feeling of what those numbers mean, Haier's brand value was ranked 68th in the world — just behind Orange and HSBC, and ahead of Pampers, Dell, IKEA, and JP Morgan [5]. Turning a company on the verge of bankruptcy into one of the biggest and most valuable in the world is quite a performance. A performance that started in the 1980s.

• • •

A Champion from Another Universe: Building the Brand
The local government of Qingdao had appointed a series of CEOs, but none had been able to turn the loss-making factory around. It was forced to take a gamble. In 1984, a 35-year-old assistant city manager by the name of Zhang Ruimin was hired. The mission to save the factory would have been a challenge for anyone, and Zhang had limited management experience. But he more than made up for this with a lively and open mind. In retrospect, this was the moment Haier was born.

Outside the factory walls, there were changes afoot that made it even harder to save the inept Qingdao Refrigerator Company. China's Planned Economy began to open to foreign investors. Deng Xiaoping, leader of the People's Republic of China from 1978 to 1992, would guide the country through far-reaching market-economy reforms, earning him the title "Architect of Modern China". His initiatives enabled the country's fast growing economy to advance on the road to prosperity, raising the living standards of hundreds of millions.

This created opportunities, but for the Qingdao Refrigerator Company it constituted a threat. Zhang Ruimin did not allow himself the dream of reforming the company to benefit from the global market. He was too busy solving problems on an entirely different scale. Zhang's first step was to ask employees to identify what they considered to be excessive or unnecessary rules. It was time, he felt, to pare back regulations

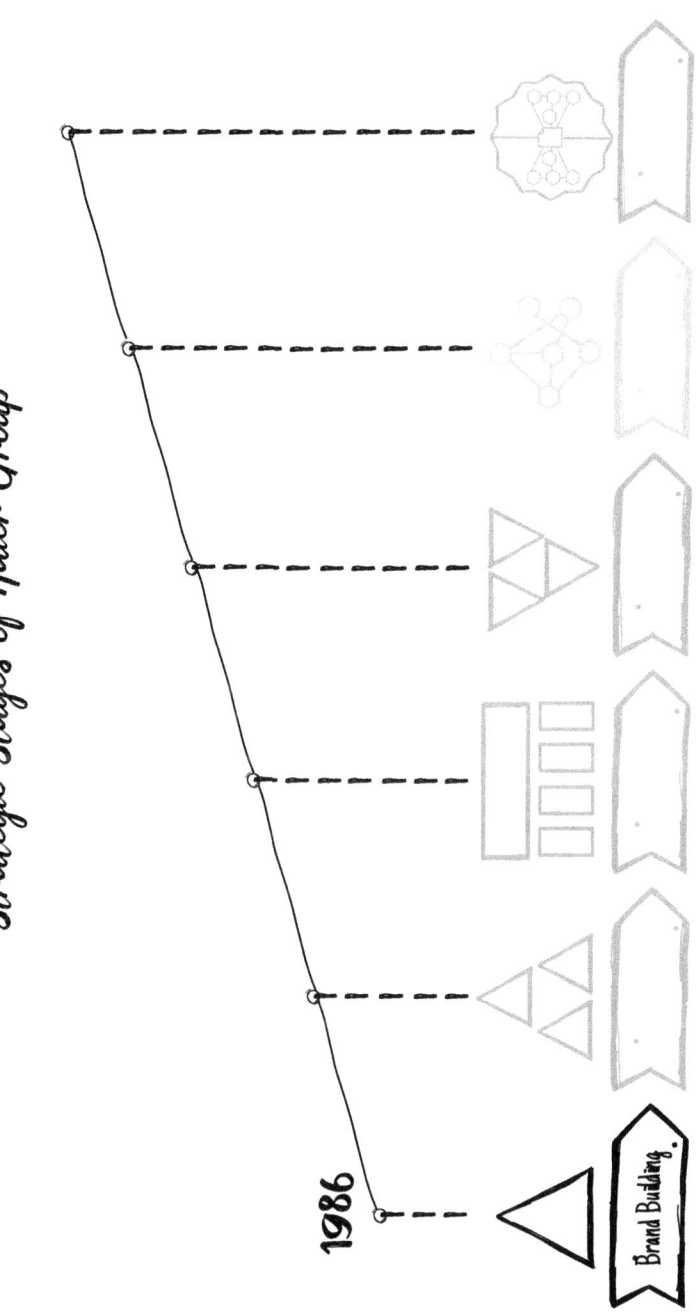

and abide only by those needed to keep chaos at bay. The resulting 13 approved rules formed the foundation of positive change. They were posted on factory walls for all to see. Rule number 10 illustrates how dire conditions were at the time. It reads: "No urinating or defecating on the factory floor."

Zhang also posted a statement of consequences for those who violated the rules. Although staff behaviour had improved, company property was still being stolen. When one employee was caught in the act and fired on the spot, a notice went up to inform all other personnel of the incident. The employees were shocked by the instant dismissal, and quickly came to understand that Zhang meant business.

A year later, he received a customer complaint regarding the quality of a fridge. It was already broken upon delivery, and the buyer was appalled. Ruimin ordered an inspection of all stock. It was discovered that one in five fridges was defective. Zhang dealt with the situation in his own direct way. His actions brought him international fame — and still make for a great story...

• • •

青岛电冰箱总厂劳动纪律管理规定
（1984年12月）

1. 不迟到．不早退．不旷工．
2. 不准代他人划出勤卡
3. 工作时间不准打扑克、下棋、织毛衣、干私活等
4. 工作时间不准串岗
5. 工作时间不准喝酒
6. 工作时间不准睡觉
7. 工作时间不准赌博
8. 不准损坏工厂的设备
9. 不偷工厂里的财物
10. 不准在车间里大小便
11. 不准破坏工厂的纪律
12. 不准用棉纱柴油烤火
13. 不准带小孩和外人进入工厂

Qingdao Refrigerator Factory, Disciplines & Rules, (1984 Year, 12 Month)

1. Do not arrive late to work or leave work early and absenteeism is not allowed
2. Do not punch attendance cards on behalf of others
3. Poker games, chess, knitting, moonlighting, etc. are not allowed during working hours
4. Do not leave your post and go to others' during working hours
5. No drinking during working hours
6. No sleeping during working hours
7. No gambling during working hours
8. Do not replace components of factory equipment
9. Do not steal anything from the factory
10. No urinating or defecating on the factory floor
11. Do not damage the public property of the factory
12. Do not use cotton and diesel to build a fire for warmth
13. Do not bring children or unauthorised personnel to the factory

REBEL LOG, ON THE SURFACE: There's a man with a hammer... We appear to be in a peaceable place, albeit one with occasional eruptions which can be seen from afar. There is more emphasis on creation, but sometimes — just sometimes — there are sudden outbursts of destruction. Could it be, though, that this destruction can be creative at the same time...?

Rebel One, out.

Creation, Destruction, and the Birth of a Star

Back in the day, it was normal practice for factories in China to sell faulty products on street corners, or directly to employees. For most Chinese people, buying broken appliances at lower prices and carrying out repairs themselves was the only way to own a fridge, air conditioner or TV. Owning them immediately changed how your neighbours looked at you, even if the products were second-hand and broken. Zhang knew this did not make long-term sense. "If we start selling bad products, even at low prices, what message does this send to the public?" he demanded. "What would prevent us from producing 760, or 7,600, bad fridges? We must solve this problem immediately."

Another, more dramatic, option was required.

Zhang ordered that all 76 defective fridges be rounded-up and placed in the middle of the factory floor. He gathered around him the workers responsible, gave each a sledgehammer — and ordered them to destroy their sub-standard handiwork. At the time, a fridge cost the equivalent of two years' salary for a factory worker.

Then, Zhang and his employees embarked on an orgy of destruction. Even though the picture marking that event is blurred and has faded with time, the workers' faces reveal their emotions.

It was the start of a new era, and the introduction of a philosophy still central to the company's operational ethos: a sharp focus on quality. This avowed intent represented the core principle behind the implementation of Zhang's Brand-Building stage. The strategy differed from that of most

other Chinese enterprises. Competitors focused mainly on volume rather than quality or customer satisfaction. Their concern was for short-term profits. Zhang and his employees worked to create a brand that would become known for its quality. The goal: zero defects. It required major changes to the factory, and the underlying corporate culture.

Barack Obama's iconic "Yes, we can!" has become a rallying call for those who believe in change. Zhang didn't have a catchy slogan for his campaign, but he would have agreed that confidence is vital for success. In an interview on organisational development, Zhang said that if there was no money, he could borrow, and if there were no products, they could be made. But if the employees lacked confidence in themselves, or in the changes that had been proposed, it would be impossible to create a successful business.

Zhang had a secondary reason for destroying those refrigerators. There was something wrong with the way his employees viewed their products. They were comfortable with production in two categories: good work, which could be sold in foreign markets, and lower-quality products that were good enough for domestic consumption. That sense of inferiority was something that Zhang hoped to change by providing only products of impeccable quality — and making them available to all. He tried to bridge the inferiority gap and make his employees more self-confident. If that meant the destruction of 76 fridges to drive home the message that no one deserved inferior products, he was more than happy to oblige.

Another demonstration of that commitment to quality came when an employee found a rogue screw on the production line just before clocking-off. This surely meant that one fridge had a screw missing, and — since Haier had adopted the goal of zero defects — something had to be done. Instructions were issued that all inventory produced that day — some 1,000 units — should be checked. No problems were discovered, so where did that screw belong? It was two hours past midnight when they finally figured out that an extra screw had been delivered to the workshop. Panic over — quality assured [6].

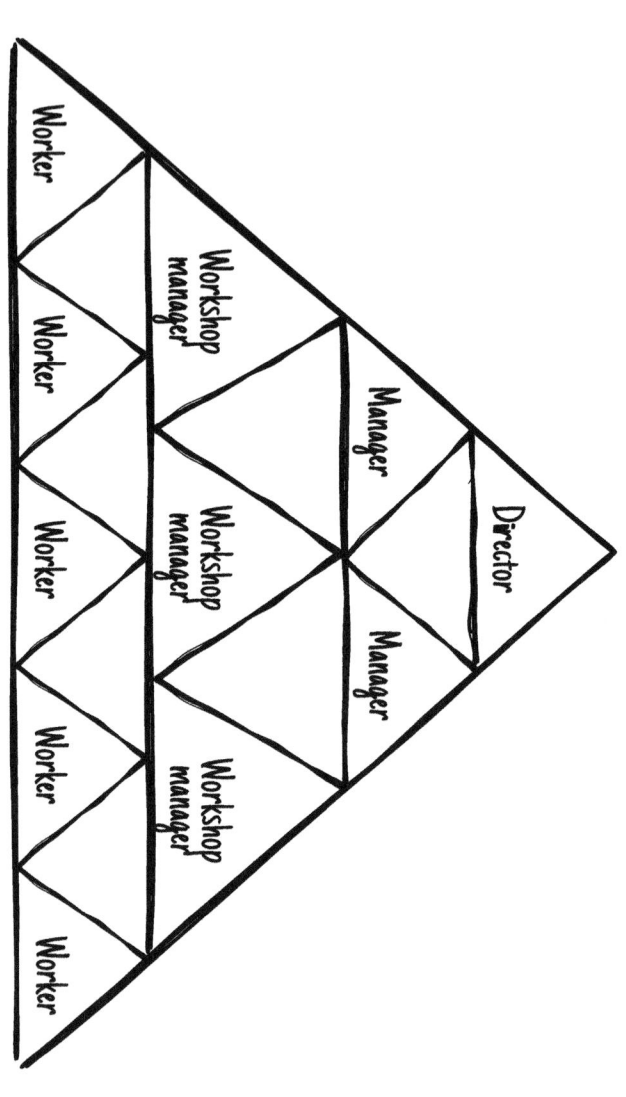

Throughout brand-building, Haier was organised — like many of the traditional hierarchies still out there today — in a pyramid structure. All authority and decision-making power lay at the top, making Zhang the person with most formal authority. He was the one charting the course. But while the management model was wholly traditional, there were signs that Zhang was not your everyday chief executive.

Instead of making decisions on their behalf, Zhang had empowered employees to create the rules they felt were necessary to turn the factory around. He had also shown that there were consequences for breaking those rules — and he wasn't interested in excuses. Zhang was indeed the boss. However, by inviting employees to be part of the rule-making process, they became "owners" of the rules. Empowered employees came to see that they could influence decisions, which motivated them to play the game. They learned that Zhang was a man who followed through.

Middle-managers had the authority to control communication and make decisions — up to a certain level. But most of all, they were responsible for co-ordination and telling employees what to do. For most of that era, employees would receive a fixed income — if they achieved what was expected of them and did not break any rules. During this period, Haier sought to improve its management style. The main goal was a method for the company to increase its execution capacity while maintaining quality.

Execution is Key
The answer proved to be the OEC model, (an abbreviation for the wordy "OVERALL/Everyone/Everyday/Everything Control and Clear" model). It was introduced in the '80s and is one of the few things to have survived the test of time; it is used in a refined form to this day. To discover how this works, go to Appendix 6. For now, let's just say it's an execution system which provides insights into what is being done, and what needs to be done. It helped employees at Haier to know what was expected of them, allowing them to complete their daily tasks, and making it easier to see who needs help and who is excelling.

Each day, every employee would fill in an evaluation form, that was connected to the targets of their team. They would hand the form over to their superiors for grading, and they would receive points based on their performances. Points were given for the successful completion of tasks or deducted for targets not reached. "Forgot to clean the floor? Minus one point for the members of the team, minus 10 for the responsible individual, and minus five for the team leader."

Besides using this to identify problems, the measurement of work and the completion of tasks, it also allowed the introduction of a new reward mechanism based on performance. In those early days, such a system was unheard of in China. Employees were habituated to getting their salaries — provided they didn't screw up. Zhang had always been a fan of performance-based rewards, and with the OEC model he found a way to make that possible.

The principle was easy to understand, at the end of each month scores were counted. If your score was good enough, you'd receive your full salary. If you failed, you would receive less. "To deliver quality product, Haier had to change the mindset from one of indifference to motivation. This was done by employing simple daily output and quality metrics, and directly tying daily wage-earnings to them." [7]

The OEC model has developed over time, but some of the core principles are still valid, and applied. Haier believes that the competitive advantage of the model is not based purely on reward and punishment. The real added value comes from the resulting transparency. The model stimulates each employee to learn everything there is to know about their goals, their performance, and the true causes of problems. Maintaining transparency over responsibility, sharing daily progress reports, and identifying urgent problems: these things still happen daily. But the tools to measure performance and activities have changed over the years.

Survival in a Tough Environment

Zhang was the first Haier CEO who managed to survive for any length of time. In just a few years, he succeeded in turning around the loss-making factory and created a brand that gained a leadership position. Haier attracted a great deal of publicity nationally (especially after the hammer incident) and even internationally, winning a global bid organised by the World Health Organisation in 1987. This was a first for a Chinese manufacturer. Also unprecedented was the way Haier managed to pass on responsibility to the workers by introducing the OEC management system.

But there was no time to rest on laurels. Haier's top-down management structure — creating products to build a powerful brand through an innovative execution model — was about to face a new challenge.

• • •

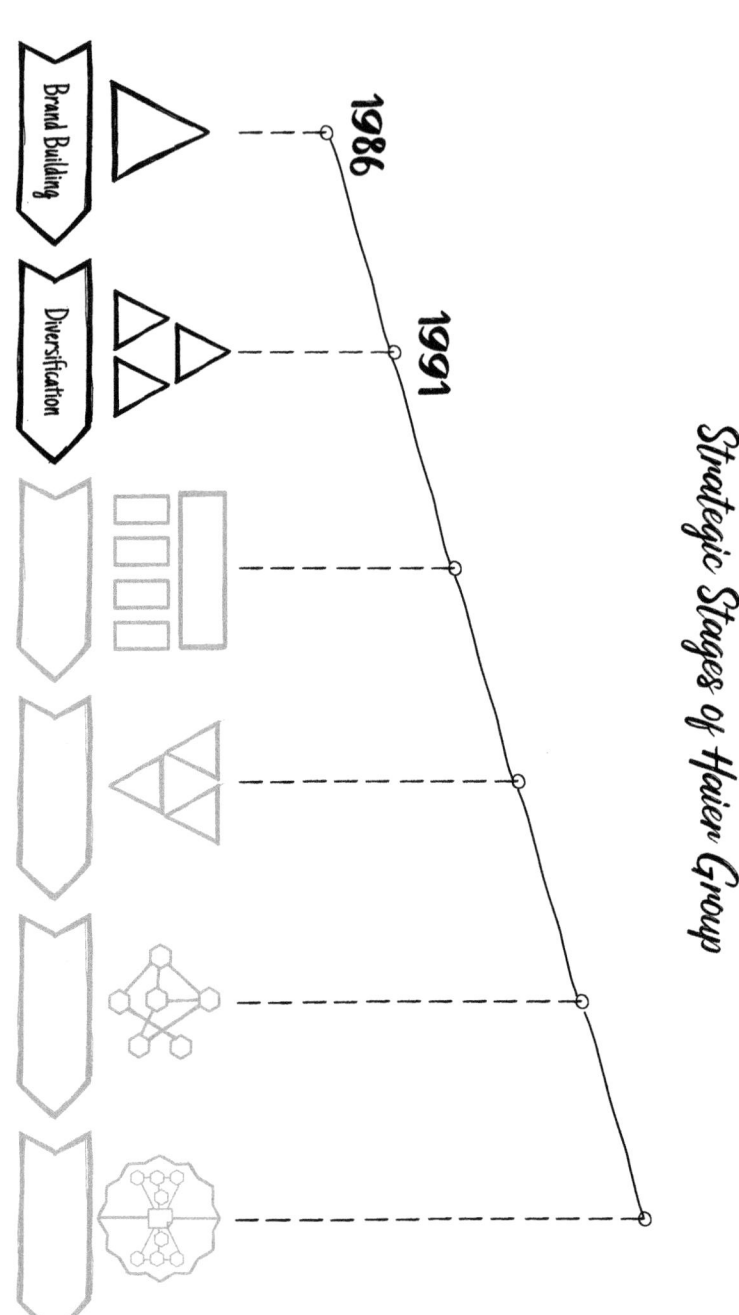

REBEL LOG, APPROACHING THE OUTER CIRCLE: There's talk of re-animation... Little is known about the local flora and fauna, but someone just mentioned fish — between mealtimes. Not just fish, but stunned fish. What could this be about, we wonder...?

Rebel One, out.

Recognition, Diversification, Threat and ... Fish?

By 1991, Haier was listed among China's Top Ten Well-Known Trademarks, and revenue climbed to $75m. Other white goods were added to the product line and Haier would soon acquire the lion's share of the national market. It was able to do so because of consumer trust and satisfaction. The traditional pyramid structure was incapable of meeting the company's needs. Rigidity was slowing things down, and Haier needed new strategies.

Beijing had taken note of the extraordinary success of the Qingdao factory, and realised that Zhang and his people were well-placed to educate and reform other businesses. The government's paternalism, concern about weakness and pervasive influence, meant that such suggestions were best heeded. It was time to diversify by taking over competitive companies.

Zhang focused on likely candidates which he referred to as "stunned fish": loss-makers with good products but lousy management. Zhang introduced Haier's management style and culture to reactivate them. It acquired 18 companies, rapidly expanding in scale (size, not fish skin) and moved into other consumer product lines including washing machines, air-conditioners, freezers, and TVs. Products from the acquired companies would take on the Haier brand only once they reached an acceptable standard of quality.

In 1992, Haier qualified under ISO 9001 and began to export. Four years later, the company set up production facilities in the Philippines and Malaysia. In 1998, Harvard Business School invited Zhang to lecture on management theory: its MBA students wanted to know more about reinvigorating those stunned fish. During this period, and with China opening to foreign investors, General Electric eyed the exemplary Haier brand as a vehicle for expansion. This didn't sit too well with Zhang; his company was no stunned fish. GE responded to the snub by saying it was going to enter the Chinese market, and announced its first objective: to eliminate Haier.

That backfired: Jonah swallowed the whale. In 2016, Haier purchased GE's appliances division for $5.4bn. There were no hard feelings, just a sensitive and highly beneficial transfer of GE into the Haier corporate fold.

In a bid to make the organisation more flexible, Haier shifted to a functional structure and broke the organisation down into several silos like R&D, Finance, Marketing, Manufacturing, HR and Legal. Underneath these silos Strategic Business Units (SBUs) were formed based on the products they made. Some of those products were previously created by companies Haier had acquired and incorporated into its structure. Those SBUs were further divided into more specific product divisions. The new structure allowed the management team to grant the SBUs authority and decision-making power, freeing-up their time to focus on strategy.

Reporting was made clear on a grid, or matrix, showing relationships between functional managers (who manage people) and project managers (who manage resources). Divisions were given the autonomy to operate and co-ordinate independently, and Haier benefitted from the flexibility to manage a fast-growing business. In a period of contextual change, Haier managed to export what had made it successful — its culture and way of working — and use that to turn around the companies it had acquired. Perhaps even more remarkable, it proved to be the right tool for those companies it had been obliged by the Chinese government to acquire. Haier's culture and philosophy helped to turn them around.

• • •

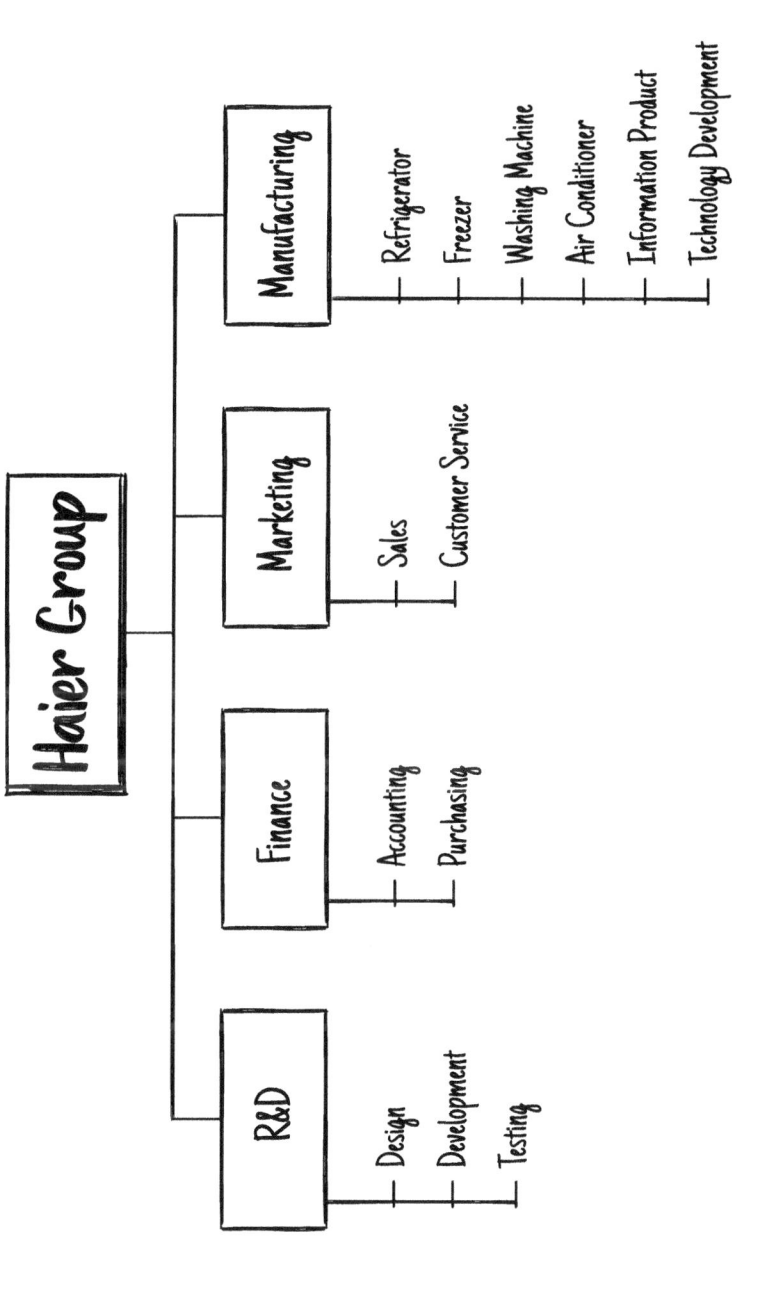

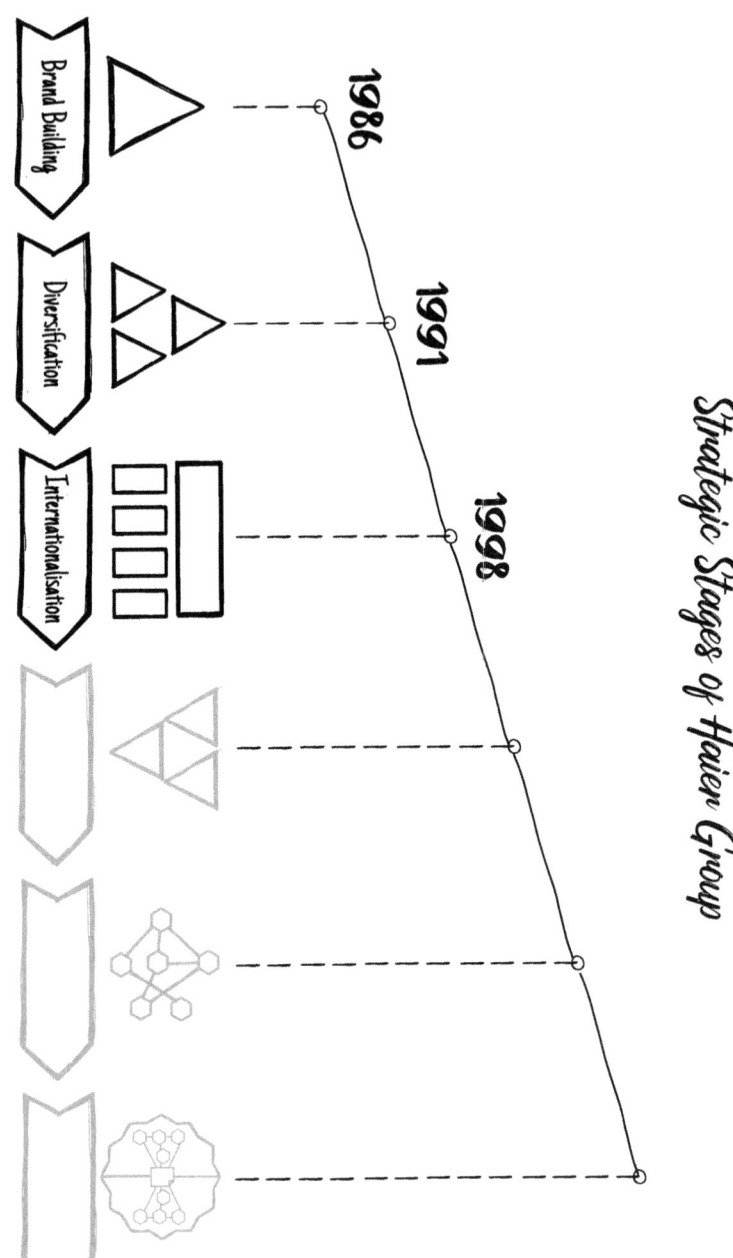

Moving into a New Orbit

With the millennium drawing to a close, Haier — at that time an employer of over 30,000 people — was China's largest fridge manufacturer. In 2001, the country joined the World Trade Organisation and opened its doors to foreigners, creating many new opportunities — and a few challenges. Zhang knew that Haier needed to react quickly to the developing situation, and the management model was re-engineered to better cater to market expectations. He hoped these changes would further spur innovation and improve Haier's reaction time to domestic consumer preferences, which were becoming more sophisticated.

Moving to a strategy of responsiveness from one of intense quality control and superior branding requires a significant change of corporate culture. Haier believed that responding to customer needs faster than the competition would not only reinforce brand image, but also justify charging a premium for its products and services.

An Example of Responsiveness: a Potato-Washing Machine

Haier was initially puzzled by the number of washing machines in rural areas that were breaking down. It turned out that farmers had been using them to clean their fruit and vegetables, knowing that attractive produce would stand out better in the markets. Instead of telling them not to use the washing machines for such activities, Haier was quick to respond to this user need. It adapted existing technology to do the best job possible for the farmers, resulting in a clothing washing machine specifically designed to double as a vegetable washer. This initiative was much appreciated. But the existing corporate structure would not help Haier to respond as sensitively to the needs of rapidly developing markets.

During this internationalisation phase, competition inside China was fierce. Foreign multinationals were targeting the domestic market, forcing Haier to develop a global strategy. Instead of focusing on less competitive regions such as South East Asia or Africa, Haier chose to enter — and would come to thrive in — the ultra-competitive markets of the United States and Europe.

In 1999, Haier opened an industrial park in South Carolina. At the time, there was no cost advantage in setting up production facilities in the US, but Haier was convinced this was the best way to meet the needs of American consumers. Following the acquisition of the Italian Meneghetti Refrigerator Factory two years later, Haier's creative studios in Lyon and Amsterdam, and its marketing office in Milan, worked together to design, manufacture, and sell locally.

• • •

Massive Attraction and Corporate Obesity
Close to the end of the diversification era, it was clear to Zhang that Haier was suffering from corporate obesity. He knew that the company would need to be nimbler and more flexible to expand into foreign markets: a change of focus would be required. A crash diet may have had some temporary effect, but to get properly back in shape, Haier decided to rethink its lifestyle.

Strategic Business Units had shown potential, but something was lacking. Inspired by Michael Porter, Zhang sought ways to integrate a market-chain. [8] His goal was to link employees to customers. But to turn into a customer-orientated operation, Haier would need to completely reinvent itself.

Zhang felt that SBUs should become smaller. A lot smaller. Instead of just working for supervisors and trying to reach the daily goals, each employee would become an SBU. Zhang was about to create 30,000 self-managed SBUs that were still organised in silos.

In practice the "shape" of the organisational structure didn't change too much, the difference was that larger SBUs were broken down into smaller ones.

Removing the command-and-control structure and transforming it into a transactional and contractual alternative was the way forward. Zhang hoped to create equality, because each SBU was at liberty to negotiate with its peers rather than wait to be told what to do.

By making everyone responsible for their own performance and allowing them to profit if they exceeded their targets, Zhang hoped his employees would develop a sense of ownership. This initiative brought major change. Employees were given autonomy to decide how best to complete their tasks, but they were also directly affected — positively or negatively — by outcomes. In the previous structure, your job may have been to carry a box from point A to point B, and you would collect a salary at the end of the day. Now your target is to move 100 boxes. If you succeed, you'll get a bonus. Come up with a quicker or more efficient method that allows you to move 150 boxes, and you will do even better. The difference from previous methods: employees were free to decide how they would do their jobs.

This was when Haier's employees started to think of themselves as entrepreneurs, and that changed everything.

Instead of employees toiling away to the orders of their supervisors, without bearing any personal responsibility, the new SBUs would work for themselves. They would decide how best to do their jobs. In the past, a shipping clerk might have thrown boxes into a truck without concern for their condition on arrival; it now became vitally important that those products turned up undamaged — because otherwise their clients wouldn't hire them anymore. Success or failure directly affected the results of the SBU, and outcomes determined earnings. Every individual was truly responsible for their tasks and results (under the same basic system as before) and empowered to profit from superior performance. Zhang wanted them to feel and behave like owners, or as he put it: "Everyone is a CEO."

• • •

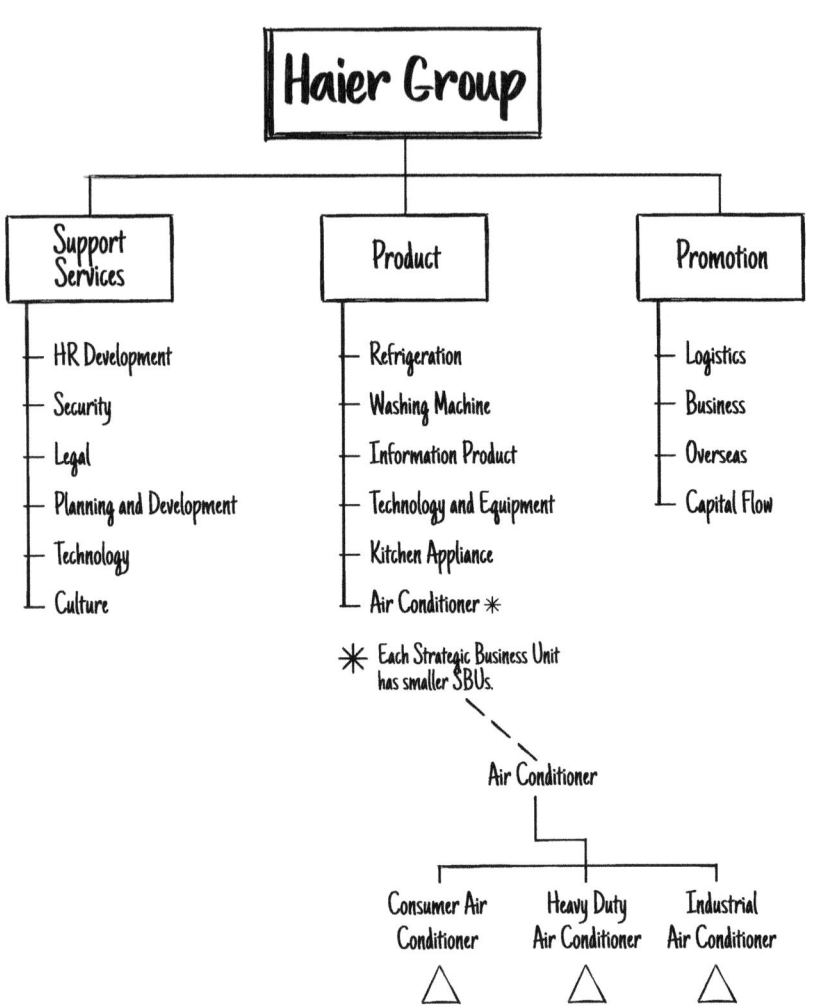

Approaching an Information Flow Zone

According to Zhang, the turn of the century was witnessing a shift. "Before the internet, it was all about mass production, but now it's all about mass customisation," he observed. He reasoned that consumer needs had changed rapidly because of the dramatic increase in information flow. And given these rapidly changing requirements, there was a need to fully customise products. The slow, stuck-in-a-rut traditional management style wouldn't allow sufficient time to react to changing needs. The updated SBU structure introduced employees to market dynamics and made them truly responsible for their work. They were free to choose how they fulfilled their tasks, and were aware of the potential rewards and consequences. It proved to be another step towards turning employees into entrepreneurs. Zhang's approach cut away at Haier's corpulence. It became more adept at delivering on the dreams of its customers.

• • •

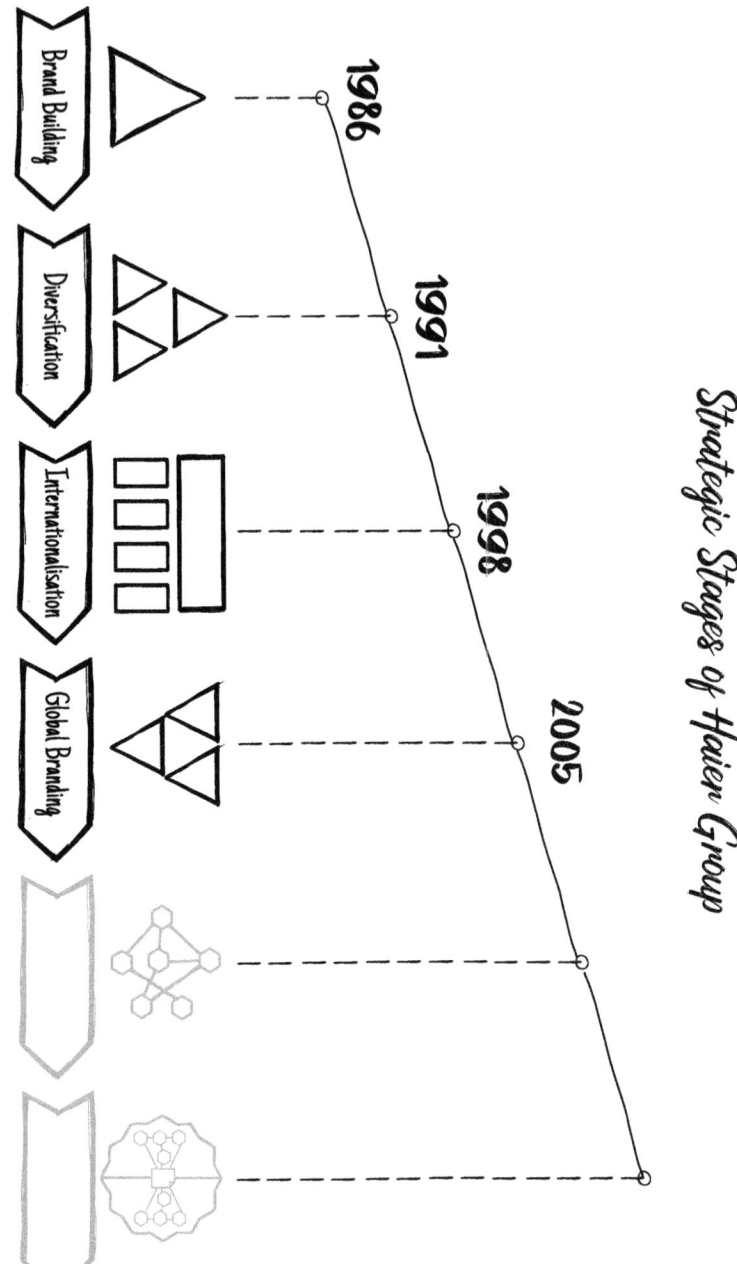

Global Branding Stage: New Ideas, New Worlds

The shift into the Internet era brought with it a need for further transformation. Zhang was committed to the Global Branding stage. The goal, once again, was to improve the capacity to respond to sudden change.

Zhang explains: "The internet means you cannot be complacent. It reduces distance to the customer to zero. Traditional continuity is broken, and the outdated structures vanish. Avoiding new ideas is effectively giving up. Not using the internet means death."

The new business structure created users loyal to the brand. This is the basis for its "win-win model". Haier acquired new insights and best practices — but there was still much to be learned and improved upon.

Like any reasonably sized company back in the day, Haier acquired new IT systems each year. By 2006, it had accumulated about 600. It was a total mess. The systems couldn't talk to one another, and it was almost impossible to collate information. More problems became apparent with the introduction of smaller, independent Haier companies. Information-sharing was nowhere near the desired level.

Haier had been undergoing organisational change for almost 10 years, but Zhang realised that the process hadn't gone far enough. His response was to declare a period of Information Technology Reconstruction. Within 1,000 days, 2,500 processes were to be changed. The goal was not just to get rid of some of the systems, it was also to embed IT into the Haier fabric. This was one of the first times that the company adopted Zhang's "Internet thinking".

A visitor to the modern Haier factories would notice the results of that internet thinking. At each workplace, screens display all relevant information for employees. How many products have they made? How many have been sold? How many orders are there? How close are they to the daily target? How much money have they earned? All this and more can be established at the touch of a button. Those working in the factories aren't the only ones who can access the information; it is available to everyone. This made for better-informed choices, and since all those factors have an influence on compensation, having more information is a powerful tool. It makes better entrepreneurs.

The company had moved away from traditional hierarchy and wasn't about to backtrack. Thousands of SBUs had been tied directly to the market, increasing Haier's flexibility. At the time this was a great step forward, and the best possible solution. But time never stands still, and a couple of years later the solution was no longer up to scratch. Zhang continued his search for better ways forward.

Rendanheyi: A Force to be Reckoned With
Haier's organising model, Rendanheyi — which roughly translates as "a tight coupling of the value created for users with the value received by employees" — was developed to help the company adapt to the digital age.

That loose translation could be more precisely paraphrased to read: "What is valued most by the customer is best compensated." Through the creation of a network of autonomous teams, Haier puts itself in direct contact with its customers to improve the delivery of products and services. The Rendanheyi model has undergone multiple evolutions since it was first introduced in 2005, drawing on value chain theories. The value chain is a tool for disaggregating a company into strategically relevant activities. This allows focus to be placed on specific activities that result in higher prices or lower costs. Michael Porter had inspired Haier and the company started to organise businesses into market chains of Strategic Business units, or SBUs.

Haier intended to monetise the transactions taking place in that market chain. The result was that all SBUs became both buyers and sellers of intermediate goods. Tensions were created due to difficulties with internal transactions. That, and the corporate desire for all units to face the market, inspired Haier to replace its siloed SBU structure with a team-based organisational model called Zi Zhu Jing Ying Ti

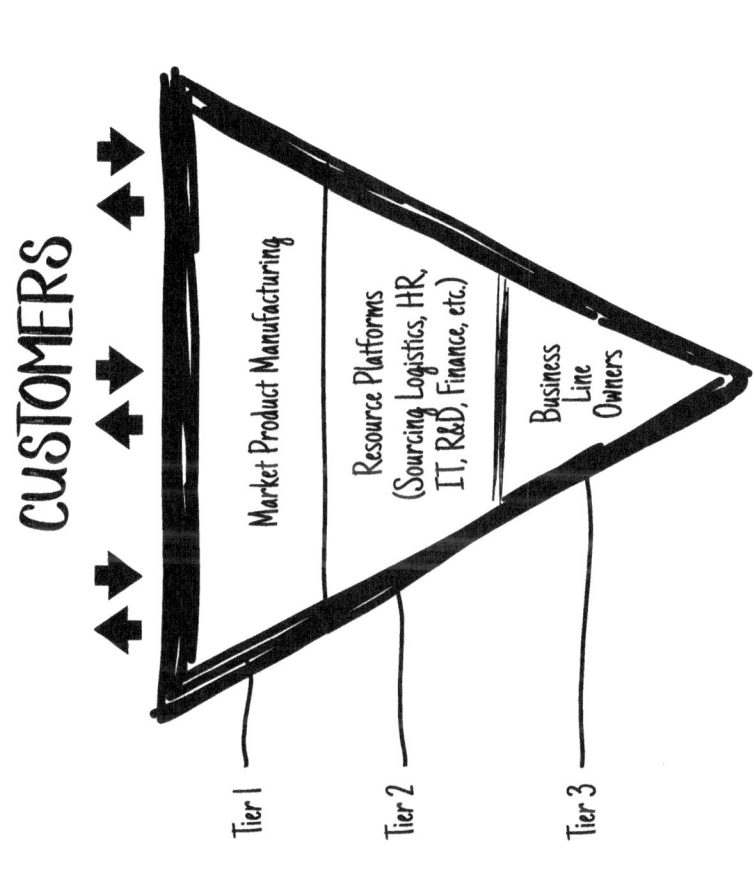

(pronounce at your own risk) or ZZJYT.

Some 2,000 ZZJYT units were created, and organised into an inverted, three-tiered pyramid. Tier-1 ZZJYTs consisted of marketing, product and manufacturing units performing core activities. They were in direct contact with the customers who provided them with input. Instead of being at the end of the creation process, the customers were placed at the start, or in a way, at the top of the pyramid. Tier-2 units delivered support services, such as logistics, HR, IT, R&D and finance. Their role was to support the Tier-1 units. Tier-3 units were intended to provide other ZZJYT units with strategic direction.

The units received decision rights favouring entrepreneurial flair and innovation. An internal labour market was created, and there were regular, transparent reviews of leadership positions. This brought about a radical change in decision-making and authority that lured employees who could sense opportunity. They would be encouraged to become entrepreneurs by bidding for work.

Haier needed to empower its employees to meet the ever-growing demands of users. The ZZJYTs operated within company boundaries, but with the autonomy to run their own profit and loss accounts, hire staff, and make their decisions. Anyone with a good idea for a product could propose the establishment of a ZZJYT. The ZZJYT model increased freedom, but units were still in the organisational silos. Each had a direct relationship with its customers and was motivated to maintain and improve that relationship by providing high quality products or services.

Employees became entrepreneurs, with earnings based on sales and created value. One simple metric was central to everything else: was the user willing to buy the product? The better the product, the more value it adds for the customer. Internal relations were also changing. ZZJYTs could identify alternative suppliers for services such as HR and legal, and take advantage of better or cheaper options. This changed the way business was conducted. Previously, it had been enough for a designer, for instance, to do their work and no more. Now, if their design ended up in a product that didn't sell, their efforts were all for nothing. If it was a winner, they stood to benefit.

It's all about keeping the customer happy.

• • •

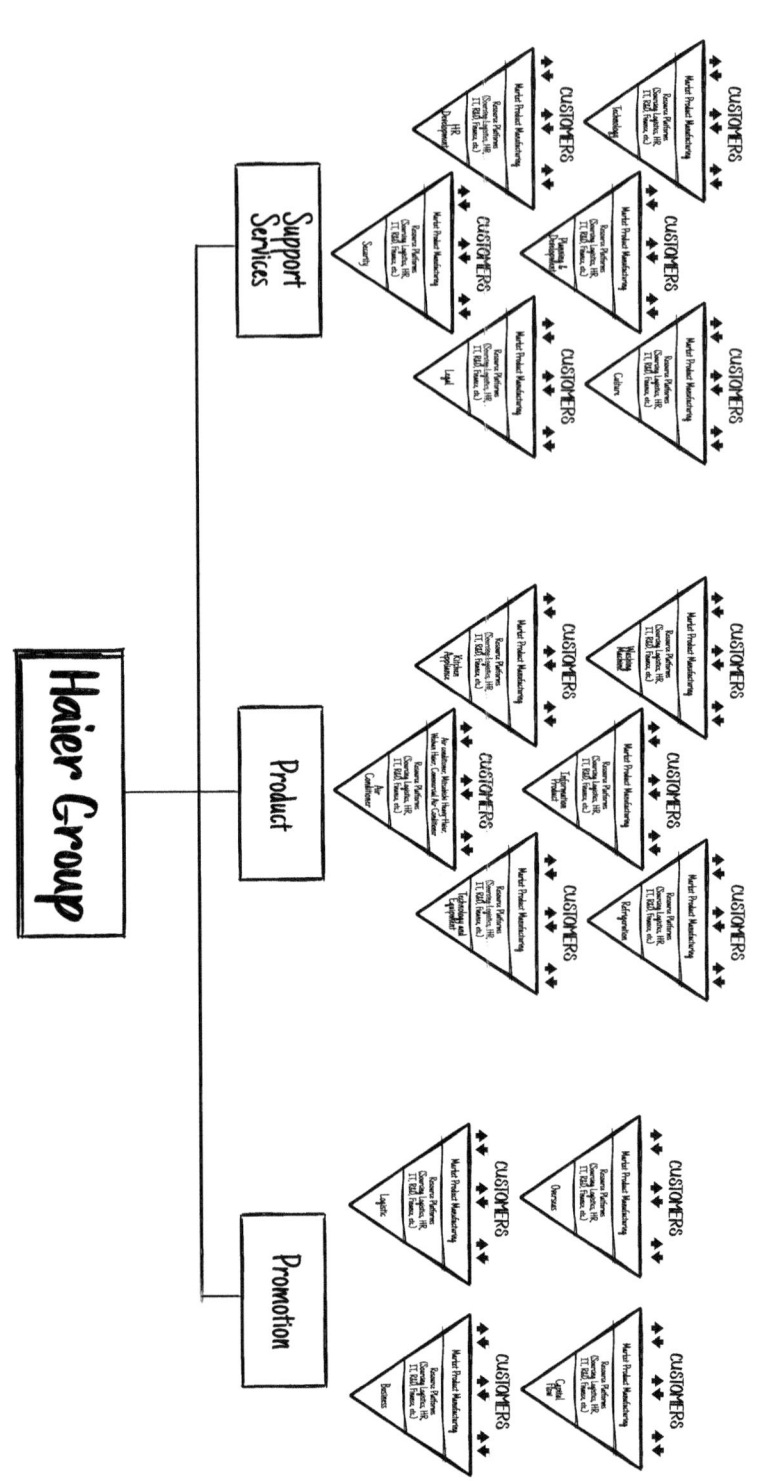

REBEL LOG, SOMEWHERE IN THE MAZE: Transparency is a concept that resonates within Haier like a gong struck in a forest clearing. The focus demands our attention, and we peer into an increasingly clear pool of wisdom. I believe we're starting to get somewhere.

Rebel One, out

Intersecting Dimensions and Symmetries

As the world became increasingly interconnected, Haier wanted to unlock more entrepreneurial energy. By creating more transparency, having systems that could communicate with each other — and by putting that information in the hands of employees — it unleashed a spurt of creativity.

To maintain motivation, reward mechanisms were fine-tuned. The more value a ZZJYT created, the bigger its share of total profits. Haier, the corporation, might receive a smaller piece — but of a larger pie. It proved to be the first iteration of Haier's innovative management model: Rendanheyi version 1.0. Zhang notes of the model's introduction in 2005: "Performance didn't pick up immediately. We had two listed companies in China and our stock price did not grow significantly. Some of the shareholders expressed concern. It took a long time for this model to succeed, because it takes time to change people's mindsets. Previously, execution had been the most important thing. But someone good at this may not be the right one to start a business. These people worked in siloed departments and didn't know who their users were, or how to engage them. As they transitioned to the microenterprise model, they needed to take time to think about their end-users."

Undeterred by the chorus of critics, Zhang stuck to his guns and went on to refine Rendanheyi. By 2016, the cumulative effect was clear: revenue and profit growth were on a tear — and the stock price doubled in 2016 and 2017.

AIR

'Today, I would like to compare Haier to a cloud. Even the most expansive sea has boundaries, but even the smallest cloud can connect a million endpoints. Open, open, and stay open.'

Zhang Ruimin, 2014*

*From essay: Break open a Dust Particle and release the three-thousand-fold Sutra Scroll
(Full essay in Appendix 2)

> REBEL LOG: Captain Zhang is toying with time travel ... in a manner of speaking. Modern is as modern does. What held true a few decades ago is laughably out-of-date now, and for Zhang there is only one sure passage through a cluttered firmament: to move with the times. Haier has done it before, will do it again, continues to do it each day — but the challenge of moving with the times was never going to be easy...
>
> **Rebel One, out.**

Unleashing the Potential of Rendanheyi 2.0 (2012–2019)

We wonder how the managers of the Qingdao Refrigerator Factory would feel if they were to revisit their old stamping ground. In less than 30 years, evolution has stepped-up apace, taking Haier from a small, poorly functioning manufacturing firm to a world-class company full of motivated entrepreneurs focused on fulfilling the "customer's need". No more pissing on the factory floor.

By introducing the ZZJYTs, Haier had managed to unleash some of the entrepreneurial energy within its employees. Haier was nimbler than ever. However, Zhang's earlier remark still held true: "There is no such thing as a successful company, only one that successfully moves with the times." And time was about to catch up with it again.

The ZZJYTs had been a bold step to leaving bureaucracy behind. In practice, it became clear the structure didn't solve all problems. After experimenting with several variations of ZZJYT, it became apparent that Tier-1 units, those who were in direct contact with the customers, especially lacked the decision-making rights needed to bring new products and services to market. The targets and responsibilities individual ZZJYTs had were still decided in a hierarchical way. Which caused a slow response to customer feedback, and was worrisome for the future of Haier. Feedback still needed to be funnelled through the (sometimes dense) hierarchical structure and silos, causing Haier to struggle to keep up with its customers.

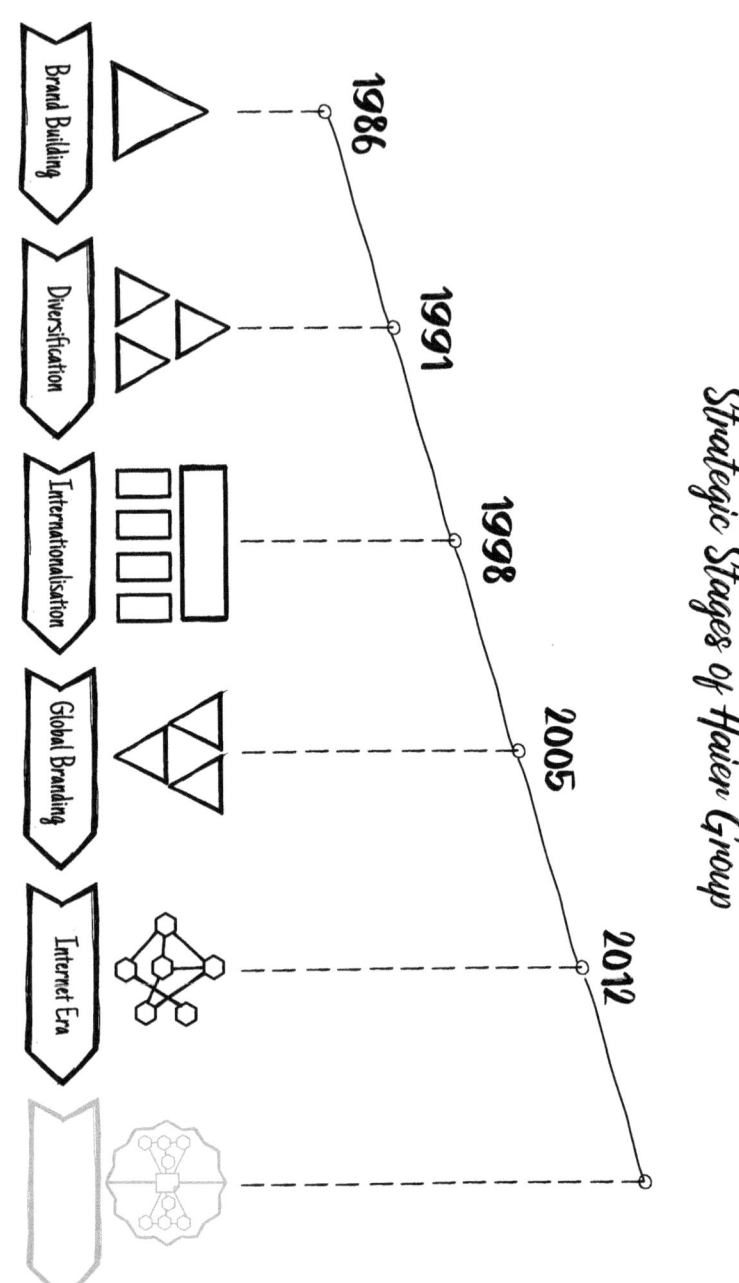

Farewell to Bureaucracy — and a Glimpse of the Future

In 2012, Haier introduced a radical organisational change, the next step in its evolutionary journey that would help it to rid itself of the bureaucratic devil once and for all. To keep up with the times, and to solve the tensions that arose in the ZZJYT model, Zhang realised the need to prepare the company for the Internet of Things, or IoT. His logic was simple: to satisfy customer needs now that the world had become more interconnected, Haier itself needed to become more interconnected. It needed to become a networked enterprise.

In this era, the management model would really blossom. And the entire Haier Group grew enormously. In the past years, 24,000 employees have joined Haier and tens of thousands more started working with the company in less direct ways. The question "How does Haier work?" has proven to be a tough one to answer. Much that has been written remains vague and intangible. Let's get into the nitty gritty and dive into anecdotes and stories shared by the employees themselves.

• • •

Turbulence, Trust, and Microenterprises

Zhang had spent years at the helm, and in rough seas. Under his guidance, the good ship Haier had survived and transformed itself into a gigantic tanker — one that seemed unsinkable. However, like anyone familiar with the maiden voyage of the Titanic, Zhang saw reason for caution. This was to be the era in which Haier would transform the ungainly tanker into thousands of smaller craft, more able to avoid icebergs and navigate bad weather.

Even though the management structures of the previous eras had been progressive for their times, they were still quite familiar and often copied from, or inspired by, other organisations. But now the time of familiar management structures was coming to an end: no more bureaucracy, not even any managers. Haier's new structure would enable the business to operate — borderless, leaderless, and limitless — and respond to disruptive changes of the IoT.

The 2,000 ZZJYTs were transformed into 4,000 microenterprises, organised into six main platforms (White Goods, Investment & Incubation, Financial Holdings, Real Estate, Culture, and Shared Services). Within the microenterprises, employees — or, more accurately, entrepreneurs — would form miniature autonomous companies. As with any small company, those people working in it decided how they wanted to do things. They have their own profit and loss statements, and there was no more hierarchical structure.

Haier turned its giant organisation into thousands of small start-ups. Instead of having one cumbersome company, there were now thousands of energetic start-ups that wanted to compete, collaborate, and invent new products based on the needs of their customers. It was as if they changed their organisation into the start-up ecosystem of Tel Aviv's thriving tech scene.

Microenterprises had far-reaching decision-making authority to develop and market innovative products and services. They'd run the show and could decide who to hire and fire, make their own decisions, and distribute their own profits.

Within the new network-like organisational structure, these microenterprises would have the freedom to do things the way they wanted to, and still have access to internal resources. They could collaborate with any other microenterprise, with relationships based on contracts, not hierarchy.

It proved to be the fertile ground needed to transform Haier's employees into real entrepreneurs. And even though the creation of the thousands of microenterprises had caught the attention of the outside world, more change was needed. The enormity of the resulting upheaval, and the probable consequences, were hard for many to grasp.

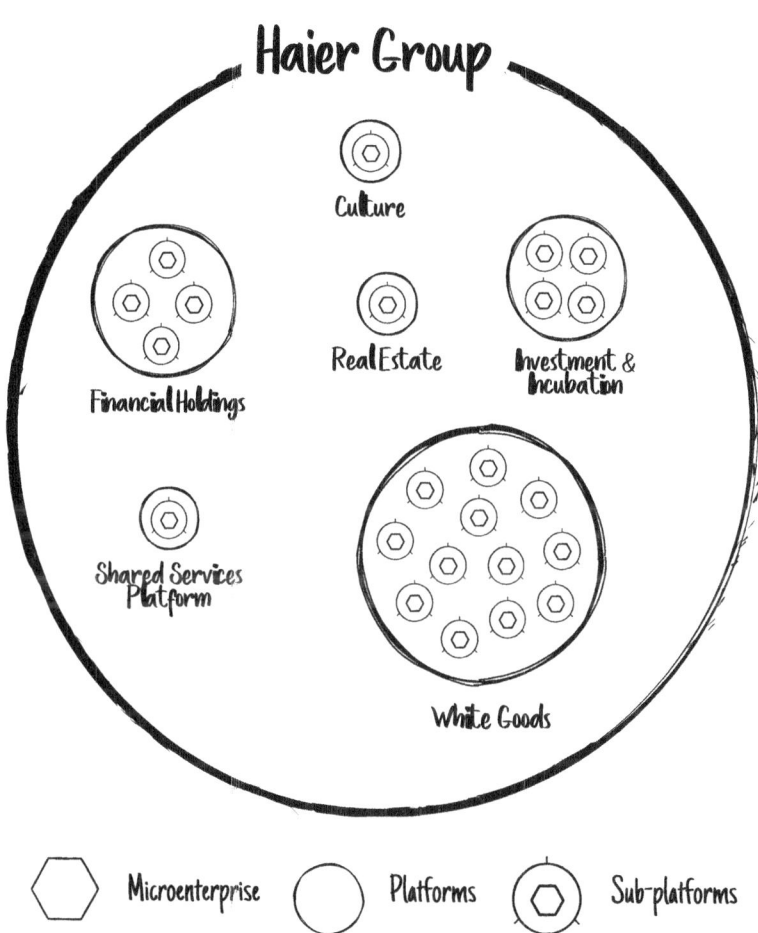

Letting Go of the Past
Things became clearer when 12,000 middle managers were given a choice: be fired, or become entrepreneurs in the new mould. Zhang has described this as the hardest decision he has had to make — but a necessary one. "I want to turn this business into an ecosystem of many small organisations," he said. "So, what would be the role of a middle layer of management?"

Qi Yupeng, one of the microenterprise leaders within the RRS Logistics platform, explained to us how big a shock this was. "In the beginning," Qi said, "I couldn't understand it. I felt a lot of resources were going to waste, we were throwing out the core. But now I can see why this had to happen. Those who stayed with the company were aligned with Haier's principles, and I think that was very important."

• • •

The Role of Top Leadership: Haier's Architects
The changes to this new organisational form had been initiated by an organ that was inherited from previous eras: Haier's board. It is the closest thing to executive management, but its execution is different to many others. Its goal is to enable the microenterprises and give them the freedom and access to the resources they need to thrive. This is achieved by setting-up the playing field and deciding the rules of the game. These leaders ensure the availability of the necessary structures, systems, and culture of entrepreneurship. You could see them as architects, and like true architects they design and shape their world. But they can't create that world on their own. It's their responsibility to respond to external threats and opportunities, and to serve as facilitators of internal operations for that design to become successful.

It's easy to interpret the role of the board as that of an authoritarian body that can decide whatever it wants, as is often the case in more traditional organisations. Haier seems to be different. The people we interviewed sketched a situation which almost perfectly matched scientific research on this type of leadership position in other progressive organisations. That research shows that for leaders to be successful, they must demonstrate a willingness to ask for input, and the ability to listen. This phenomenon is called "Emergent Leadership". The board, or anyone else, for that matter, needs to have the ability to "steer things in the right direction without the authority to do so, through social competence." [9]

Luckily for Zhang, his years of experience and bold decisions had granted him a reputation and stature that meant he did not need to worry about his ideas being heard, or people not following him. Building that reputation had not been easy.

In 1984, Zhang literally decided how the hammer was swung. But it doesn't seem that he was an authoritarian figure, even then. He was trying to do what was best for the employees — sometimes using unusual methods...

∙ ∙ ∙

> **Zhang Taking One for the Team**
> It was the 1984 Spring Festival, when the factory did not have money to pay salaries, let alone provide gifts such as the traditional presentation of five hair-tail fish. Zhang was forced to take a loan from a neighbouring village. "But this isn't the complete story," noted Yang, our guide. "Zhang had to almost beg, but the mayor would only grant the loan if Zhang would drink a glass of strong alcohol with him. Zhang doesn't drink, but so as not to offend the village head — and potentially put the loan at risk — he tossed it back anyway, and returned with the money."

Servant Leadership

Zhang isn't your everyday CEO, but he, like most of his opposite numbers in other companies, is still the one who officially holds the most power. How he wields that power is what is significant, and different. Over the years, he too has evolved from boss to coach. Initially, he had to be more authoritarian to encourage people to change. Employees came to trust his intuition. He doesn't tell people how to solve their problems, he asks questions to help them gain the insights they need. This helps them to solve future problems autonomously, and, hopefully, support others.

Yu Mingyong, one of the main researchers of the Haier Model Research Institute that aims to optimise the organisational system, clarified the role of Zhang and the board. "The top leadership team members are resource providers, and they empower and enable people," Yu said. "We call them 'servant leaders', or 'help-providers'." These supportive leaders help employees explore and develop. This calls for humility, nerve, and the genuine desire to winkle-out smart ideas from the people working at the pointy end. The servant leader is likely to understand that traditional directive leadership is mere vanity in this fast-changing world of shifting consumer preferences. Leaders are better off asking how they can help employees than telling them what to do.

It's hard to improve on his wording: "What it comes down to is this: employees who do the actual work of your organisation often know better than you how to do a great job. Respecting their ideas and encouraging them to try new approaches encourages employees to bring more of themselves to work." Leaders would do well to create a low-risk space for employees to experiment, and in doing so push the boundaries. As Zhang Ruimin says: "We want everyone at Haier to be a servant leader. Soon after we acquired the domestic appliance division of General Electric, I visited one of the plants. I told the 500 managers that we were not going to lead them. Our users would lead. It is the sole reason we need to be so close to our customers. My advice to leaders who want to make such a transformation is this: be sure you are willing to give up your power."

The role of the Haier board has, like everything else, moved to its current form over time. It has been transformed from a top-down, co-ordinated company to one where active collaboration is the norm. That division of leadership and roles is to be found in other progressive organisations as well [9][10].

By refusing to set the course, top management freed employees from bureaucratic structures. It has created a scenario where microenterprises could set a course for themselves. It wasn't enough. To really make the microenterprises thrive, enablers were needed. At Haier, those enablers are called platforms.

• • •

> REBEL LOG, WE APPEAR TO BE ON SOME SORT OF PLATFORM: *There are many levels here, and we sometimes have trouble locating our position regarding the Haier nerve centre. But this is mostly down to our linguistic limitations. We are starting to appreciate that the communal intelligence and collaboration of this organisation are vital to its ongoing upward trajectory.*
>
> **Rebel One, out.**

Zhang Ruimin believes that "either you own a platform, or you will be owned by a platform". But what exactly are platforms, and what are their roles?

What defines them is their role in value creation. Platforms facilitate partnerships and enable others to create value — and charge a small fee in the process. Companies which have taken a more "platformish" approach have often proved successful. Uber, Amazon, Airbnb and Apple have benefitted from it. Whether the actors operate a transport system, a delivery website, help you to book your next vacation or create an app marketplace, the platforms have the same role. They facilitate recognition of the business as a brand that customers know and trust.

Haier platforms provide support, resources, knowledge, and guidance. It's their responsibility to create and maintain an impeccable brand. They determine consistent strategies, ensure microenterprises aren't building the same products, and allocate funds. All platforms have a leader, and as you would expect from any good leader, nobody is forced to follow. The main tools to influence strategy and direction? Inspiring others to follow or invest in initiatives that fit their strategy. The latter option entails the formulation of specific goals and allows entrepreneurs to bid on them via the internal marketplace. It's not taken for granted that these plans will be accepted. It's important that ideas and philosophies are supported by entrepreneurs. Whether that is the case becomes apparent during the bidding process, which we'll come back to later.

Haier's platforms can be divided into two categories, Industry Platforms and Shared Service Platforms.

Industry Platforms

Industry platforms bring together microenterprises working on similar products. They incubate and support the microenterprises.

The industry platforms form a bridge between microenterprises that work in similar sectors by facilitating the exchange of resources.

The leaders of the platforms have their own goals, formulated to become the best within a certain industry, such as the Refrigeration platform "becoming the world leader in smart appliances". The head of the platform reached out to those microenterprises that could provide specific technology thus far lacking, such as app developers and network experts. Besides acquiring these additional resources, leaders help microenterprises to identify new market opportunities, and/or new ways to collaborate or integrate with others.

Platform leaders cannot fall back on the old standard practices; they do not have formal authority. Instead, they convince others by demonstrating the benefits of their strategy. When the refrigeration platform leader tried to introduce frost-free technology — which required a hefty investment — he could assume only a facilitating role. The microenterprises make the final decisions. "I helped," he said, "but they planned and executed the job."[11] The platform leaders must listen to the needs of the microenterprises. If the suggested strategies don't align, they are free to start looking for other work. A new strategy will usually emerge.

Hamel and Zanini noted that co-ordination often means sacrificing speed and responsiveness for greater efficiency. Zhang believes that such trade-offs are best made close to the customer, by microenterprises that are free to choose when to collaborate and when to go it alone.[11]

Platform leaders are entrepreneurs and facilitators. This option to switch roles based on context — instead of what has been written in a job description — enables Haier to be quick to react. Yu compared it with other management philosophies. "Other organisational structures are mainly about employee and employer," he said. "Rendanheyi is about platform and entrepreneur. The idea is that everyone can be a CEO. Within bureaucracies, mobility and co-operation are usually low. Their organisational structures allow people to have some flexibility to move around a bit, but Rendanheyi encourages employees to keep adjusting to their surroundings."

RRS Platform

These Industry platforms have often gradually evolved from a microenterprise that produces to a platform that provides. Or, as Zhang would put it, they transferred from being owned by a platform to owning a platform.

This is an evolutionary journey that has been accomplished almost entirely by RRS Logistics. Hu Qingmin shared his story. "When e-commerce came in, we entered the second phase: becoming a logistics company which provides services to other brands. It's mainly about supply chain. Later we built a platform that is also about interaction with users, such as delivery installation. We specialise in the 'last kilometre', the place where our company interfaces with the users. We're trying to create communities and provide better user experience."

RRS Logistics, which evolved from Haier's logistics department in the bureaucratic days, became a microenterprise, then a platform. Nowadays it consists of smaller platforms such as Warehouses, Truck Lines, Distribution, Delivery, and Installation. All these platforms do the same thing: they facilitate business as the brand that customers know and trust. Whether those customers are other platforms, or customers waiting for their packages, doesn't affect that.

The RRS platform directly employs over 2,000 people, but they are not the ones that create the largest part of value or income. That lies in the provision of services, and facilitating business. It's an open platform, an incubator. The users place the orders and make appointments, and the products are moved out to a smaller warehouse nearer to the end-user's location.

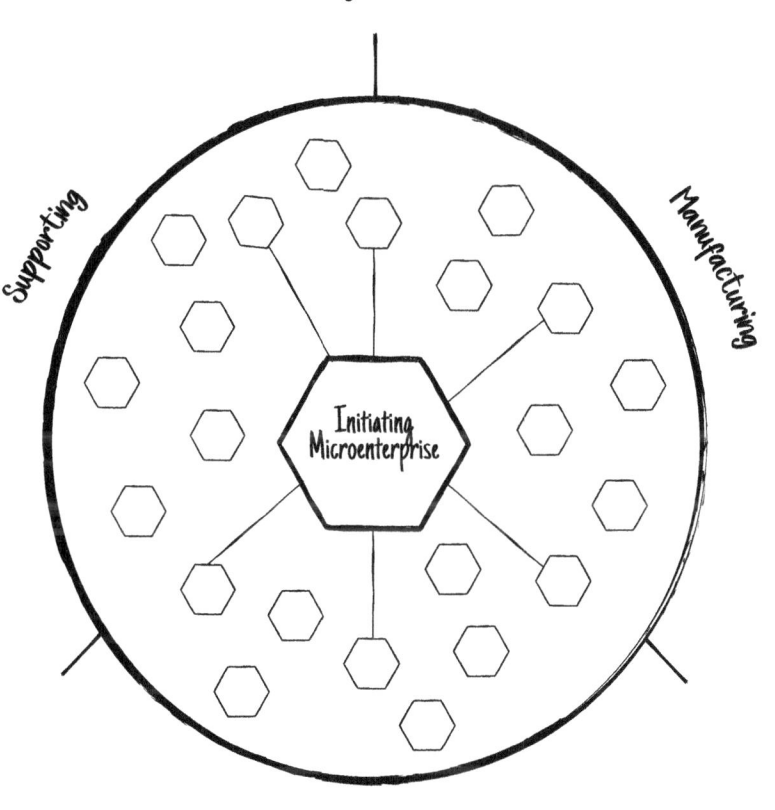

From there, one of the 100,000 external vehicle microenterprises — or one of the 200,000 delivery workers and installers connected to one of the RRS platforms — picks up the product and delivers it. If required, they will install it as well.

It's like Uber: entrepreneurs have an app and can select suitable "rides". With more experience, they can expand their services and become salespeople as well. RRS Logistics ranks microenterprise progress using feedback from end-users about the quality of service. The duty of microenterprises and platforms to communicate and interact with one another does not slow the process. Since all microenterprises have skin in the game and depend on good reviews, motivation is guaranteed. Swift delivery is one of the surest ways to a user's heart. Delivery time depends on the region, of course, and in the e-commerce stage it could take up to 96 hours. Now, the delivery arrives within 12 hours — 24 if the customer doesn't live in the city.

RRS Logistics enables others to start and grow business, but it doesn't distinguish between internal and external companies. It isn't about who does what, it's about who does it best.

Any money earned by RRS flows back to the platform, and is used to finance expansion and investment in new platforms, microenterprises or other business opportunities. Hu explains: "We do not have real competitors. Some specialised microenterprises are better at providing certain services — delivering medicines, for example. But they probably won't beat us, because we have a better business model. If they should turn out to be better, Haier would probably invest in them instead of us."

Investing Role of Platforms
Investing is one of the most important roles these platforms have. Platform leaders often act as venture capitalists and strive to invest in microenterprises that can help them realise their goals. By setting clear targets and offering rewards and resources, including funding, platform leaders try to encourage existing microenterprises to help them. And

if such a microenterprise doesn't exist, entrepreneurs within Haier can create one.

The investor-investee relationship between platforms and microenterprises usually entails a Value Adjustment Mechanism, or VAM, contract. These form a core element in Haier's remuneration mechanism, something we will dive into later in this book.

More experimental and innovative investing agreements prescribe basic living expenses, employee share creation, and exit and dissolution strategies. To minimise risk and incentivise competitiveness, a common requirement is for new microenterprises to bring in funding, either their own resources or from outside investors.

Shared Service Providers
The other category of platform at Haier: the Shared Service platform. It provides administrative, finance, HR, and legal services. That way, microenterprises do not need to worry about creating their salary system or recruitment department, they simply sign a contract with one of the service providers for said services instead.

Of course, these platforms have their own growth targets, and will be held accountable for the services they provide. Normally they focus on internal delivery — but that can change.

From Back Office to Thriving Business
We spoke to the friendly and smart Sun Lei, she had joined Haier in 1997 and had witnessed many of the changes that occurred, and to Chen Jiao, a more reserved 38-year-old who joined in 2008 and quickly found his way around. Both work on the Haier Financial platform. It has become a strategic partner for the microenterprises instead of a number-crunching department. It provides services to almost all Haier's Smart Home units. Almost all? As Sun explains: "If they don't like our product or the quality of our services, they can find someone else to help them — and even look outside Haier." In practice, this rarely happens, and most are happy with the Finance Platform.

By automating the system, making agreements with preferred suppliers, and using blockchain technology to increase the transparency and speed of transactions, an attractive resource has been put in place. "Entrepreneurs can use our system to reserve a car, for example," Sun explains. "The system can review whether a project or microenterprise still has enough money, and this can all be checked and approved more swiftly than before. There is no need to pay in advance or worry about reimbursement. We have a Three Zero Goal: Zero Distance from our users, Zero Signatures, and Zero Delay."

By keeping these principles in mind, Sun Lei, Chen Jiao and their colleagues managed to make financing a smoother operation, more convenient and efficient. At a regular company, finance staff usually handle 3,000-5,000 receipts or bills per person, per month; the Haier platform handles 30,000. Haier uses this to its advantage. As with RRS, the Finance platform has started offering its services extramurally. It now has over 1,000 client companies across 31 countries, and has become a profit-making entity in its own right.

Haier's HR Platform

Microenterprises are connected to Haier's HR Platform, providing services to other microenterprises. It's as if a start-up hired an outside HR expert to help them with certain tasks. Hu Wang Hongwei, leader of one microenterprise, provides HR services to the Xingchu Internet of Food microenterprise. The cheerful 45-year-old has been working for Haier for 19 years. "Our microenterprise supports others with all sorts of HR tasks," she said. "We help set up talent pools, design the right incentive schemes, and help microenterprises to experiment." Service providers may well come from outside Haier. When Xingchu and Hu's microenterprises decided to collaborate, they signed a contract in which the incentives of both parties were aligned. Hu: "If we create a talent pool, we'll try to find the right people to join us. When those people end up joining a microenterprise and eventually reach their goals — perhaps even outperform them — we share in the value that is created."

The HR microenterprise has an incentive to help others. "Our members join with other microenterprises to find talent and coach for success. In a way, we benefit from the success of other microenterprises." As their contacts are aligned with the success of the HR microenterprise, all are motivated. They are quick to help a struggling member. Sharing progress and ascertaining how colleagues are doing — taking relevant financial information and the root cause of any problems into account — helps to stimulate positive behaviour. Individuals and microenterprises such as the HR microenterprise are connected to different parts of the organisation. This allows information and best practices to spread rapidly.

'The World is Our HR Department'
Haier's approach to HR avoids centralisation. "Haier used to have HR and compensation departments with 2,300 employees," Zhang told us. "Now there are fewer than 100. We'll soon be down to 20. They are now simply providing a platform as a service. Previously, one would ask HR to recruit certain talent. The search would begin, and the pay scale would be set. This is no longer needed. The value created for the user is aligned with the platform's income. In traditional companies, there's a disconnect between value created and value received, because compensation is predetermined."

Some of the old HR tasks have been taken over by smaller microenterprises. Some have simply become obsolete. Haier is getting closer to the point where there is no traditional HR department, but the work will still be done — just in a more flexible and dynamic way. Or as Zhang puts it: "The world is our HR department."

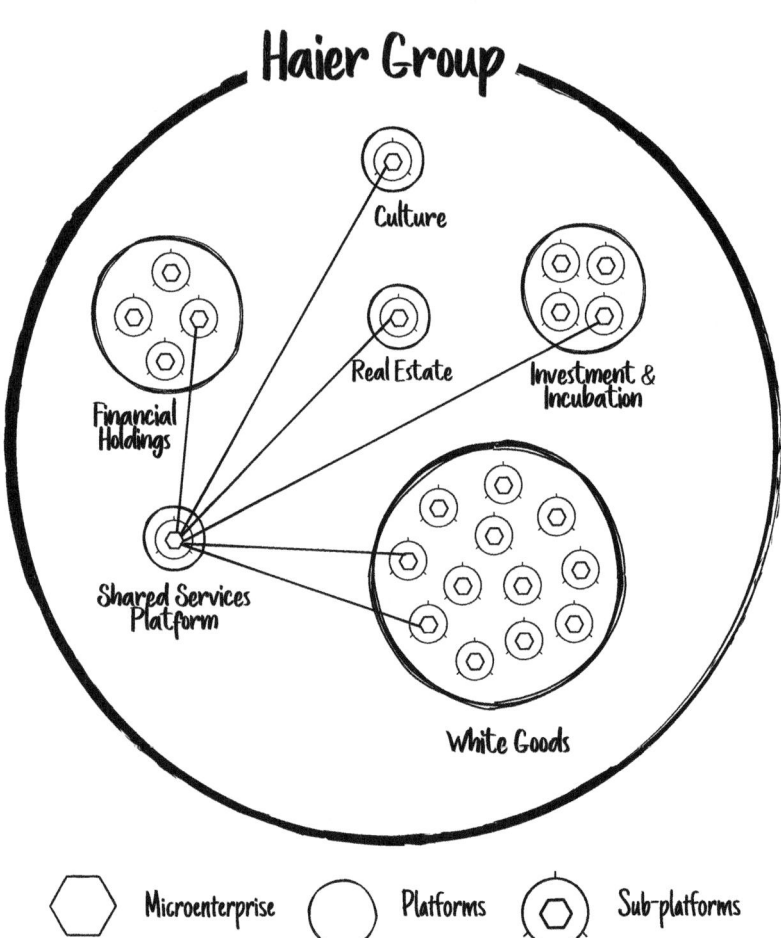

UX Platform

Some of the Shared Service platforms operate in similar ways to HR & Finance. Others, however, provide more specialised services such as Smart Manufacturing and Cloud Services. These platforms merit in-depth study, but let's focus on one for now. The actors have a major influence on the rest of the organisation and are critical for maintaining that all-important "zero-distance to users".

In the User Experience (UX) Cloud platform, the "cloud" refers to online servers that connect the various IoT devices. "It connects the enterprise with its users," UX platform leader Li Huagang explained. "It's a place where microenterprises can interact with their users, and where they can grow their user base. In the past, the relationship with a customer ended when they completed their purchase. Today, we try to turn them into lifelong users of our brand." The User Experience platform combines market intelligence, direct communication with customers and data gathered by the smart products sold to better understand user needs. In some cases, there is improvement even after a product has been sold — because some things can't be foreseen. "During the Covid-19 pandemic, we learned that our users had different needs. They wanted to wash their clothes and facemasks on a short drying cycle for disinfection. We hadn't equipped our machines with such a programme — because nobody needed it. Since our washing machine has been connected to the Experience cloud, we have added the programme. The platform helps us to understand and respond to such emerging needs."

• • •

> REBEL LOG, HOMING IN ON A BEACON: More on the wildlife… or so we thought. After being thoroughly confused by the fish, birds have now been brought into the equation. Or rather, their accommodation has. We are no longer surprised — by anything — so we are keeping our eyes and ears open, hoping to learn more.
>
> **Rebel One, out.**

Examples are plentiful, and boundaries between users and platform are sometimes invisible. This raises the question: Who really came up with the product in the first place? Sometimes ideas from users are so good they just have to be implemented. A customer once shared an idea for a new product on one of Haier's forums. The user didn't like the way most air-conditioning units looked: too big and lumpy. An elegant shape would be more pleasing to the eye, and he had a suggestion. The Olympic Games were due to be held in Beijing — and the Bird's Nest stadium could be a useful model.

The Bird's Nest — the Beijing National Stadium — became a symbol of Chinese pride and prestige when it was constructed for the Summer Olympics. The idea to incorporate its features into an aircon unit gained traction on the forum. Within months, an air-conditioner sharing design features with the iconic stadium was on sale. It was a huge success; thousands were sold within days. Haier does not simply look at its customers as buyers, it recognises them as co-creators and resource-providers.

The User Experience platform actively searches for that sort of information and shares it with the network. User needs arise, and microenterprises fulfil them. In some cases, the platform takes a more active role, that of opportunity creator, and formulates goals for other microenterprises to bid on. They basically say: "We know what users need. Who wants to build it for them and share the profits with us?" The UX and other marketing platforms can be seen as the company's biggest enablers. Without their ability to connect to users and build relationships, Haier would not be the powerhouse that it is today. The platforms further close the gap. Haier makes sure of market validation before anything is built, whether it's an air-conditioning unit or a shop that transforms into an online store. The variety of services being offered by microenterprises on the platform is wide, no matter if they provide blockchain technology, market intelligence, host platforms, create crowdfunding campaigns or gather insights while repairing a clogged-up washing machine. They all focus on building relationships and learning from users to take advantage of their feedback and seize opportunities.

An example of just that is COSMOPlat. Haier has invested in developing automated, mass customisation capabilities to manufacture bespoke products at scale. Through COSMOPlat, customers purchase appliances in a variety of design and colour combinations, and watch them being built on a live-streaming app. A single automated process logs the order, designs the appliance, requests components, manufactures the unit and delivers it to the customer, providing remote performance tracking.

• • •

The Haier platforms have replaced many traditional middle management and functional roles. They provide microenterprises with access to resources and expect the same microenterprises to ensure brand quality. They are responsible for the co-ordination and communication needed to build successful partnerships. The platform leaders aren't involved in how microenterprises do their job. Instead, they listen to their users, the microenterprises, and try to take away any "pain" they are experiencing.

REBEL LOG, IN THE HAIER IDEAS LAB: There is no fear of failure here, only a fear of stagnation. Boldly trying out radical ideas is standard practice — and it's increasingly evident why...

Rebel One, out.

Microenterprises, Haier's Entrepreneurial Units

Now that the playing field was clear and level, and the supporting systems in place, the microenterprises could make their appearance. Some 4000 of these virtual companies were created when Haier first moved to this new iteration of the Rendanheyi model, Rendanheyi 2.0.

These microenterprises would become the entrepreneurial units that allowed Haier to thrive. Their main objective was to find opportunities, and the best way to do that was by getting as close as possible to the end-users. It's vital to know what problems are being experienced. Only then can units start experimenting, innovating, creating and refining products. If this is done successfully, the product could achieve "hit" status, meaning that sales go through the roof, bringing big profits to that microenterprise, the platform — and Haier.

Within those thousands of microenterprises are tens of thousands of entrepreneurs, the people closest to the customer, and according to Haier's philosophy of being as close to the user as possible, they are the most important actors in this play. According to Zhang, introducing the microenterprises was just the ticket to fully unleash the pent-up creative power of the workforce.

Haier has transformed itself into a "start-ups ecosystem" that is performing very well. [12] The success rate of start-ups in China is on average 10 percent; those incubated by Haier have a success rate of 49.

Two Types of Microenterprise

Microenterprises are geared to fulfil the needs of their customers — whether they are people buying their products or other microenterprises buying services. There are two types of microenterprise: User-facing microenterprises and supporting microenterprises.

Back in 2012, there were roughly 200 of these user-facing microenterprises. They are in direct contact with outside customers. The remaining 3,800 or so supporting microenterprises (internally referred to as Node microenterprises, but since all microenterprises are technically nodes within the networked organisation, we'll stick with the term supporting microenterprises.) provide design, production, R&D, and logistics services.

Together these groups unite via contracting and form smaller, internal networks to collaborate on product creation.

User, or customer-facing microenterprises, could be shops in rural areas or shopping mall franchises. They could be market intelligence experts, repair specialists, or the hosts of online forums. They are responsible for identifying problems and solving them by initiating a new product and delivering it to the user. And to do that, they sometimes go to extraordinary lengths.

> ***Mosquitos ...***
>
> *Microenterprises are known for going the extra mile to make sure their customers are happy. When the Ministry of Health of a certain country conducted an epidemic survey and needed laptops with built-in microscopes for on-the-spot analysis, the necessary microenterprises gathered to create a prototype. When the customer came to Haier for a demonstration, the test called for a live mosquito. It was winter in Qingdao, and there were none to be found. Most companies would have asked if there was a suitable substitute. Not this microenterprise. They found out that the Shenzhen epidemic prevention station had stored some mosquito eggs — and sent a courier to fetch them. The eggs were duly hatched, and the customer was able to test the product. The laptop passed the test, the microenterprise won the bid, and a bulk order was placed, meaning a lot of work for all the microenterprises involved. Mission accomplished [6].*

Structure and Rights of a Microenterprise

Even though there are thousands of microenterprises, you'd struggle to find two that are the same. All of them have their unique quirks and do some things their own way. Nevertheless, there are some shared characteristics.

As with the Platforms, each microenterprise has a leader. Their role is to facilitate processes in such a way that the microenterprise reaches its goal. Other than that, microenterprises can organise themselves however they see fit. Sometimes that means they're run by one person, and sometimes by many hundreds. The entrepreneurs decide what works best. And if their customers are better served if their microenterprise employs 150 people... well, they do just that.

And they can do that, because microenterprises have their own profit and loss statements. This enables them to spend money without having to get approval. They, and only they, are responsible for making sure enough money comes to pay salaries and buy resources. They are free to decide how to distribute rewards. If a microenterprise doesn't manage to find enough income, it ceases to exist, and the entrepreneurs move back to the talent pool. More on what that is and how it works later.

Microenterprise Lifecycles

When Rendanheyi 2.0 kicked off, the ZZJYTs were directly transformed into microenterprises. But since then, many new ones have emerged, and others have ceased to exist. After the first batch was created, for historical reasons, new microenterprises came about in two ways.

Either a group of entrepreneurs would come together, find an opportunity in the market, and pitch their ideas and approach platform leaders or other microenterprises to invest in their idea. Alternatively, platform leaders would see an opportunity in the market and place details on the internal marketplace, allowing entrepreneurs to bid on them and formulate a plan on how to seize the opportunity.

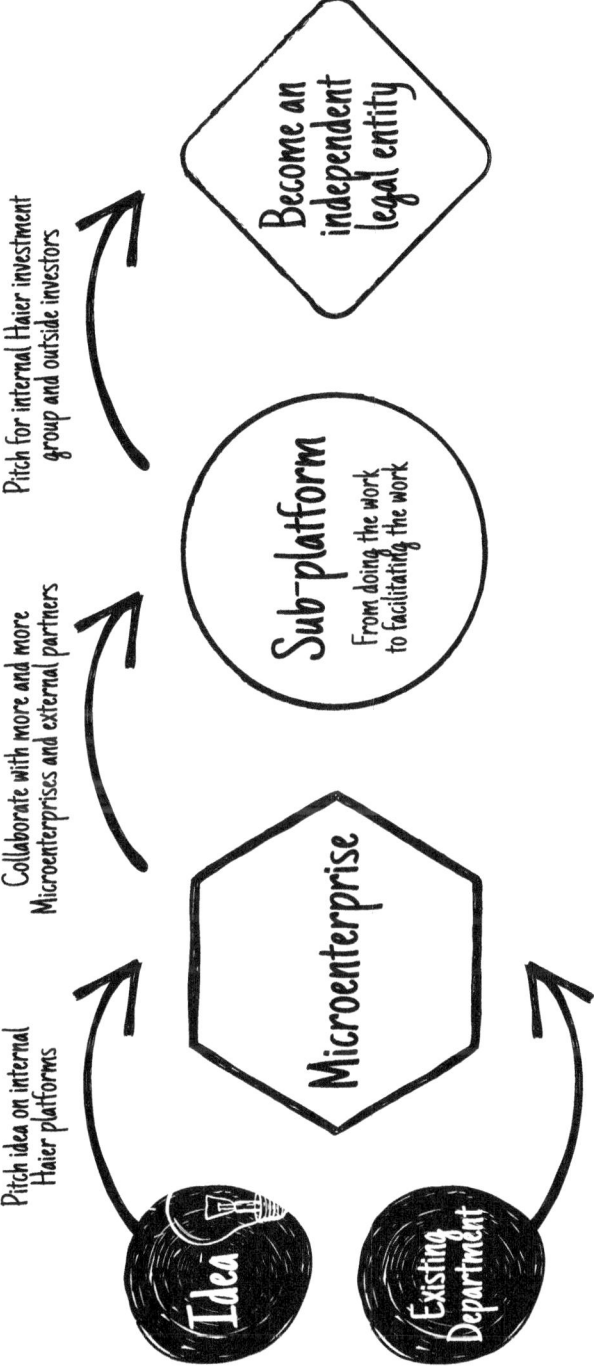

Once a microenterprise was established and managing successfully, its goal would be to develop and eventually evolve into a platform. This changed the role of doing the work into one of facilitating the work — by connecting with microenterprises and helping them become successful as well. This was the case with RRS Logistics, which steadily grew its business.

The next step in the evolutionary journey would be to move outside Haier and become a spin-off company, often with the platform the microenterprise was part of, as one of the main shareholders.

Entrepreneurs managed to turn their ideas into profits, and became "real" business owners.

Bound Together via Internal Contracts

The completion of the evolutionary process requires a good deal of collaboration. Thanks to internal contracts, it is possible to bind many microenterprises from both types and form a network based on contractual, rather than hierarchical relationships. The difference is that nobody tells anyone else what to do. Both parties collaboratively decide what they want to do, and for what reward.

Entrepreneurs of a supporting microenterprise can, if they wish, temporarily join other microenterprises, and provide services of their own. In most cases, tasks such as production and logistics are outsourced, and to get a better understanding of how such contracting works, it's good to remember that almost everything at Haier can be directly connected to a microenterprise — even inanimate objects such as office buildings. Microenterprises can be provided with a desk, or meeting room, in one of the Haier offices available for rent. Office space needs are addressed by Facility Management (a supporting microenterprise). If it runs out of room, becomes too expensive, or the services aren't up to scratch, chances are a new microenterprise will step in. Any microenterprise is free to contract, or terminate a contract with, any of the others, or with outside resource providers. This allows them to find external service providers, should they better suit their needs.

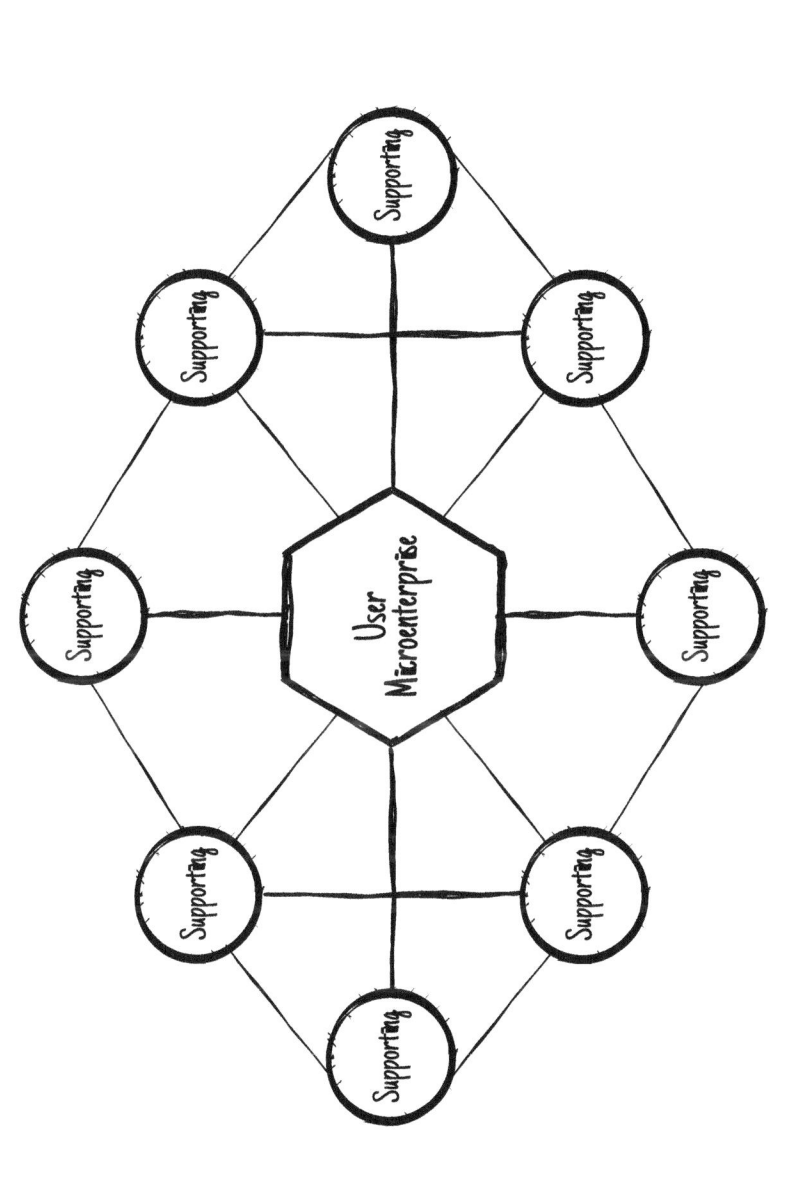

Preventing Internal Monopolies

In many traditional companies, departments tend to turn into virtual internal monopolies. No matter how badly they do their job, they can't be fired by the units they serve. Many act as if they were untouchable — and often they are...

Normally, whenever a company comes close to a monopoly, governments step in and either break them up or ensure a measure of competition. In companies, the exact opposite can happen, with encouragement for a monopoly mindset. This is usually bad for all concerned: services become more costly, quality falls, and motivation flags for want of incentive.

At Haier, all units are exposed to market dynamics such as competition, requiring them to be sensitive to the needs of the units they serve. Without those happy customers, the units would lose business and see a decline in income. This form of economic feedback informs those units whether their efforts are appreciated, and if their pricing structure is correct. It teaches employees the business of business.

Haier's architects made sure such an economic feedback loop was in place for the entrepreneurs as well. They developed the customer-paid salary system. The principle is simple. Microenterprises are directly influenced by customer evaluations; the more customers appreciate the product, the more likely the products are to be sold. That means customers will be willing to pay more. And the more a microenterprise earns, the more the entrepreneurs receive.

In a way, the customers pay the entrepreneurs' salaries. For such a system to function, it is essential that entrepreneurs can influence the outcome of their work [13]. They need decision-making power, the right to negotiate contracts with potential clients, and the ability to develop new products without having to convince managers three layers up. Microenterprises have the right to attract talent. They know what skills are lacking, and whether to invest in another member. They'll make sure to choose someone who adds value to the team.

Frontline Employees Need to Decide

Frontline employees often know best what the customers want, but in many companies, they have limited autonomy. Not at Haier. An often-heard argument is that these frontline employees do not know enough about the broader context to make the calls. At Haier, information is easily accessible and actively shared. Entrepreneurs are educated and trained to understand the value of information that allows frontline employees to quickly respond to sudden changes in customer needs.

Zhang had learned this was a necessity back in the pre-Haier days when productions targets were being set by the Chinese government, and pay was dependent on the number of machines manufactured; quality was a secondary consideration. He realised this effectively turned his employees into machines, instead of people that think and act to overcome problems. Instead of getting the sledgehammer out again, Zhang figured out that empowering employees to sign-off on certain decisions wasn't enough to ensure they made the best ones. To encourage their frontline employees to behave as entrepreneurs, they needed to reward them as entrepreneurs.

Hello Kitty

That those ideas sometimes lead to the development of some extraordinary appliances is a risk Haier is happy to take. The only stipulation is that it fulfils a user need. Even if the need is a bright pink, Hello Kitty-styled washing machine. (Don't believe us? Google it.) The Hello Kitty washing machine was borne of collaboration with users, and partly funded by them. Crowdfunding is becoming common at Haier. After creating a prototype, the usual practice is to pre-sell and ask users to make an initial payment for an early version of the product. Invariably, first versions are cheaper than the final ones. The goal is not to make a huge profit, but to test the waters and make it relatively safe to start production.

Pre-selling lets the microenterprises gauge public interest in a product, and they benefit from feedback. Crowdfunding also lowers the risk for the microenterprises. They know that the capital required is at least partly covered by the pre-sell.

From Talent Pool to Microenterprise

At Haier, everyone is an entrepreneur, and each entrepreneur needs to find, or create, a microenterprise. New hires start by joining a talent pool. Everyone in the pool receives a basic salary — often the minimum required by law, which is usually not enough to live comfortably. If someone fails to find a place, or their old assignment comes to an end, they go back into the pool. In this way, the pool acts as a safety net. Entrepreneurs know that if their endeavours fail, they won't lose their job.

On top of the basic, there's the dynamic part of the salary which is directly tied to individual and team performance in a form of profit-sharing. This is based on how much customer value an employee creates, irrespective of position or experience. The more value, the bigger the reward. Customer value is highly subjective. The amount someone would pay for a glass of water while lost in the desert differs from what they'd expect to pay at a city cafe. By rewarding its entrepreneurs for creating value, Haier attempts to create benefit for all parties. It honours Peter Drucker's philosophy by making sure that the organisation is correctly focused.

This moves decision-making about salaries from management to customer. It avoids internal politics, nepotism, and sycophancy. Instead of being rewarded for how you negotiated at the interview, you're rewarded for the value you create. Whether the customers deciding your salary are inside or outside Haier boundaries makes no difference. Microenterprises can decide how to spend their funds, how rewards are formulated, and how the added value is determined.

The microenterprises make Haier dynamic. They are bound only to those with whom they do business. Microenterprises are sometimes created on a whim — and if they aren't successful, they are just as easily disposed of. It's survival of the fittest. Some microenterprises remain small, others turn into multi-million-dollar companies that see their role change from entrepreneur to enabler of other microenterprises.

• • •

Loosely Coupled Networks Sharing Space...

We've looked at Haier and identified the main actors, each with their specific roles. The top leadership team has the role of architect or servant leader for the microenterprises, and the platforms enable those endeavours. If it were possible to zoom-out, you'd see a network of thousands of loosely coupled nodes: the microenterprises. Relationships based on contractual agreements create mutual benefits and make Haier a profoundly entrepreneurial company.

And we are now ready to take a good look inside.

> *REBEL LOG: This voyage is a strange, but very interesting one. While you are trying to unfold the plot of Haier you will find many answers to your questions, but you will never uncover all its mysteries. The answers you will find might not always seem obvious and you might not understand all things directly, but you need to stay alert because clues that you gain at any point might be vital to understanding the plot...*
>
> **Rebel One, out.**

Now that the main actors of Rendanheyi 2.0 have been introduced and you understand how Haier is organised, it's time to have a closer look at what's going on behind the scenes. What practices are used, and what rituals and rhythms does the company have? In other words, what is it like to work in a company like this?

Joining Haier

Liu Junxiang is a 39-year-old who joined Haier six months before we interviewed him in Qingdao. He is a product manager of the Smart Kitchen microenterprise, and one of 24,000 new employees to have joined Haier in the past five years. Some joined en masse due to acquisitions — GEA and its own complement of 12,000 employees, for example — but suffice it to say Liu wasn't the only one to figure that Haier was a good career step. He ensured all kitchen appliances were interconnected and could communicate with the broader Haier Smart Kitchen platform, so that the same app could interact with user's IoT devices. "I wasn't used to how Haier worked at the beginning," he said, "it was really something new for me. Before I was just a product manager and focused on software, now I had to consider the entire product: software, design, user interface, everything. Luckily, there were colleagues to help me find my way."

Liu read about the plans for Haier's Smart Kitchen, and immediately knew he wanted to work there. But first, he had to join the talent pool.

The Talent Pool
Hu Wang Hongwei, the leader of an HR microenterprise that is active on the Shared Service Platform explains how her unit helps to create talent pools. "The other microenterprises are our users; we build open talent pools to find people that can help them. We search and select talent to join the pool. Once someone is in, they'll sign a contract and officially become a Haier employee. The entrepreneurs-to-be are hired for their potential, and not for any specific role."

For any traditional company, hiring without having a position to fill might seem ridiculous. But the risk the HR microenterprise is taking is limited. Nobody in Haier has a traditional job anyway: they have goals.

When an entrepreneur joins the talent pool, they have three months to find a suitable goal. If they can't, out they go.

The HR microenterprise will, however, do anything it can to prevent that from happening, and for good reason. It needs to find the right entrepreneurs for other microenterprises to ensure the livelihood of its own. To help entrepreneurs succeed, Hu and her colleagues motivate, educate, and coach them. Hiring for the talent pool is much more than looking at a resume; it's a search for certain skill sets. "We look for courageous people," said Hu. "They need to be brave enough to do what it takes. Working at Haier means developing yourself, and not everybody is open to that. People need to be innovative, and able to find solutions. And they need to be highly motivated. Being an entrepreneur isn't easy. You

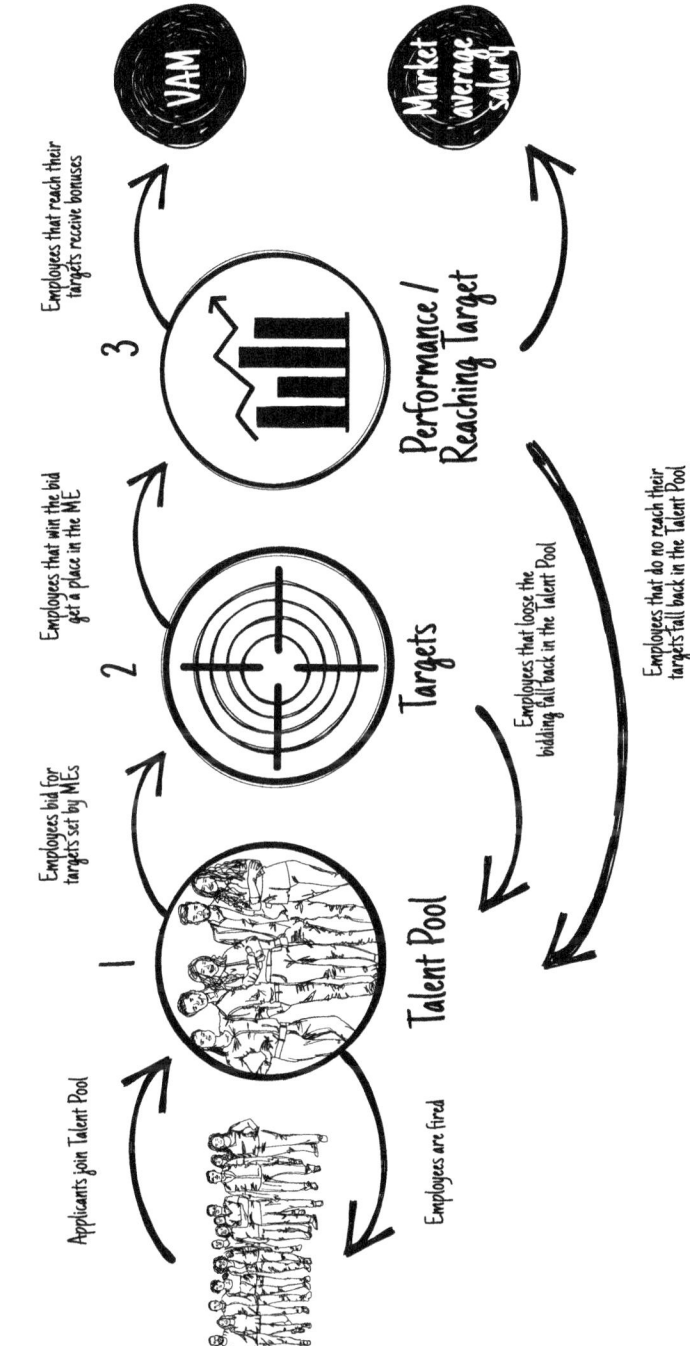

will encounter setbacks and you need drive to help you through. That's not something you can judge based on a resume."

Figuring out how entrepreneurs do their work, which skills they possess and where their talents lay is a complex task. The struggle to quantify what it takes is real. To help, Haier developed a transparent performance ranking system.

Peer-Performance Ranking

Like many other large organisations that have adopted more flexible ways of working [14], Haier has developed a transparent peer-ranking system to assess performance. Unlike the performance systems in more traditional organisations, it allows for self-monitoring and motivates internal collaboration — and competition. At Haier, all individuals and teams are measured on productivity, profitability, and customer satisfaction, with peer ranking based on these metrics, available to all staff via digital tools.

This system allows entrepreneurs to give direct feedback on their colleagues' behaviour. It provides them with the opportunity to recognise effort and performance, and at the same time correct any unacceptable behaviour.

Although this might seem hard to envision in a work context, it contains elements all of us will recognise. Amazon, Airbnb and Uber have similar ranking systems run by their users. You're likely to be barred from those services if people let it be known that you've made a mess of somebody's house, or otherwise misbehaved. To avoid reputational or financial loss, people tend to play it safe. In most cases, the best course of action is to abide by the (un)written rules. An Uber driver will not drive like a maniac, partly because there's a critic in the back seat. And what that critic says could impact the driver's future income.

On these platforms, transparency is key. You might read reviews of a hotel that you would like to stay at. If it got a bad score for hospitality, you'd want to know why — even if a comment was made 10 years before.

The same holds true for Haier's peer-ranking system. If there is a lack of transparency, it's almost impossible to understand the scores. It could also potentially allow colleagues to give ridiculously low scores if they don't like someone.

By opening-up this ranking system, employees can see which scores were given, and why. Outlandish scores will stand out, and probably attract direct feedback — or a lower score for themselves when the time comes.

The exact metrics to measure performance can differ from platform-to-platform, or between microenterprises, but often the principles are the same.

"We use a star system," Wang explains. "If you receive three stars, you're at the bottom line, and will receive only a salary that conforms to the market. If an entrepreneur overachieves, they will get four or five stars, and a bigger reward. If they underachieve — two stars or less — their salary can be cut. And, since some jobs require a minimum level of performance, it could mean that that person can't apply for high-end goals in the future. In a worst-case scenario, it could be that an entrepreneur or a microenterprise consistently gets low ratings. If that goes on for too long, they'll go back to the talent pool, dissolve the microenterprise, or leave the company." Firing people after a few bad ratings might sound harsh, but in practice colleagues are usually keen to help one another. That drive to help is something that can be partly explained by the collective esprit — which is quite common in Eastern cultures.

But there is something else that stimulates the caring behaviour. Since microenterprises and entrepreneurs have aligned incentives, they collaborate. Having a failing colleague in your midst is not beneficial and might directly influence the achievement of your goals. On top of that, helping your colleagues to be successful will often lead to higher peer scores as well, so that actively assisting one another is something that is clearly beneficial.

So, what happens if you get a lower rating? Wang Jian, leader in the refrigeration realm, admitted that this had happened to him. "It has happened to almost everyone," he said. "But the others help you. Let's say that it's the middle of the month and my goal is to get a five-dollar reduction in production costs. The others will pitch-in, since all our targets are tied together and the star evaluation is at the end of the month, my ranking will not drop." Another Wang, Wang Jie, who specialises in refrigeration solutions for young mothers, added: "Monthly or more frequent new contracts are signed. For example: we're collaborating, but you didn't get your star rating, which influenced our overall performance. I wouldn't want to collaborate with you again, or at least not on the same deal. So, we'll create a new contract, or find someone else from the talent pool."

We wanted to know more about that mutual aid. We asked some other employees why they would bother to help a struggling microenterprise. It was difficult to get the question across; Haier workers couldn't understand why we would ask. "We help the microenterprise to be successful because they are connected to us," replied one. "Sure, if a microenterprise consistently fails to meet its targets, we could try to find a replacement. But it's better to help the original because that microenterprise knows us. Getting a new one up to speed will take time and delay the whole process."

The reasoning is something you hear often in small or medium-sized enterprises all around the world. Haier's entrepreneurs must constantly find a balance and decide if the people they're collaborating with will help them reach their goals. They also need to decide if the reward they're getting in return is fair compared to the others, and most of all if it's enough to keep their microenterprise running.

At Haier, about 50 percent of employees get a score of four stars or higher, meaning that they are eligible for higher rewards. About 10 to 15 percent eventually must leave for underperforming. The application of this latter outcome can differ, depending on the microenterprise. Each of the microenterprises has the right to decide matters for themselves.

Learning, and Trying Again

Members sent back to the talent pool will get the chance to find new opportunities, follow various programmes and attend workshops, but most of all evaluate their performance. Or as one of our interviewees described it: "Reflect, reflect, reflect!"

This eagerness to learn from mistakes is part of Haier's culture. It's one of the secrets of its success, and a stimulus throughout the company. By combining peer-ranked performance systems to create insights into one's behaviour, and having a culture in which learning is seen as a vital element, Haier enables and facilitates personal and professional development.

Even though there are many positive things to say, we also have some more critical observations. Ranking systems can lead, and have led, to stress for employees who feel they are constantly being judged. Some of our interviewees did acknowledge that stress, but — they quickly added — that was greatly reduced because they felt that the system was at least fair. They knew where their scores came from, and why they received them. The system saved them the stress of having to please an individual manager, or having to worry about nepotism or other political games.

Haier's solution might not be perfect, but it does avoid the trap of making a manager responsible for judging your performance. Scores are given in more transparent ways by everyone in the organisation, and most importantly, the scoring is seen as equitable.

Bidding for Goals

Young people enjoy working at Haier because they are not judged for their experience or background, but on their performance. It came as no surprise to us that 62.6 percent of all microenterprises are led by people under 35.

The talent pool is just the beginning, as Liu Junxiang explained. "Before I could really start working, I had to bid on a goal," he said. Bidding for goals gives the entrepreneurs-to-be the freedom to choose what they want to work on.

In an internal marketplace all these goals, which can best be described as business opportunities, are gathered, and shared with the rest of the organisation.

They are formulated by other microenterprises or Platform leaders. The goals (known as "dan") describe what the creator hopes to outsource.

They are well defined, with contextual information, in-depth analyses, and a clear description of what needs to be achieved. There are various performance thresholds, an indication of potential gains, and sometimes, as with the Bird's Nest air-conditioning unit, a ready solution. Goals come in all shapes and sizes. Some could be minor projects — such as helping a bunch of Corporate Rebels conduct their research. Others are larger, such as building a state-of-the-art factory or achieving a 10 percent market share in a specific region.

Formulating these goals* in the right way can be seen as something of an artform. If they aren't clear, or the potential rewards aren't attractive enough, or the microenterprise concerned has a bad reputation, the entrepreneurs won't bid on them.

---

* *More details about formulating goals in Appendix 5, about the budgeting process in Appendix 6, and about the OEC method in Appendix 7.*

> REBEL LOG, DAY UMPTEEN: We're settling-in nicely in our new environment, feeling more and more part of this community. One thing we have noticed is the comforting spread of support offered to us — and to all. Co-operation is key, and the benefits seem to be exponential.
>
> **Rebel One, out.**

Customer-Paid Salaries

Liu was guided, in his first weeks at Haier, by his colleagues. They wanted to get him up to speed fast; the sooner he was able to start adding value, the better. The tale of Liu's early days drew some chuckles from the assembled company in the meeting room. When these more senior workers had joined Haier a decade before, onboarding was a less gentle and supportive affair.

"All of that has changed," one told us, "and nowadays, it's more about coaching and personal development. It's much better." Liu has been brought into the Haier fold; his life as an entrepreneur can begin. As well as having autonomy, he has a career with promise. It can be a profitable one, thanks to Haier's remuneration system.

This is a driver of innovation — and success. It motivates employees to keep pushing the organisation forward. Haier is growing quicker than many of its competitors — and that was true even while the world was being shaken by a pandemic [15].

Perhaps the best part, stressed by many we interviewed, is that it's fair. "If I work hard and add value for the customer," said Liu, "I know I'll be rewarded." This sense of fair play is engraved in Haier's culture; people are judged on their ability, not on their working relationship with people in the right places, or their negotiation skills at interview. The reward mechanism is built around performance, and more precisely around the value they add for the customer. Value will be determined, along with the size of the stake for those who manage to add that value, during the bidding process. The thresholds one must pass to receive a higher income will be clearly outlined.

Haier's remuneration system consists of two parts, the first being basic income. Even if an entrepreneur is in the talent pool and in search of a goal, they'll receive a basic wage. This acts as a safety net, but is often not enough to live comfortably.

The second part is dynamic, known as the Customer-Paid-Salary. It comes into play when an entrepreneur has won a bid. This salary is often built up from several thresholds defined in the bidding process.

There is no guarantee that the thresholds will be reached. Nor are the rewards a sure thing. A bottom-line target must be reached for the first threshold. Often this means an entrepreneur will receive a bonus, but that may be below the market average. Failure to reach that lowest criterion means a significantly lower salary — possibly just the basic.

The next threshold is set at market average production. Entrepreneurs who reach it get a "market-conform" salary. After that, things get interesting, and more profitable. This is where Haier's interpretation of the Value Adjustment Mechanism (VAM) comes into play.

Whiz, Boom, Bam ... VAM!
VAM originates from China and has proved popular with private equity investors interested in domestic companies. It is an especially defined shareholder agreement. The goal is more safety for investors; it works like this:

An investor selects a company or project to invest in and receives shares. A set of specific conditions is added to the agreement. These conditions usually fall into one of three categories: financial, non-financial, or specific events. Financial performance indicators include revenue, profits, sales growth and market share. Non-financial covers quality of products, acquisition of new patents or successfully applying new technologies. Specific events are things like mergers and acquisitions or initial public offerings (IPOs).

The investor specifies what the conditions are, and what should happen when they are reached. They influence the direction of the company. Companies are usually obliged to buy back some of the shares, offer extra shares to the investor at a discounted price, or allocate them for free.

Investors have a certain guarantee. If a goal is not met, the company needs to buy back a certain percentage of the shares for a fixed amount. The investor is protected, and the company is motivated.

Reverse logic can be applied, and works as a motivator. This is the case when there is a condition to sell back shares for a lower rate should the company become worth more than anticipated.

The value adjustment mechanism works in a similar way to America's convertible preferred stock, and aligns investors and entrepreneurs. Success for one means success for both [16][17].

Haier has adopted and integrated VAM for just those reasons. To understand how it works, we need to take a step back and forget everything we know about traditional reward systems.

Imagine Haier as a gigantic incubator with thousands of investors. They invest all sorts of resources: time, skills, knowledge about the customer or products. Some even invest money. The goal is to facilitate as many start-ups as possible, gathering all those investments and making sure all investors are aligned in such a way that they overlap with user needs. Where formulating the goals in specific ways helped align them, the VAM contract brings extra focus and motivation to achieve increasing rewards.

VAM contracts include specific objectives and events that — should they happen — trigger bonuses. In many cases it could be paraphrased: "Do better than the market average, and you'll get a share in the profits."

Profits are shared when an entrepreneur outperforms the market

VAM CONTRACT EXAMPLE

1. Basic information of the microenterprise & platform
2. Strategic goal and ecosystem path of the microenterprise
3. Resource needs
4. Leading targets
5. Microenterprise valuation adjustment mechanism

equivalent target, and he or she enters the Added Value realm. This value has been added by the efforts of the entrepreneur and distinguishes their individual performance. If the market average sales volume is 1,000 washing machines and you manage to sell 1,100, the added value is 100. This is where the entrepreneurs can start to earn big time, because VAM contracts often specify the situations in which entrepreneurs create added value. Success means a percentage of the profits over the added value they helped create, in this case a percentage of the profits from the 100 extra washing machines.

That incentivises more product sales above market average. There is no upper threshold, because the reward grows in tandem with the added value. Usually there are several thresholds in the VAM contract that further increase the percentage of the profits that go directly to the entrepreneur.

In the image you can see how that works. The horizontal axis shows performance, the vertical axis shows income. The better an entrepreneur performs the higher their income will be. Up until the market average production often means a fixed step in income. After that, the next threshold is where things get interesting. The entrepreneur enters the added value realm which means that on top of their salary, they will receive a percentage of the profits on anything that is created above the market average threshold. That percentage can increase even further after new thresholds, causing a steep climb in income.

The conditions call for a predefined distribution of profit, and usually mean that one of the goal initiators will have to give away a percentage of their profits or shares. And they should be happy to do so, because if those events are triggered, it means that the product was a success. The initiators will get a smaller cut of a bigger pie.

In practice, most microenterprises do not become separate legal entities, and the shares represent no more than a stake in the financial outcome for the duration of the contract. This means that entrepreneurs can receive a percentage of the total profits made by their microenterprise.

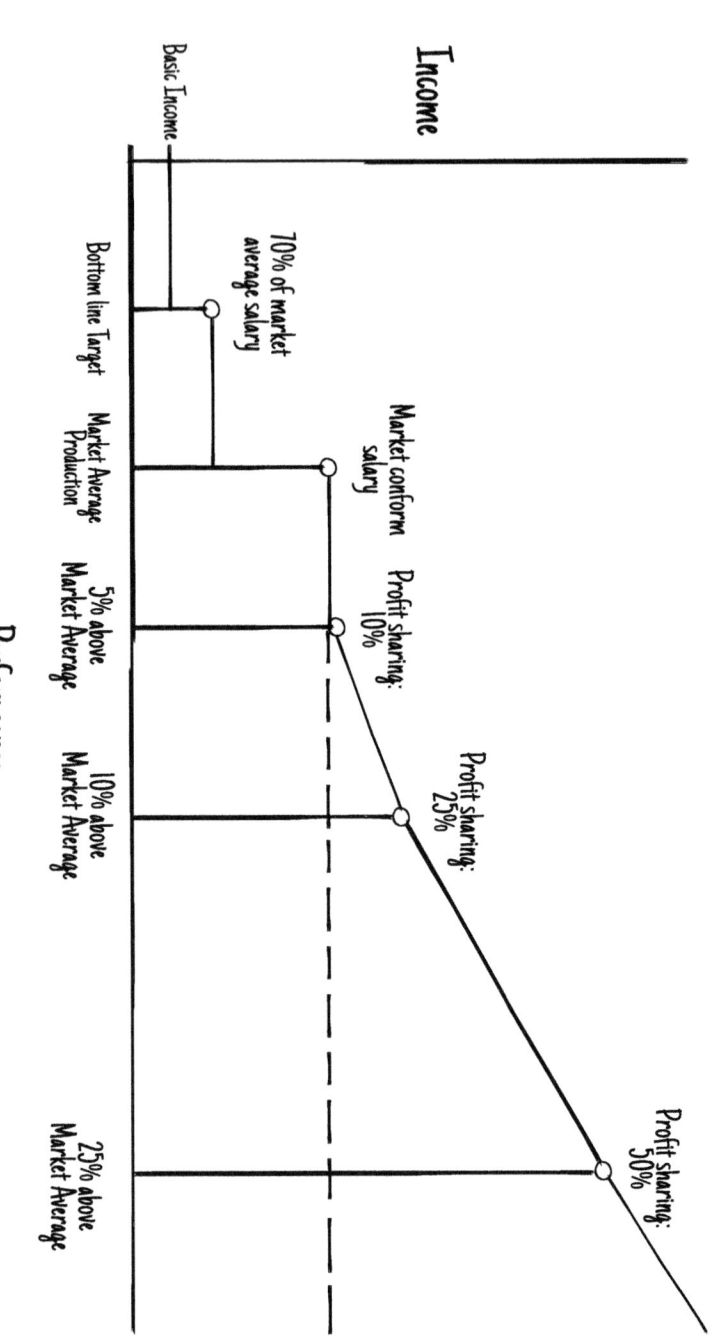

By ensuring the meshing of goals and happy users, the remuneration mechanism is designed to be beneficial for all, including customers. The happier the users, the more income the entrepreneurs receive, and the higher the return for investors. Which is probably why the document in which these agreements are captured is referred to in-house as the "Win-Win Value-Added Statement".

Finding this state of equilibrium is an enormous challenge. If a microenterprise formulates simple goals, and gives away too much of the potential profits, it won't see much in return. If it doesn't give enough rewards, it might end up with the wrong entrepreneurs — or none.

There is no such thing as a one-size-fits-all. Negotiation and discussion mean microenterprises have autonomy, and can come up with solutions that fit their needs. This makes it possible for new ideas to emerge. More on that later.

Comparing New and Old Ways of Doing Things

The unique qualities of Haier's VAM interpretation are perhaps easier to understand when compared with more traditional systems.

Let's say that company ABC & Co hires someone to do a job and pays them a fixed salary. Due to some errors or misunderstandings, that job isn't adding much value to the company. In a small organisation, that quickly becomes visible, and leads to swift action. However, ABC & Co is one of the larger ones, where value is harder to ascertain. People are doing their jobs, and they get paid. People are being judged based on whether they do their job correctly, not whether that job adds real value. [18]

What happens if an employee is doing a job that falls into this category? Well, usually the company is in trouble. Now it has an employee who is not creating value and is wasting time doing unnecessary things. Even more troublesome, the employee will, very understandably, try to hide this. They don't want others to know theirs is a bullshit job because they worry about being let go. Keeping your job is key. Of course, there will always be companies and people that will not follow this pattern, and a motivated employee could be proactive and come up with an alternative plan to keep the manager, and the customers, happy. In reality, this seldom happens.

And let's be fair, it's not that strange if you work in an environment where you have almost no freedom, extra effort is seldom rewarded, or the rewards are not perceived as fair. Any profit that has been created by an employee does not automatically flow back to them, but gets added to the company coffers, or those of its shareholders. This is unlikely to inspire workers to focus on cutting costs or taking extra steps to bring in a customer or help struggling colleagues. Quite often, they do not have the authority to make such decisions, which causes delay and frustration.

To overcome this, many companies have found other methods of motivation. Some give bonuses, status symbols, promises of future benefits, reserved parking spots, impressive job titles and corner offices. These things create a sense of importance and give employees something to aspire to. All these things were, of course, invented to inspire those who are not intrinsically motivated.

Rewarding Haier Entrepreneurs
Haier tries to step away from these struggles and stimulates its employees to behave as entrepreneurs by rewarding and treating them as such. It motivates them to be "owners". Instead of rewarding previous success, negotiation skills, good attendance or (even worse) popularity with the right people, Haier sticks to its guns: rewards are linked to added value. The value is determined by the customer. Trust is essential. Employees must be counted on to make the right decision, and that is most likely if what's good for the company is also good for the employee. With that in mind, Haier developed its customer-paid-salary system.

Giving employees a cut of profits and more autonomy takes away many of the costs of bureaucracy. The system helps to attract and retain staff by placing the issue of salary setting in the hands of the customer. If no value has been created, it will quickly become apparent. This economic feedback has proved to be a vital motivator of change — and makes employees more innovative.

Potentially, this combination of market-driven contracting and salaries based on performance could lead to toxic situations. The base salary helps to counter that. It gives employees some breathing room to find opportunities that fit their needs. Goals are plentiful at Haier. Whether an employee is prepared to take some extra risk to profit later, or they are more cautious and looking for opportunities with a higher base salary and more certainty in the short term, there is choice. Like the products it creates, Haier places the goals on the internal market to fulfil user needs, and those of the entrepreneurs. It is vital to customise agreements and attract the right person for the job. All this has made Haier buzz: entrepreneurs are eager for success.

Haier's customer-paid salary system is an important part of its entrepreneurial culture. It's not a case of giving employees a job, it is providing them with a chance to become successful. Haier simply ensures that they are rewarded when they do well — something that in other companies can't be taken for granted.

• • •

REBEL LOG, IN THE COURT OF THE KING: Well, perhaps 'king' is putting it too strongly. Zhang rules benevolently and wisely, in a regal manner in terms of his magnanimous methods. But he doesn't rule with an iron rod ... and no position is unassailable. Heads can roll at Haier — but usually metaphorically, and without bloodshed.

Rebel One, out

Hiring, Firing and Challenging the Leader

Since income is in many cases closely bound to the success of a microenterprise, having a good leader is vital to get people bidding on targets. What has emerged as a result is fascinating, and exciting.

It's something many of us have dreamed of: hiring, or even firing, the boss. In some microenterprises, entrepreneurs can choose their leader, or fire that leader if they feel he or she lacks the necessary skills. As the income of the entrepreneurs is directly related to the capability of their leader, having an influence on how they are led makes sense. If a certain majority is reached, the entrepreneurs can vote on whether the leader should step down. But it's better to focus on helping someone, rather than sacking them. It's the responsibility of the entrepreneurs to make sure their leader is the best person to do the job.

Another interesting practice with microenterprise leaders is that they can, in some cases, be challenged by outsiders. In much the same way as the Stunned Fish were reanimated, the ability to challenge a microenterprise leader optimises the organisation. If the challenger comes up with a better proposal, chances are he or she will get the chance to lead. Bear in mind, however, that just because a proposal is better does not automatically mean that the microenterprise members will agree to it. That's where trust in the leader comes into play.

We can only wonder what would happen if this practice were to be adopted in traditional corporations. Our guess is that it would radically change the way managers take care of their employees.

Is it All About the Money?

It is important to at least speculate whether that is the case for Haier. It is, after all, a profit-making growth machine. Its revenue increased, after Rendanheyi 2.0 was introduced, by more than 60 percent.

It's fair to say that the way Haier pays its entrepreneurs has an important role in motivating and attracting them. But according to those we interviewed, there is something more at play. "We are people-orientated," said microenterprise leader Wang Xianjung. "Our microenterprise is organised according to user needs. We provide high-quality products and rapid delivery services, and we bring down the cost. We have financial benefits, but there are other rewards that depend on what the employees want." Those rewards could be as simple as a gift card, but there are less conventional options. "If someone performs really well, they can invite their family to visit them at their workplace. The country is large, and families often come from far away — their travel is paid-for by the company. It's like a short holiday for them, and they can see how their relative is doing. In China, most people consider it a great honour — but of course they are free to decide."

During the several Rendanheyi forum events, Haier's yearly management gala in which the latest ins and outs are presented, Zhang invites his management heroes to share their wisdom. After a couple of interesting lectures, the event morphs into an awards ceremony. Besides delivering monetary compensation, Haier is known to think laterally. There are numerous categories: Best microenterprise, Most Innovative ... you name it.

We noted that recipients were given a sash and a gold medal to mark their exemplary performance. They were publicly praised for their efforts, and the pride was evident on their faces. Some of the awards were extramural, for individuals or institutes that had collaborated with Haier. Several of the winners looked a little bemused by the whole affair.

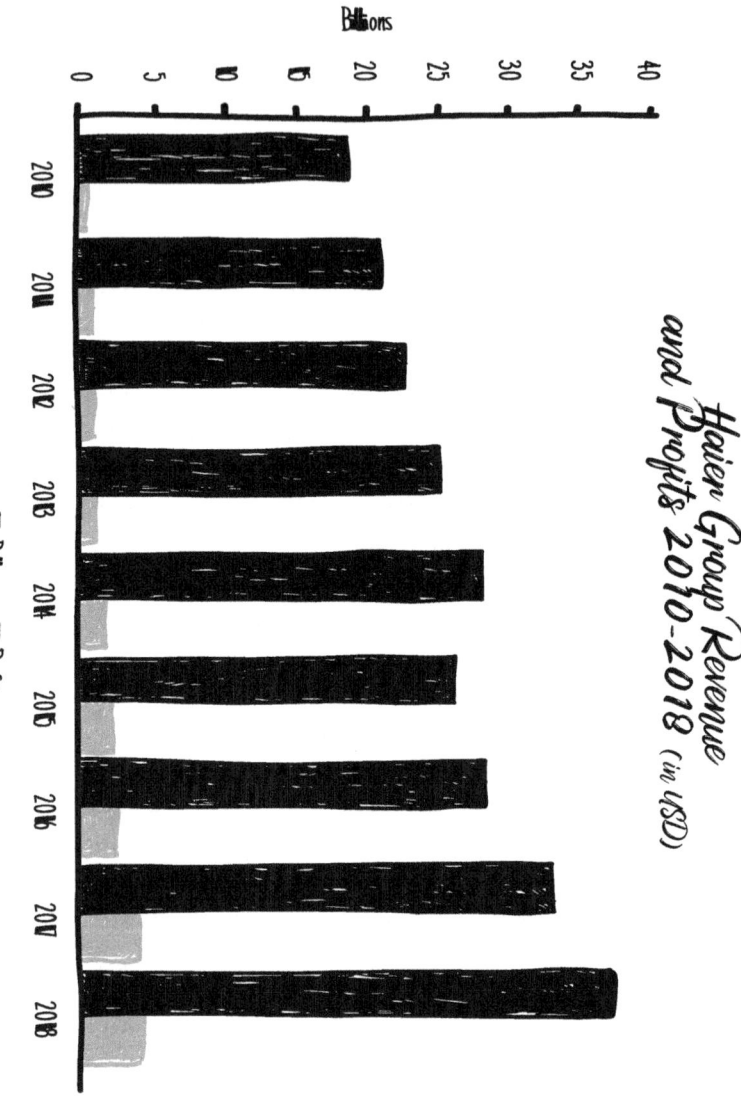

Also invited on stage was the board of the newly acquired General Electric Appliances (GEA) company, headed by Kevin Nolan. The board members were recognised for adapting and implementing Haier's philosophy in US workplaces. The speech sounded promising, and we couldn't wait to find out just how much "Haier" GEA managed to adopt.

There are still more ways for employees to receive a non-monetary reward. The Golden Hammer, for example, is given each year to the entrepreneur who dares challenge conventional wisdom. This reward system has been adopted to stimulate production process improvements. One of the welding torches used in Haier factories is called the "Qiming torch". Its inventor, Li Qiming, noticed that existing tools weren't effective in hard-to-reach places. At that time — the late 1990s — no suitable welding torches were available on the Chinese market. Li got stuck in and created one. His invention is showcased in the Haier Museum, right next to the Xialing wrench, the Yunyan Mirror, and some Shenqiang hooks.

The reward system has proven to be a true catalyst for entrepreneurship. It may seem straightforward, but it is still unknown in many companies. With a tight coupling of user happiness and higher rewards, this system creates a bridge. Entrepreneurs are, for more than intrinsic reasons, motivated to do what's best for the users. Again, it's a matter of finding what is wanted. Extra income? An invitation for a family visit? What's the best motivator? While this might seem like another management game, tricking people to run as hard as possible, it's as well to remember who bids on the goals, and who chooses which results to strive for: the entrepreneurs themselves.

Haier strives to help entrepreneurs and microenterprises to be successful and get the rewards they're hoping for. In the talent pool, entrepreneurs receive coaching and learn new skills. On the job, other entrepreneurs will help them, but there's more that transforms the business plans of the entrepreneurs into something actionable.

• • •

Access to Information

Sun Lei and Chen Jiao, who we met before, both work on the Financial platform. The platform provides financial services within and without the boundaries of Haier, and has become a strategic partner for the microenterprises rather than a number-crunching department. And this is yet another way that Haier helps entrepreneurs to become successful.

"Traditional financial statements are usually created at the end of the month," said Chen. "They only show you what has happened during that period. By then it's too late, you can't do anything about it. We wanted to make sure our financial data could be used to improve our performance throughout the month." The pair reasoned that having "live" financial data would make it easier for microenterprises to respond to sudden changes in customer behaviour or rising costs. Re-engineering the financial systems boosted the company's transformation, as more information became available.

By having more detailed information and making it accessible by practicing Open Book Management, entrepreneurs are enabled to make better decisions. It helps them feel more engaged, motivated and sparks innovation, all of which help the company to stay sustainable [19]. At Haier, employee motivation is partly driven by the fact that salaries are determined by the financial success of the microenterprises. Realising at the end of a month that your team has been spending too much money isn't a welcome scenario.

New information systems have made it possible to do more with the data to hand, and revolutionised the way employees interact with those data. Near each workstation on the assembly line, screens display all relevant information. Everything can suddenly be found at the touch of a button, and in a sense, this turns all employees into financial experts.

Knowledge-Sharing and Personal Development

Knowledge-sharing is appreciated company-wide. Chen Jiao believes it doubles as a motivation mechanism: "If your microenterprise shares information about effective practices and others take it on board, you have the chance to win an award. You get to hoist a flag with your name on it."

This often happens at the Saturday Meetings — one of the few practices shared throughout the entire organisation. Financial Services group member Sun Lei explained that she often gets the chance to speak to top leaders, including CEO Zhang. "We have a group meeting each week." In China, working on Saturdays is cause for some controversy, but in many companies it's the norm. At Haier, Saturdays are precious. Zhang is a fierce protector of the process. He attends every session and adjusts his schedule to suit. "If he has a long journey ahead, such as an overseas tour or a series of international meetings, he will normally depart on Saturday afternoon and return to Qingdao the following Friday. One can only imagine how difficult this is for a busy executive." [6]

The meetings' structure, reporting and follow-up means that every session has meaning. There are glaring differences between this in-house speciality and traditional management meetings. The focus is an activity summary: a good, hard look at the week's progress, with an emphasis on systems, strategies, and philosophies. Zhang introduces best practices he has seen elsewhere, and encourages attendees to follow his lead. He encourages experimentation — and the sharing of results, whether those are good or bad.

Participants aren't reviewing tasks and financials; they are building the future. There is sometimes a single-topic focus, and an atmosphere reminiscent of an academic seminar. Challenges, brainteasers, and possibly even koan will be thrown up, along with plenty of out-of-the-box thinking. The objective is to improve mechanisms using the daily activity reviews. Leaders of microenterprises and platforms are expected to stimulate excellence.

What's so special about the Saturday meetings is that everyone is invited. It's not just leaders talking to each other, all entrepreneurs can be present. No other system could spread important news as swiftly. Microenterprises are invited to present a case study. No one is overlooked, although only one or two microenterprises are invited each week. Jiao explained why he likes the process: "Maybe your work hasn't been going too well, but this is a learning process, and you can expect some helpful instruction. People are challenged, but never laughed at — and the others will help." Microenterprises' success and failure stories are grist to the mechanism's mill. Attendees can put forward potential solutions — and challenge approaches if they think that will help.

These regular encounters are more than talk-fests. Haier abhors the concept of meetings without specific agenda or meaningful follow-up. Resources are in place to ensure the implementation of resolutions. Ideas that emerge will be covered by the Corporate Culture Centre and published in Haier Ren, the staff newspaper. Information is also disseminated via platforms and the company's in-house TV channel. Senior leaders convene meetings for their microenterprises to decide on courses of action.

Knowledge transfer is the pooling of wisdom; entrepreneurs often have multiple roles, and this process is a natural form of corporate education. It stands or falls with the motivation of employees to learn and share experiences. These are vital steps for creating more value for customers, and motivation is not lacking. Zhang, who doesn't speak English, hires translators to work on entire management books for his personal edification. Haier puts an emphasis on acquiring knowledge in any way possible. Data are analysed, and experiments constantly undertaken. Initiatives that add value are adopted; those that don't simply cease to exist.

As Wang Xiangjun explains, "When you have something that is exciting, you want to share it. You are part of a bigger network that can benefit from the knowledge you have. If you want to reach your goal, all microenterprises must perform as well as possible. Sharing knowledge helps them improve." This has enabled Haier to transfer practices swiftly, without the need for enforcement. Those who feel that a new practice is useful are free to adopt it. Entrepreneurs figure out what needs to be done, saving Haier time and money without any loss of quality. The company trusts and encourages its entrepreneurs to educate themselves. Platforms provide suitable options, but they work only when aligned with entrepreneur needs.

Experimentation

Haier's favourite method of finding new solutions or best practices is by performing experiments. Some are small, others large, some methodical, others less so. Crowdfunding, prototyping, or selling first generations of products at a discount — to gain feedback — have all been used. They reduce risk, as actual production often starts once the crowdfunding goal is reached. This avoids the manufacturer being stuck with unwanted products. A great example of such experimentation is... Thunderobot.

Robots Like Games, Too...

According to industry experts and users, the Thunderobot is a top-value gaming laptop. It is well-equipped to handle any game — and is a triumph of design and functionality.

Thunderobot dates from 2013, the brainchild of Lu Khailin and three of his colleagues. Business laptops at the time didn't cut it with the Chinese gaming community, the standard of living was rising, and tech costs were falling. A Haier team rolled up its sleeves to figure out what was wrong with the current crop of PCs. A lot, it turned out: 13 significant user needs had to be addressed. The team approached Zhou Zhaolin, head of the platform that includes laptops. After expressing some initial scepticism, he plunged in, and came up with $270,000 in seed funding. By the end of the year, it was time for a Thunderobot product-launch on JD.com, a domestic e-commerce site. Thunderobot was one of the first to raise money on the JD Equity Crowdfunding Platform, which also offers training and support to start-ups.

Thunderobot benefitted from Haier's resources in supply chain, logistics, and after-sales service. The initiative attracted leading software and component suppliers. The first 500 Thunderobot PCs sold out within a week — the next 3,000 in minutes. Further funding was secured. The company took on a 72.5 percent stake. Lu and the three founders had invested some $65,000, giving them a 15 percent stake — with the option to acquire more. By December 2014, $800,000 had been raised in a Series A financing round, with more to follow. The enterprise was profitable and did not require further funding — but Haier was not in the gaming industry. It needed external help to gain access to top-notch resources.

The importance of the support and mentoring by Zhou can hardly be overstated. The team had come up with a great idea, but he could see that the members were young, inexperienced, and needed help. They soon got it.

In 2017, Thunderobot was listed on China's NEEQ market with a valuation equivalent to $180m. Thunderobot is now a leader in its field, famous at home and making great strides overseas. Haier developed, removed, shifted, or eliminated boundaries to ensure a co-operative process.

Experiments are constantly run in-house. In combination with the motivation factor, this has proven valuable. This culture has been active throughout Haier's history, and it makes good sense. Even the transformation of one company into thousands of microenterprises started with smaller experiments. The results were analysed, adapted, and improved. A successful experiment is quickly shared and rolled out, and if the results are good enough, it can lead to the entire organisation moving in that direction.

What We Saw Up-Close
We've zoomed-in on life at Haier, looked closely at how microenterprises and platforms are bound through contracts, and how other mechanisms and practices help entrepreneurs to do what they do best: find and seize opportunities. By balancing the roles of investor, resource provider and business owner, everyone can influence what work to do, how they carry out that work, and how they are rewarded. It provides autonomy.

The practices and mechanisms described here are often applied in a slightly adapted form throughout the organisation, but hold true for all layers. Whether entrepreneurs, microenterprises or platforms place a bid on a goal, the process and logic will be the same.

Repeating principles allows understanding of processes. The entrepreneurs come to feel at ease with the diversity of their working lives. With over 4,000 microenterprises, no two alike, Haier benefits from the application of clear guiding principles. No need for strict handbooks telling people how to behave. Instead, trust is placed in the entrepreneurs' judgment.

It works, so why change it?

FIRE

'The enterprise will eventually go up in flames, while the ecosystem will become an eternal living fire. The microenterprises converge and disperse, whereas in an ecosystem the entrepreneurial spirit will be passed on like a torch.'

Zhang Ruimin, 2018*

*From essay: A New Year just adds a Number; a new me welcomes new prospects (Full essay in Appendix 3).

REBEL LOG: Researching Haier is like playing an adventure game. You spend time in a different world and lose yourself in the plot. The story unfolds through what you discover on your travels. Just like any adventure game, Haier is based on a good story and a set of engaging characters. There are puzzles to solve and riddles to answer. You must seek out clues to progress. There are subplots, side plots, and dead ends, and the main plot reveals itself bit-by-bit. Clearly Haier builds on success by addressing problems and embracing change.

Rebel One, out.

Rendanheyi 3.0 (2019-present)

When Haier first adopted its network structure, there was an immediate and welcome effect: less resistance to the flow of resources. Each microenterprise could freely collaborate with any of the others. Its way of working became the envy of many. Haier was ranked by Euromonitor as the world's top brand for large home appliances for 10 consecutive years. The China Market Monitor has named it China's most valuable brand for the past 17. A decade ago, it was active in 124 countries; today it's 186. Those figures would be reason enough for many companies to rest on their laurels. But these great results were born of challenge and change, and the benefit from those strange bedfellows has been embedded in company strategy since 2005, when the Rendanheyi model was introduced. By giving its microenterprises freedom, Haier has come to rule the white goods world. However, behind the curtains, things weren't as perfect as they seemed....

Changing a Winning Team?

Most companies are unwilling to forsake a winning formula, but at Haier transformation for the better is seen as an ever-present possibility. Even with the success that had come from initial changes, entrepreneurs and microenterprises began to realise that the revised structure had its boundaries.

In short, the company was again facing problems. And at Haier, problems are there to be solved.

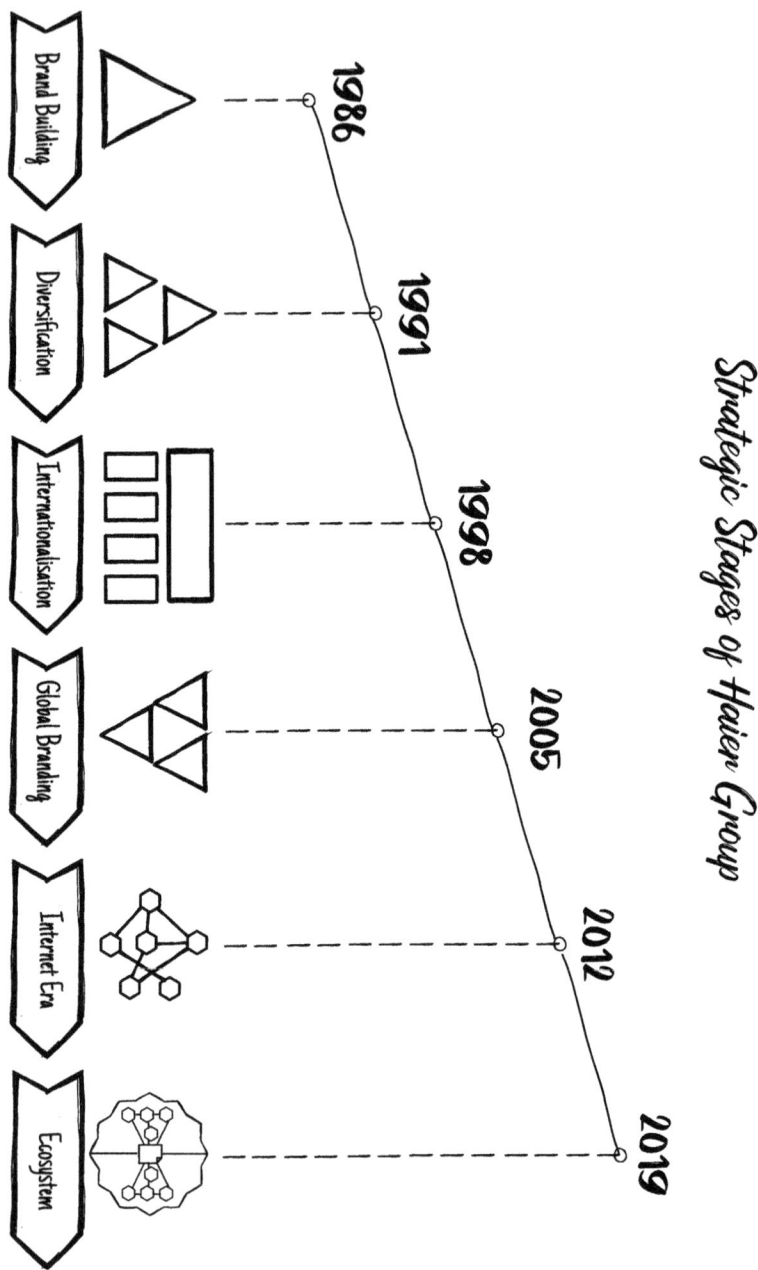

There were two major issues, the first related to complexity, the other to competition. In recent decades, there has been enormous growth in product complexity. A refrigerator that looked nice and did a decent job of chilling food was, at one time, enough. Today's consumers want more than that — and more than just a refrigerator.

It still needs to be smart in appearance but should be smarter in other ways: connected to the Internet, and usable via an app to which users can connect their other appliances. The thinking extends to all other white goods needs, and expands to include kitchen furnishings, user needs and desires that go way beyond household equipment.

Microenterprises were finding that there was only one way to consistently give customers what they wanted: closer and more effective collaboration. And that's where the second problem came in: competition, not from outside, but from within: other microenterprises.

The ever-increasing complexity of products and services demanded more collaboration. One microenterprise would be responsible for designing the microwave housing, another the motor, a third the app. The specifics of these duties were captured in contracts, which clearly defined roles and responsibilities, as well as the share of profits.

For some products, this worked just fine; for others, it was terrible.

The logical step of creating contracts to divide the work had some unintended consequences. Competition came to the fore. Each member knew that their salary was directly related to the whole team's performance. There was a tendency to try to create contracts which would be beneficial to one's own microenterprise. The effect soon became noticeable. Entrepreneurs became more concerned about their microenterprise's interests and lost focus on the most important thing: customer satisfaction. This led to a form of competition known as "shading".

> ### Shading
>
> "Shading," observed Oliver Hart, "happens when a party isn't getting the outcome it expected from the deal and feels the other party is to blame, or has not acted reasonably to mitigate the losses."
>
> "The aggrieved party often cuts back on performance in subtle ways, sometimes even unconsciously, to compensate." Hart knows what he is talking about; he was a Nobel Prize Winner for Economics in 2016.
>
> He explained that the way contracts were being negotiated was having negative effects on the end-product, the end-user, and all parties in between. Shading can be found in many organisations, in every industry, on every continent. Its deleterious effects can be seen in the quality of products, motivation of employees and success rates of companies.
>
> The concept can best be understood by analogy. Let's say you're a supplier with a contract to deliver a specific metal housing, for a certain price, for the period of one year. The contract states that late delivery incurs a fine. You were okay with that initially, because you negotiated a small profit margin.
>
> Then something unforeseen happens, something nobody could have anticipated: a trade war, or Covid-19. And this affects your ability to deliver the housings at the cost you had calculated. But you must honour the contract or be fined. So, you cut costs, fire a few people and hire cheaper labour, use raw materials of lower quality, focus on timing rather than craftsmanship. Anything you can do to live up to the agreement.
>
> This kind of intentional under-performing is petty, but common. According to Hart, it's impossible to define the quality of a product in the wording of a contract to preclude under-performance. It has a net-negative result for all concerned; you, as supplier, are frustrated that you must live up to a contract in a world that has changed. The factory is frustrated about the lower quality of the product. The end-user will probably be disappointed in the final product. Lose-lose-lose.

Targets not Aligned with the Goal

The problems Haier encountered weren't unique to them. Shading, and perhaps more precisely the miss-alignment of targets, happens to companies around the globe. Targets that aren't aligned with the goal cause trouble, regardless of good intentions.

Success is often simplistically defined as reaching targets. Do X, and you'll get a bonus and a good performance review. Or in Haier's case, produce this and your microenterprise will get a chunk of the profit.

The problem is that targets that aren't perfectly aligned can cause more harm than good. The same is true of targets that aren't using the correct criteria, or fail to recognise the essential work that somebody is doing. Customers and employees often suffer because of these shortfalls.

Nurses receive targets for helping a certain number of patients a day. Too many, and quality of care falls and stress rises. Call-centre employees use their mobile phones to ring their own number and hang up immediately so average call-handling quotas are met. In both these cases, targets were probably set for good reasons, but left room for people to hack them and find loopholes.

Goodhart's Law, as proposed by the economist Charles Goodhart in 1975, states: "When a measure becomes a target, it ceases to be a good measure." A faulty measure leads to the focus shifting from the goal to the measurement. And to be fair, it's hard to blame people for chasing rewards.

Haier noticed that microenterprises were in some cases showing similar behaviour. Competition and trying to benefit at the cost of other microenterprises took precedence over collaboration.

In its previous incarnations, Haier's microenterprise structure unleashed potential by allowing employees to benefit from their solutions. That ensured motivation and benefitted all parties — including customers. It was inspired by Peter Drucker's insight that "the purpose of business is to create and keep customers". Although that alignment was functioning and helping them be successful, time had caught up with them once again.

With this increased need for collaboration, the old method of formulating internal contracts wasn't working as well as it once had. A fresh solution was needed, and fast, if Haier was to retain its leading position.

The EMC-Contract

From an outside perspective, the solution Haier found seems rather simple: a new type of contract that avoids internal competition and provides flexibility so that microenterprises can work together. These EMC-contracts tie together the more continuous microenterprises by forming temporary alliances called Ecosystem-Micro-Communities, or EMCs for short.

As you have probably guessed, in practice things aren't that simple. The new evolutionary step would require major changes, in organisational structure, and had even more consequences for the interaction with customers and product creation. It was the start of Rendanheyi 3.0: The Ecosystem Era.

> ***Business Ecosystems***
>
> *Ecosystems are open systems in which living organisms have struck a balance between resources and consumption. In nature, resources are transferred by organisms consuming one another, or benefiting in other ways. A cow eats grass, takes a dump, and adds nutrients to the soil; grass grows. The same is true when organisms die: it's not so good for the individual, but the ecosystem benefits from its passing.*
>
> *The concept of business ecosystems, as was defined by James F Moore, is different, of course, but similar principles apply. These should enable companies to evolve together and focus on co-creation rather than competition. As Zhang puts it: "We want to create a rainforest, not a walled garden. In a rainforest, a tree may die, but it adds to the health of the ecosystem and enables other species to thrive." In a walled garden, a few crops may grow, but they can be destroyed if snails find a way in.*
>
> *Vint Cerf, VP and Chief Internet Evangelist at Google, argues that ecosystems need to be a "harmonised group of elements". He used Lego as an example: although the pieces are different, they fit together. Google is*

trying to emulate this in its cloud services, making the clouds interact with each other to offer users more choice. It is important to question the benefits for all ecosystem stakeholders, as this may simply be a strategy for a single company to acquire more than its share of available resources, disturbing the balance. Haier's scenario calls for the acquisition of many resources — and that's where ecosystem-thinking comes in. Changing the business model to better serve the customer was the catalyst for organisational change.

The ecosystem metaphor is helpful but let's not labour it. Nature does not design systems that exhibit long-term stability across interconnected structures (the goal of business ecosystems) [20]*. They do not result from forethought, or the hand of authority, nor are they designed to be resilient or maximise the success of their component parts. Many would argue that they are not designed at all, but are emergent properties of individual organisms interacting — processes that involve a hierarchy.*

Organisms that under-perform are shaped by natural selection. Interactions between organisms may lead to failure; one may be consumed by another. Biological ecosystems include keystone species, which, if removed, would cause the collapse of the entire system. Certain actions are profitable to only one party, and some are detrimental to both.

The rate of change can be slow. On the other hand, there are similarities that are not always recognised. Both sorts of ecosystem emerge and become established via ties that link components. Many features conferring resilience in ecosystems are true of the organisational, as well as the biological. Within both systems are actors that are specialists or generalists, and the one interacts with the other. This nested system improves overall resilience and guards against the collapse of the ecosystem following the removal of one part. In both cases, mere existence is no guarantee of general health, functionality, or persistence.

Haier's Ecosystem Approach

Haier didn't copy an existing philosophy, it created its own. The EMC model stimulates collaboration by providing a shared goal, and creating a contract in which each microenterprise is connected to it. Every microenterprise that becomes part of the EMC will receive income only when the entire ecosystem succeeds at creating added value for the user. Profit will then be divided based on predetermined agreements on the value and size of the individual contributions. These binding agreements are embodied in the EMC-contracts.

A contractor hires sub-contractors to help build a new shopping-mall. All get paid for their services. Once the building is completed and sold to the highest bidder, the main contractor earns the profit. Using the EMC-model, things are done differently. The contractor still seeks assistance, instead of selling the building the sub-contractors exploit it, put in a shop, rent out apartments or open a restaurant. Profits from all these businesses are pooled and divided based on the influence the contractors (in Haier's model, the initiating microenterprise) and sub-contractors (other microenterprises) had in the eventual success.

Microenterprises were encouraged to evolve from selling transactional hardware to one-time customers to building smart products and services that would generate recurring revenues from interactive users. The development of such smart products and services required not only new organisational resources and capabilities. It also created a need for existing microenterprises, which had operated independently, to collaborate with one another and outside partners to collectively create products and services that could fulfil the needs of a specific user group: "user scenarios", in Haier-speak.

Haier restructured its five main platforms (White Goods, Investment & Incubation, Financial Holdings, Real Estate, and Culture), that had been organised according to traditional market segment, into six new groups, or "Fields": Smart Home, Touchpoint Iteration, Thousands of Links Sharing, Industry & City Integration, Culture, and Smart Connection, all with their own sub-fields based on user scenarios rather than specific products.

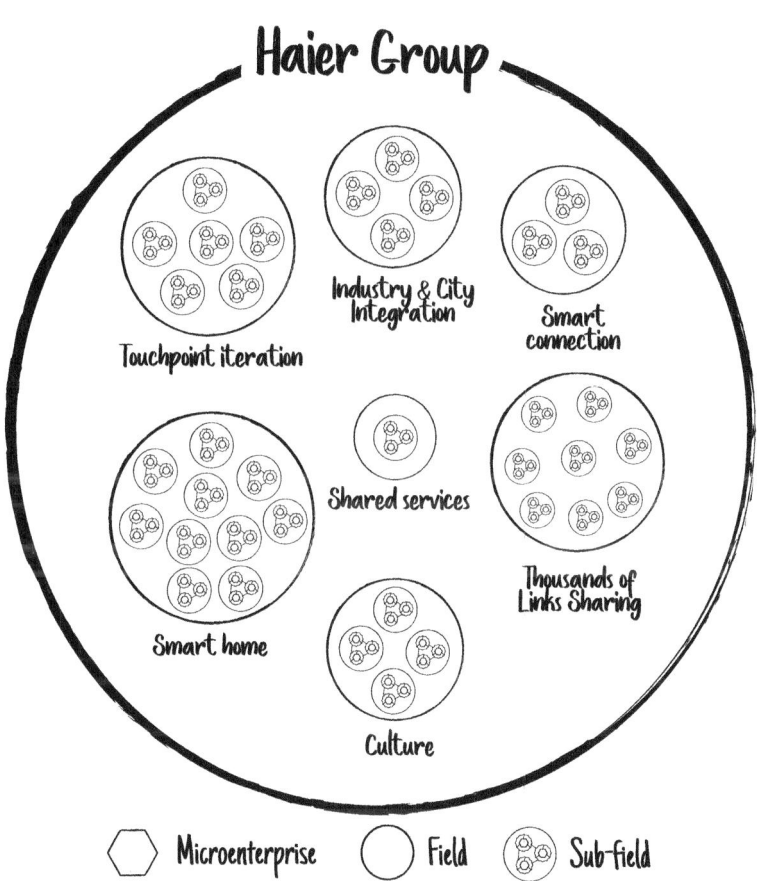

Internet of Food: Scenario Thinking

The emergence of the EMC model was not a centrally organised event, and not something that began when the new fields and sub-fields were created. Like so many solutions at Haier, it emerged from within the company itself, and grew larger when it proved successful.

In Qingdao, we interviewed someone who knew more. "I was working for a microenterprise that was making refrigerators," Sun Hang told us. "I realised that the products we were making would at some point become outdated. I needed to come up with something else, and that's when we initiated the Internet of Food Ecosystem."

Sun, 32, has worked for Haier since 2011, and is the leader of the Internet of Food EMC. The transition is from a microenterprise that created just a few stand-alone products to a thriving, collaborating ecosystem full of products that could communicate and collaborate with each other. It had integrated parts of a larger solution, and each product had a function complementary to the other parts. Haier called it Scenario Thinking.

Scenario thinking means moving things ahead while thinking laterally instead of going for the most obvious solution. For instance, there was a shift to viewing the customer as integral to the creation of a device. Some of Sun's colleagues found that many young people, newly living independently, were lazy when it came to cooking for themselves. This is a consumer problem that Haier chose to take on — and provide not just a solution, but a better product. It was no longer just about selling an oven, it was about finding out how the user wanted to use that oven.

"People, not products, are at the core of our thinking," said Sun. "We are always looking for resources to help them. Take the refrigerator as an example. At the beginning, we think about food — the product most closely associated with the appliance. Then we think further: could it also be connected to music, or movies? If we're talking about ecosystems, we don't think only about the refrigerator. Users need 'whole kitchen' scenario solutions.

Sub-Field: Internet of Food

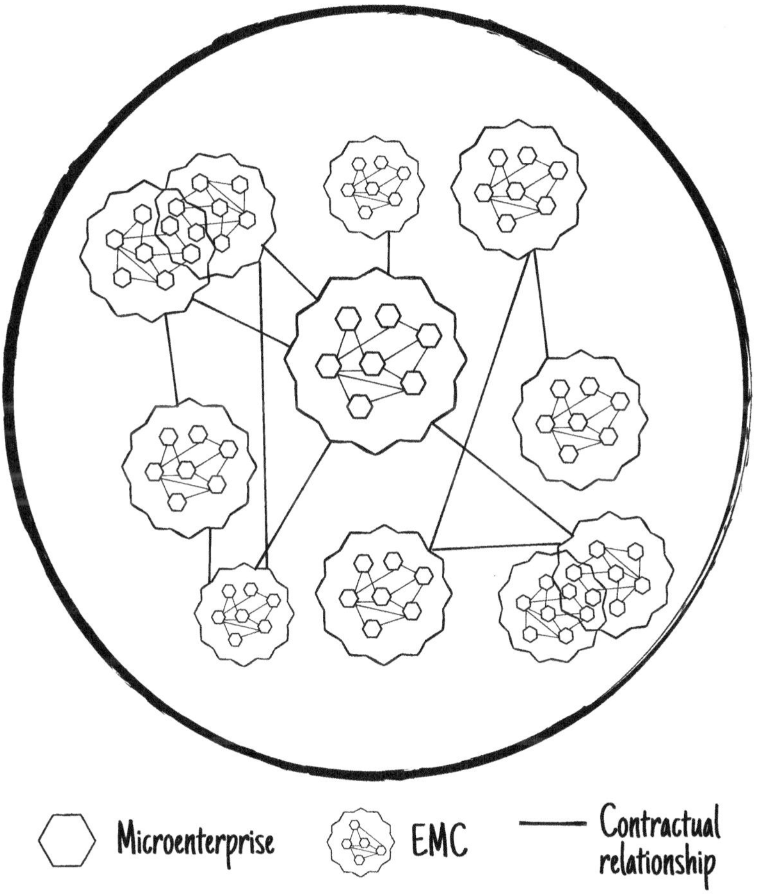

"We realised we could also provide home furnishings, a one-stop service to help users customise their homes and Haier to break new ground. We could let the user make 'whole set' choices, integrating services by working with partners. Through communication, we create a community. If it's people-orientated, the road will be wider. If it's 'thing-orientated', the road will be narrower. We analyse various needs."

Based on those analyses, Hang initiated the launch of Ecosystem Micro-Communities. These EMCs closely integrated all the autonomous parts and partners that were needed to deliver integrated solutions to the customers. Five EMCs were designed and created, all related to behaviours they had identified. They related to buying food, to storage, to washing, to cooking, and to eating.

These dynamic EMCs are future-proofing Haier's business by creating unique partnerships, as was the case with the Peking Duck project.

Created by the Cooking EMC, the project enables anyone to enjoy a Peking duck meal as served in a fancy restaurant. The Cooking EMC had learned that many of their users loved food, had all the equipment they needed, but lacked skills. To make a complicated dish like Peking duck, you need more than equipment. Knowledge, skill, and high-quality ingredients, for a start. After realising that the chefs in five-star restaurants often use semi-finished dishes, the EMC set out to find external partners. Many partners joined the EMC: a duck farm, a processing plant, chefs that had made the recipe, storage units, smart oven manufacturers, logistics and many more. All were bound via the EMC-contract, giving every partner a share of the profit of the ecosystem.

The unusual approach to user problems allows EMCs to focus on a broader range of challenges, and work with their partners for the ongoing provision of tasty, healthy food. It even led to the Cooking EMC trying to sell entire kitchens to the inept (or lazy) home chefs, and provide additional services like grocery delivery or easily accessible recipes.

The case of the Smart Cooking EMC also shows how Rendanheyi enables Haier's entrepreneurs to be so close to their users that they can develop and launch new products and services. Soon after the launch of the original "One-Bite Crisp" Peking Duck came a low-fat version of that same dish. This authentic version attracted foodies — and received high praise.

But some users pointed out the high fat content. Being health-aware, they said they felt obliged to exercise to offset the calorie intake.

After communicating with the user communities and figuring out the pain points, the EMC acted. It discussed the issue with ecosystem parties: chef Zhang Weili, Yanqi Lake Duck Farm, and the processing plants. Finally, the EMC decided to put the duck dish on a diet; enter the "Sports Fitness" Duck.

Haier's previous experience indicated that the research and development cycle for new products usually takes at least six months. But thanks to the joint efforts — via the IoF sub-field and various ecosystem parties — the Smart Cooking EMC successfully developed the low-fat version of roast duck in just three.

The concept of EMCs was shared in 2019 by Zhang Ruimin. It was not his invention, but his thinking was instrumental to its development. It proved to be the perfect greenhouse for such initiatives. Sun was one of the first to start thinking about collaboration in this way. The Ecosystem philosophy had already been in the ether for a couple of years. Microenterprise heads were shifting their stance on problem-solving.

It is still possible to simply buy a fridge from Haier, but this appliance is unlikely to be the endpoint of the transaction — the EMC is ready to go further. As Sun Hang said: "We should let the user choose the whole set. Based on this, we can integrate other services such as meal suggestions and food purchasing by working together with partners. We think from the users' point-of-view. They all have different needs, and by communicating with them we create a community. And there will be more needs to be met as we go forward."

• • •

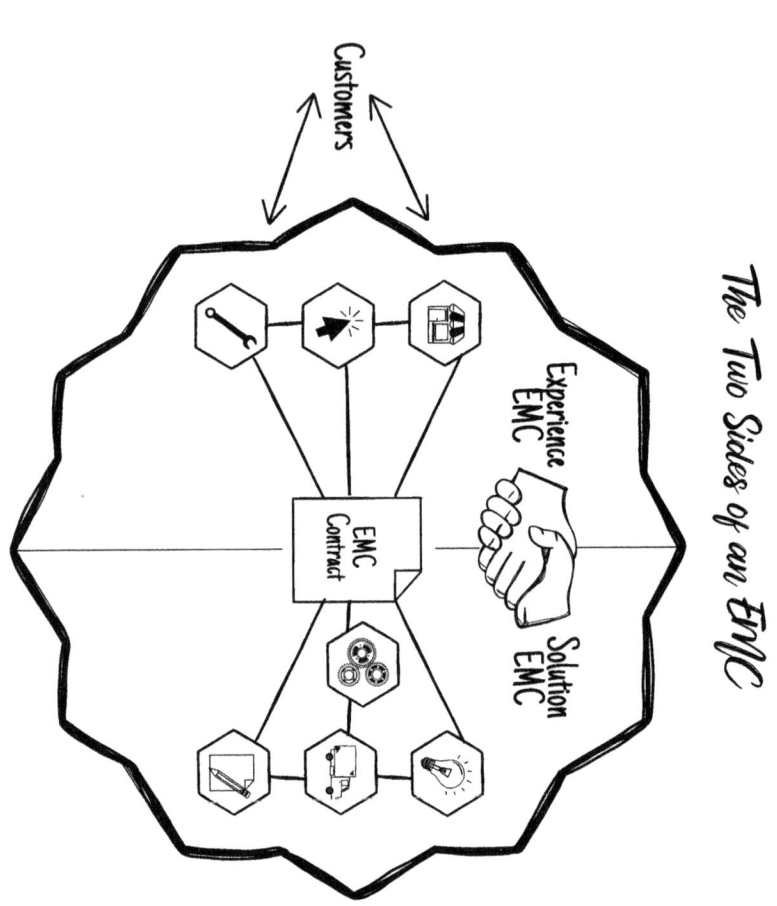

Two Sides of an EMC: Experience & Solution

Simply put, microenterprises are bound together by contracts, and form an EMC. They form temporary alliances that focus on the needs of a specific user group. Each EMC is comprised of two parts. These two smaller ecosystems complement one another: The Experience EMC and the Solution EMC. Their focus points are different. One creates value, the other transfers it. Together, they thrive.

Experience: Part of the EMCs

All Haier product ideas originate from the Experience EMC, which consists of microenterprises that interact with the user, or in Haier-speak, "user touch-points". The Experience EMC members must know who and where their users are, what they want, and how to get in touch with them. It's their responsibility to develop the scenarios that meet their needs.

The importance of information acquisition to EMCs throws up some unusual business ideas. They may offer free repair services to better understand customer needs. Specific user knowledge is a precious resource, and there are myriad ways to benefit from these insights. The interactions can take many forms: microenterprises can be repair companies, local stores, online communities, market researchers. Some even act as hosts of live-streaming in-store broadcasts, where potential clients can pose questions about the products on display.

• • •

Into the Goldilocks Zone

An example of how microenterprises can add value to the Experience part of an EMC can be found in the way the Baby Home Solutions Package set out to research the concerns of young mothers. Their job was to find out what the problem was. It quickly became clear that a typical concern was how best to prepare milk formula. Like the bears' porridge, it is invariably too hot or too cold, and bubbles could upset the infant. Now that China's one-child policy had grown into a two-child limit, births increased to 18 million each year. That presented a major opportunity, provided Haier could come up with some answers.

The microenterprise canvassed Babytree, China's largest online discussion platform for mothers, with 10 million users and close to a million daily visitors. Haier then constructed a website of its own, sharing its customer base and synching with Babytree. Young mums were able to consult with specialists online and share their concerns about infant health, and get advice on healthy nutrition. A specific need was identified, and a temperature-controlled milk maker was produced. This digital development was a first, with 56 million mothers showing interest. It resulted in 30,000 pre-launch product orders.

Haier obtained creative ideas and information via the platform, co-created value with customers, satisfied their demands, and was able to come up with the desired products. This innovative new model allowed the company to transform the knowledge of customers into valuable intellectual resources [6].

Haier moved on to develop a complete process. "We have 200 million users throughout China," reports Wang Jie, leader of the Haier Mother & Infant Refrigerator EMC. The translation suggests that this EMC specialises in cooling mothers and their small children, but that is not the case. It reacts to the pain points of a specific user group, and you have already guessed which one.

Wang Jie, not to be mistaken for her direct colleague Wang Jian, joined Haier in 2016, working on smart refrigerator planning. "Soon I moved from management of things to healthcare, particularly for mothers and children aged up to six."

Wang Jie explained the services her EMC provides. "Baby food preparation advice comes free-of-charge," she said. "Then there are some mums who want to lose weight after giving birth. A nutritionist will suggest a programme and track progress. This service is still at the trial stage, so we are not charging for it, but we will do so eventually. The nutritionists advise on breastfeeding and share information on baby food. They send out notifications and explain how best to use the milk warmer."

By being in direct contact with the users and these people sharing their experiences, Wang Jie and her colleagues could quickly see changes or opportunities by analysing user needs and sharing those insights with the rest of the EMC. This allowed them to improve existing products, or create new ones.

Examples of such innovation are legion. We encountered a different form of Experience EMC in the live-stream sales channel. This was introduced to us when we met Leng Heli and Sun Danfeng. Their live streaming platform tries to combine the easy access of an online store and the customer experience of an offline one. And because more than 10 million people have used the platform, you could say their attempt has been a success. Information is shared online, and more client interactions are arranged offline for optimal design and installation.

Sun took out her phone and fired up an app connected to a webstore. With a click of a button, we were watching a live stream in which two presenters talked about the products on display. We were not alone; the screen informed us that over 10,000 others were watching. Comments and questions came flooding in, and even though our knowledge of the Chinese language is limited, it was clear the presenters were fielding all queries. All this to help the connected EMCs to sell more products...

The microenterprises that form the Experience EMCs know who their users are, where they are, what they want, and how to get in touch with them. It's their responsibility to understand user experiences and needs.

The higher the quality of this knowledge, the greater the chance of becoming a successful entrepreneur. All you need to do is share resources with the microenterprises in your Ecosystem.

• • •

> *REBEL LOG, IN QUEST FOR UNDERSTANDING. There is no effort to keep us in the dark here; we are allowed access to pretty much everything. Our understanding, however, is sometimes limited by context. Haier has an answer for that, as well. Solutions are its stock-in-trade...*
>
> **Rebel One, out.**

A Whole World of Solutions

The Solution EMC, as it says on the tin, creates solutions. The microenterprises in it design, create, produce, and transport products that address user pain-points based on the information gathered by the Experience EMC. The sole judge of their efficacy is the end-user, and a sub-standard product will be rejected — putting at risk the income of all microenterprises. The Solution EMC and the Experience EMC must collaborate on creating an affordable and acceptable product.

The Interconnected Factory

Haier's Shengyang Interconnected Refrigerator Factory is the Solution EMC paradigm. A long drive from Qingdao this "lighthouse factory" lies amid architecture strangely reminiscent of Germany. There is a Teutonic heritage here, and some of the neighbouring factories even have German names.

> ### *Liebherr and Haier*
> *Haier's eagerness to collaborate with external partners can be traced back to 1984, when Zhang was appointed to run the Qingdao General Refrigerator Factory.*
> *He may have had an impressive moment of destruction with a sledgehammer and those defective fridges, but the firm was by no means out of the woods when he contracted with Germany's Liebherr to introduce the first four-star refrigerator in Asia. Zhang had purchased production lines from the German company, but domestic issues delayed implementation of the plans. But the time was right, given Chinese government reforms and the open economic policy of the decade. Zhang had chosen a powerful partner, but had real difficulty when it came to funding.*
> *A Haier contingent was sent to Germany for training, led by chief engineer Yang Mianmian. Zhang told the group that, because of investment costs, this was "death or victory". Head of Quality Control Han Zhendong was part of the team. He felt under pressure and was concerned that a month may not have been long enough to become familiar with the technology. The team took notes, made drawings based on blueprints, and generally tried their best. The representatives of other Chinese companies on the trip behaved differently. Some poked fun at the Haier team's studious behaviour and treated the trip as a holiday.*
> *This was the first time that a Western brand was able to get to know its Chinese counterpart, and for Haier the technology transfer went smoothly. Its reputation for reliability was reinforced. Haier's journey to success began with the Liebherr collaboration. It saved the company — something Zhang has never forgotten.*

> Ecosystems have allowed Haier to flourish in today's business environment, but the company's enthusiasm for co-operation and collaboration has been evident for over 37 years.

There's a Light Over There...
We visited the Shenyang Interconnected Refrigerator Factory, one of three owned and built by Haier to have joined the World Economic Forum (WEF) Global Lighthouse network.

They are called lighthouses because of the guidance they provide for those navigating the Fourth Industrial Revolution [21]. Lighthouse selection — just 18 factories are included — is based on the successful deployment of intelligent manufacturing technologies including AI, big data analysis, IoT and 3-D printing.

Wang Xiangjung is wearing a brown work jacket when we meet, not exactly the outfit you'd expect to see draped across the shoulders of the leader of one of the world's most prestigious factories. Chinese businessmen tend to dress rather formally; Haier seems to have broken with this tradition. His colleague, Hou Tingyi, is bespectacled, wearing a similar work coat, and is also of short stature.

Wang and Hou lead the way. We start the tour at the almost fully automated assembly line to see this Solution EMC in action. Sheets of metal move via elevators to their starting positions. We lose sight of the sheets as they go around a corner; when we see them again, the machines have done their work. The metal has been turned into refrigerator housings, and the further along the line we go, the easier it becomes to recognise the emergence of an embryonic refrigerator. The workers instantly know which part to grab, and how to manipulate and mount it before the line moves on.

"All the teams working here are different microenterprises," Wang explains. "One is responsible for installing electrical wiring, another one fits motors, a third takes care of insulation and installs the doors. Each is responsible for their part of the process, and only by collaborating can they complete a product." Each team has access to live data and can gauge whether the process needs to be faster, slower, or left as is. If one of the members finds a way to do their work more efficiently, bigger rewards are on the cards.

Along the factory hall there are signboards showcasing some of the Haier landmarks and innovations, for example "Zero Work Fixture, Zero Tape". The plaque includes a picture of the proud inventor, Wang Zhe, and a description explaining the worth of his innovation. Wang's microenterprise was responsible for fitting electrical motors and wiring. To ensure those wires didn't untangle and get stuck in anything, they were taped in place. A couple of steps down the line, another employee would have to remove the tape before connecting the wiring loom. Wang Zhe's solution was to replace the tape with rubber bands. This speeded the process, saving 10 seconds per unit and five seconds of process turnover. Costs were brought down by 0.2 yuan: three cents per unit, the going rate for a half-metre of tape.

Miniscule improvements can be crucial to improving everything by one percent per day. Even in one of the most prestigious factories in the world, where 5G operating systems allow computers to track the complete process of each product, where AI is used to take preventive measures, using a rubber band is celebrated with a plaque.

We love that. And we can see similar signs honouring innovation every few steps of our tour, all the way to the far side of the factory.

• • •

REBEL LOG: At the heart of the ship. The factory's control room is like the bridge of the Star Trek Voyager. Without the aliens, of course. Gigantic screens display a real-time map of the factory: assembly line progress, production data, team progress. The decision can be made to tap on the brake pedal or, perhaps, the accelerator. Heading for warp speed, captain.

Rebel One, out.

End of the Line

We are at the end of the production line, having completed a circuit of the factory. Here we find hundreds of boxes, filled with various refrigerator models lined up and waiting to be shipped. "Before we had the EMC structure, we had to wait for other departments to pick up our supplies," says Wang. "If they didn't have room in their warehouses, they would simply not collect. Now, because the income of the whole EMC is at stake, the other microenterprises find us."

Most Haier refrigerators are built on-demand, and to-order. From the time the metal sheets begin their journey down the assembly line to the collection of the finished machine, not more than 24 hours will have elapsed.

"We are a Solution EMC," says Wang, keeper of this Lighthouse. Compared to the more user-related Experience EMCs, their Solution EMC is different. They need to plan, do research and development, and eventually create the products that form the best solution for users. Wang explained that to create the best, outside resources can be acquired.

"For R&D, we usually try to make things as open as possible. We like to say that 'the world is our R&D department'. We discovered that Americans prefer iced water to cubes, so we integrated GEA's ice-water module into our EMC. Their solution was better than ours."

• • •

Making the Impossible ... Possible

Wang and Hou told the story of the factory's construction. "Our target was to start production within 13 months. Both of us had relevant experience and had invested in the factory ourselves, so we really wanted to meet the deadline. Work slowed because of a three-month delay for permits. We had just 10 months to build the factory and get it up and running. We were all highly motivated, and we succeeded. Production started at the appointed time.

"We had to be inventive. We used heating to ensure that the foundations dried at the correct pace. When we started production, the roof was half-finished: in some places it was snowing indoors. Nobody cared; we were only thinking about fast and efficient production."

• • •

> REBEL LOG, EXPLORING: *Not just us; Haier is on a constant quest to find undiscovered riches and seams of value. This is promising territory, and claims have been staked by the EMCs — sometimes outside of the empire. We watch with interest...*
>
> **Rebel One, out.**

Across Boundaries to Resource-Rich Terrain

Those microenterprises on the solution side and lacking resources can search outside the Haier ecosystem. In most companies that would be hard to imagine, but Haier has porous boundaries. Resources come in many forms: specific parts, specialist knowledge, or — as with the Hello Kitty Washing machine — money to start production.

Haier has always been keen to remove boundaries between management and employees, between supporting-roles and end-users, and between company and competition. Haier's organisational boundaries would best be traced with a dotted line. With big spaces between the dots.

Haier always seeks collaboration with the brightest minds in the innovation community and established the Haier Open Partnership Ecosystem (HOPE).

In most organisations, there is no infrastructure to enable, or motivate, employees to problem-solve or create products inter-departmentally. Sure, marketing and sales automatically share insights from their survey with the design department. A better design will make it easier to sell the product. In a large organisation, it's sometimes hard to get knowledge to the place it's most needed. Researchers don't have direct access to the problems of others, so it can be difficult for them to pick up on developments which may help.

At Haier, microenterprises are comfortable to admit that they don't know how to fix the "whole problem". The firm understood that given the extraordinary expansion of consumers' personalised demands, enterprises needed to co-innovate with users and world-class resources. This platform displays Haier's areas of interest and represents an invitation to individuals in the wider world to come up with solutions, contacts, and resources to fulfil needs. This is a company that is truly designing and creating the future. There is no looking back, and Haier helps its collaborators identify opportunities and access strategic options. This platform encourages innovative resources and develops talent, culture, and systems to drive projects forward.

According to management guru Gary Hamel, "No company is promoting innovations on such a large scale, and in such a systematic manner." [22] Haier is seen as a company which, in the new realities, is producing an alternative to bureaucracy. "Bureaucracies are insular. Typically, they make sharp distinctions between insiders and outsiders, and are characterised by secrecy and a reluctance to tap external partners for mission-critical tasks. The problem with a closed system is that it doesn't adapt — it atrophies. Recognising this, Haier sees itself not as a company but as a hub in a much larger network. The implications of this view are profound."

Haier products and services are developed in the open — the bureaucrat's nightmare. Haier used a social media site to identify consumer preferences when setting out to build a new home air conditioner. It worked; there were more than 30 million respondents, and 700,000 were invited to delve deeper and reveal pain points and share their thoughts on features. More than 200 problems are shared annually on HOPE, and 400,000 technical experts and institutions are the solution-finders helping Haier. The firm once made a request for design assistance for air conditioner blades; the challenge resulted in several proposals delivered within a week. The winning design came from the China Aerodynamics Research and Development Centre, and the 33 institutions that contributed to its development. When the resulting Tianzum Wind Tunnel was launched, it was an immediate success. In that same year, a consumer complained that commercial refrigerators could not keep produce fresh. Haier's big-data analysis picked up on that. The problem could not be solved internally, so the call went out on HOPE for seven-day freshness. Two technical providers co-operated with the platform — one an institute specialising in food preservation technology, the other a manufacturer of the defined containers. Problem solved. Haier creates a pool where its partners confidentially share patents and are financially rewarded, or added to an EMC when their ideas figure in the final product.

In moving the development process online, the time from initial concept to sales can be reduced by upwards of 70 percent. All stakeholders work in parallel throughout a project. HOPE introduces talent to Haier too, as many microenterprise leaders' first contact with the company comes via the platform. HOPE's income is generated mainly via its network of customised services, including tech intelligence and management consultancy. The HOPE initiative has adopted the philosophy of "Wikinomics" successfully. The idea behind it is that mass collaboration changes everything. By opening the doors for others to help innovate and share knowledge, world-class resources and wisdom can be exchanged easily while at the same time tapping into a global pool of creative thinkers. The combination of that drives technological innovation forward at unprecedented speeds [23]. As you probably know by now, this is exactly what Haier is hoping to achieve.

• • •

Ambiguous Microenterprises

When reading about the different roles of microenterprises, one might think it would be a simple matter to classify a microenterprise or individual on the Experience side or the Solution side. These roles can be ambiguous, with certain microenterprises having multiple roles within the same ecosystem, or even within other ecosystems. Think of a microenterprise that offers repair services to customers with defective goods or appliances. That would make its members part of the Solution EMC, because they solve a user problem. But in many cases, they are also part of an Experience EMC. Repair employees can, for example, gather information about user needs, or even sell other products. Such ambiguity is perfectly acceptable. It allows those repair microenterprises to add even more value for the EMC and customers.

When Haier adopted the network structure, the resistance to flow of resources was reduced. But there were still problems to overcome — and one of the biggest was that the form of collaboration sometimes led to internal competition and shading. The EMC model makes it easier for microenterprises to share resources, because they have a common goal.

Profit will be divided between microenterprises of that specific ecosystem, based on those predetermined agreements. In most cases, these are based on the amount or quality of the resources a microenterprise has provided, or on how successfully each of the microenterprises has completed its share of the work.

Remember: Failure is Impossible

The principle of these contracts may seem logical and easy to understand on the small scale. But Haier finds ways to use principles such as this to create something momentous.

We spoke to Yu Mingkai, one of the entrepreneurs at the Smart Kitchen Scenario Planning microenterprise. "We develop different scenarios," he said. "We have 37 now, and we make sure that they play out in the best way possible." We were not surprised by this, as we had seen this principle in action. "One of our scenarios concerns young urbanites with demanding jobs," Yu continued with a grin. "They can't cook. They don't have the time to shop for groceries, or maybe don't have the skills to prepare proper meals."

You may think these are not the people who would want to buy a kitchen, but Yu and his team thought otherwise. "We try to help by making cooking easy. Earlier on we would have sold them an oven, but now it's a complete ecosystem. Using a screen on their oven, or an app that connects to it, they can access all sorts of recipes. They make a choice, then order the groceries and have them delivered by one of our partners. The app can preheat the oven to the desired temperature, close down when the dish is ready — making failure almost impossible."

Profits are shared throughout the ecosystem. The Oven-Microenterprise benefits when a user orders groceries through the system. One of the latest developments is that users can become vendors. "If a user doesn't feel like creating a meal, they can order through the app. Meals can then be produced by another user who loves cooking. They can sell their meals on our platform."

For each transaction made, a fee paid to the EMC enables every microenterprise to benefit, even if the oven made by the Oven-Microenterprise is used only to order a meal.

> ### Contracts on the Blockchain
> *Execution of the EMC contracts is done using blockchain technology. Blockchain enables a higher level of trust between microenterprises. To understand why this is the case, you need to understand how blockchain technology works.*
>
> *On the blockchain, information is transparent and stored in a way that does not allow manipulation. The time-stamped series of immutable data records is managed by a cluster of computers with multiple owners. Each block of data is secured and bound to the others cryptographically*

(the chain). The network has no central authority but is a shared and secure ledger with total transparency. This offers a way for two parties to pass along information in an automated and safe manner. One initiates the block, verified by the computer cluster; it is then added to the chain, creating a unique record. It is impossible to falsify a single record without falsifying the entire chain.

The technology could change the way that ownership, privacy, uncertainty and collaboration are conceived in the digital world, disrupting sectors and practices as diverse as financial markets, content distribution, supply chain management, the dispersal of humanitarian aid and even voting in a general election [24].

"Everyone can access the information stored in the ledger," Leng explains. "They can see how much value is generated, and how much will be shared with them." This transparency stimulates trust because each member of an EMC has access to information that by default cannot be manipulated or deleted. Once a microenterprise has trust in the system, it becomes confident of receiving its agreed share.

• • •

REBEL LOG, IN THE SICK BAY: But strictly in an observational capacity. Healthcare for the denizens of Haier is a priority, along with safety. But outside of the community, healthcare is affected — positively — by what goes on within it.

Rebel One, out.

The Power of EMCs: Responding to Extreme Changes

For years, long before Covid-19, China had been haunted by vaccination scandals. Shots were improperly stored, the quality questionable, and fraud was rife. By looking holistically at the problem, U-vaccine was able to restore trust.

Smart logistics at Haier microenterprise U-vaccine ensure that products are correct and valid, transparency improves, patient information systems function, and reception areas for adults and children are comfortable.

The Covid pandemic hit this microenterprise hard, and non-essential healthcare went by the board. An easing of restrictions was accompanied by what Haier would come to call "user pain points". If clinics were not perceived as safe, children would be kept at home.

U-vaccine initiated a new EMC, forming a network to find solutions to all user problems. It became responsible for attracting resources: time, funding, knowledge, special techniques, and access to networks.

According to the leader of the U-vaccine microenterprise, Mr Gong, the moment was saved by the Rendanheyi 3.0 model. Gong has been working for Haier since 2005. He started off as an R&D engineer, and in five years became head of the department. In 2018, he placed a bid to become leader of U-vaccine, a microenterprise that provides complete solutions for points of vaccination.

In mid-July 2018, China's premier, Li Keqiang, declared that the Changsheng Bio-technology Company vaccine scandal had crossed an ethical line. He promised to crack down on criminal acts that endanger lives.

According to Reuters[25], the country's drug regulator reported that Changsheng had falsified manufacturing and inspection records. Police investigated company executives, including its chair. President Xi Jinping described that company's actions as "vile and shocking". It had been reported that Changsheng sold 252,600 doses of ineffective vaccines to "inoculate" children against diphtheria, whooping cough and tetanus. Earlier in the month, Changsheng had recalled all its rabies vaccines after the drug watchdog noted that the process violated manufacturing standards, and its licence was revoked.

By the third week of July, Changsheng share value dropped by $1.8bn — more than half. In late 2019, BMC Public Health (part of Springer Nature) commented that the country's immunisation achievements had been threatened by the crisis. A survey revealed that most respondents expressed negative views about vaccines following the incident. BMC commented: "A co-ordinated effort is required to restore public confidence in vaccines, especially in China, where a nationwide mandatory immunisation policy is implemented..." [26]

In the meantime, Chinese parents had lost faith. Even if the products themselves were dependable, could the same be said of their storage? Mr Gong had something to say about that. "In China, there is a law that vaccination must not be carried out in the afternoon. By the end of each morning, refrigerators have been opened as many as 300 times, causing the vaccines to get too warm. To prevent that, a law stating that vaccinations should only be conducted in the mornings was passed, but that did not really address the root cause of the problem. We wondered if there was an alternative solution."

Scenario Thinking at U-vaccine
What differentiated U-vaccine from many of its outside competitors was its holistic view, using Haier's scenario thinking. Gong had created a new EMC for a specific scenario when he became the leader of U-vaccine. His microenterprise quickly realised that this challenge was bigger than building a more efficient refrigerator. He had to rebuild trust in the entire vaccination system. Gong analysed user needs, and likely solutions were tested. "Sometimes they work on paper, but in practice do not address the user pain point," Gong points out. "If you test a new refrigerator in an R&D lab, conditions are perfect. It tells you nothing about operations in real life. We knew that we had to come up with better solutions to ensure stable temperatures. We developed a refrigerator with eight drawers, each with its own door." The separate drawers were insulated, to be less affected by the opening and closing.

Gong's team came up with many solutions in its bid to rebuild trust. These included smart logistics to ensure vaccines were correct and valid, and improved transparency, displaying information on a screen where parents and nurses could read it. Sensitive patient information systems were established, and décor adjusted to make children feel comfortable (in time-honoured tradition, cartoon characters helped). This approach worked, and within two years U-vaccine was an important player in the market.

Virus Located ... Emergency Stations

Lockdown brought China to a standstill. In February and March of 2020, almost all companies had to close, and production plummeted. It was a pattern that spread across the world.

"When Covid-19 broke out, we were hit quite hard," says Gong. "Our production and logistics ground to a halt, and the vaccination points had to close. Hospital nurses could stay, but the others had to go, and families were not allowed to leave their homes. Non-essential healthcare came to a stop. Nobody went to the vaccination points."

After restrictions were eased, Gong and his EMC saw that things had changed on many levels. There were new government guidelines, and needs were different. Earlier solutions were no longer sufficient, but children still needed to get their shots. Parents needed reassurance that the clinics were safe, or they would keep their children home. Nurses were concerned about contact with so many people, and the hospital directors needed to guarantee their safety.

"There was an opportunity here," Gong continued, "but without the Rendanheyi model we wouldn't have coped." Haier's way of working allowed the EMC to react swiftly, and solutions were developed. Improved reservation via WeChat eased pressure on medical facilities, temperatures were tracked via infrared cameras, IoT solutions confirmed hand washing prior to appointments, and smart refrigerators made it easier to locate and use vaccines about to expire.

By applying Scenario Thinking, U-vaccine understood that help would be needed to solve all these problems. It needed to initiate a new EMC and attract resources. And, just like any new EMC within Haier would do, it took the following steps.

U-Vaccine EMC Initiation
Haier
Microenterprise
U-Vaccine microenterprise
External Companies

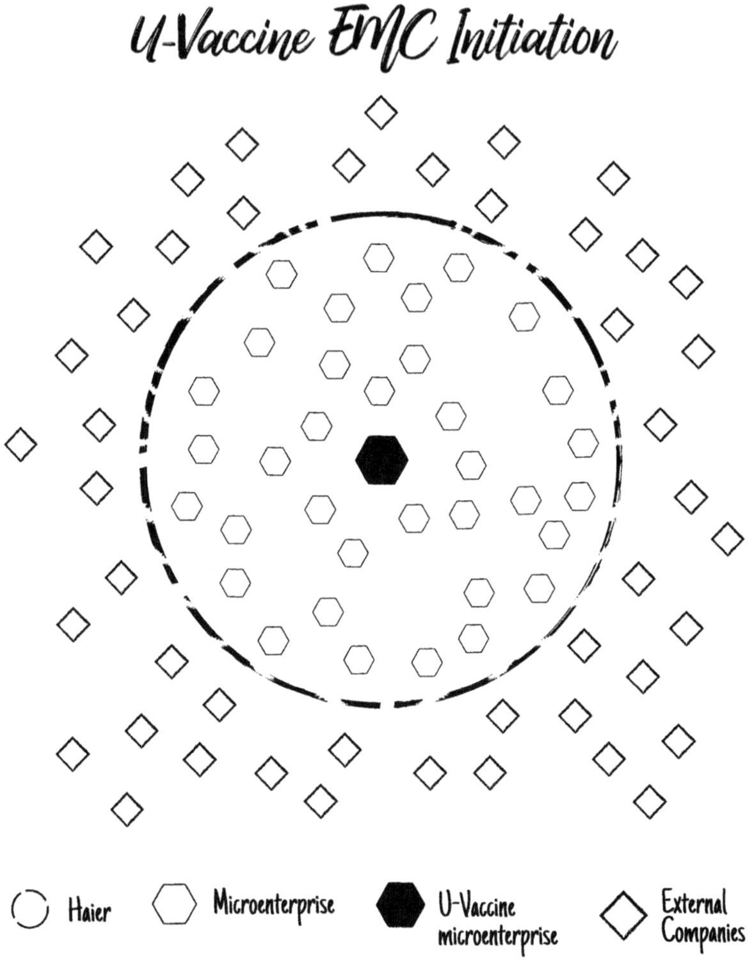

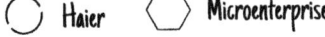

A Possible Scenario: Initiating an EMC
The first step in creating an EMC is taken by the initiating microenterprise. By default, it becomes the EMC-leader. Gong became EMC-leader. His responsibility was to ensure the availability of resources. He shared problems with the rest of the Haier community. At that point, the new EMC was really a single microenterprise reaching out for help.

Each EMC uses contract templates to ensure the inclusion of the necessary elements to align all interests. It makes sure the goal is well-formulated, the profit distribution is clear, and the roles of all participating microenterprises are defined — before work starts.

Bidding, Betting, Bettering
Individuals at Haier bid to undertake certain tasks or goals and, if successful, join a microenterprise. The same principle applies within the EMC structure. Any microenterprise that feels capable may bid on a goal set by the EMC-leader. Microenterprises formulate their goals and explain how their achievement will address pain points.

There seem to be simple rules for microenterprises formulating a goal: it must be competitive, and out-perform the market. The bid should explain how a microenterprise plans to reach that goal and how much of the profit it expects to see.

After review by the EMC leaders and the shared services platform (HR, Financial, Legal), winners are identified, and contracts negotiated. The role and goals of the microenterprise are made clear, and the percentage of total EMC profits to be distributed is stipulated. This step may seem obvious, but it's critical to the success of Haier: decades spent evolving internal processes have been a good investment of time.

Contracts are always designed to ensure that performing as well as possible is beneficial for all parties: there must be win-win.

EMC CONTRACT TEMPLATE

1. User resources

2. Sharing of profits

3. Revenues

4. Cost and marginal cost

5. Marginal income per active user

If not, it would result in a zero-sum game, reports Gong: "If the supplier did not agree with our price and delivered a sub-standard product as a result, we would not be happy." There can be no single winner. "Value created within the ecosystem is shared by all the microenterprises. Everyone stands to benefit. There is no need to make bad products; we can, and should, focus on creating great things."

Even though this sounds similar to methods used in the microenterprise structure, there is an important difference. Microenterprises were only contracting with one another, and one initiating microenterprise was involved in all those contracts. The EMC contract is focused on wider collaboration. All microenterprises in the EMC are contractually bound in a tighter formation.

EMC contracts are forged according to these rules:

1. Each microenterprise sets its own goals, and potential rewards are calculated.

2. Each contract aims for higher profitability than the industry average to out-perform the market.

3. The range of value-added sharing is defined before production starts, with lower and upper limits.

Action Stations, Action Stations: Solving Problems

Now that all microenterprises are bound by smart contracts, solutions can begin to relieve user pain points. Microenterprises all have skin in the game, which encourages them to help one another. If the microenterprise responsible for infrared temperature measurement fails, and sick people infect others at a vaccination centre, the trust in the EMC drops. Noticing that another microenterprise in your EMC is failing and doing nothing about it will backfire. This dependency leads to camaraderie. Mutual aid is normal and strengthens the whole. The approaches may differ, but all are borne from the same ideology and have the same goal: to increase transparency and improve collaboration and information sharing.

Renegotiating Contracts

The value that microenterprises bring varies over time. Each month, they meet and sometimes renegotiate profit-sharing. As Gong says: "Usually, the EMC leader will propose a new balance and hopes to reach consensus. After the Covid-19 outbreak, we lowered the percentage of profit to the Marketing microenterprise, because it could not organise events or conduct offline marketing. Online marketing is cheaper but adds less value. And the Research and Development microenterprise received a bigger share, because it was more important to the EMC."

All members know that they need each other to create a good product and get it to the users. Collaboration is the means to success and profit. In a company with a divisive culture, there could be conflict: departments blaming each other, colleagues arguing over who is at fault. The culture at Haier is different: almost every person we spoke to said they received help when they were struggling. That first-hand experience will have shown them how valuable a little assistance, or even a small gesture, can be.

"We help the microenterprise to be successful because it is part of our EMC. Sure, if a microenterprise consistently fails to meet its targets, we could look for a replacement – but it's better to help the original because it is already part of our EMC. Getting a new microenterprise up to speed will take time and delay the whole process."

U-Vaccine EMC Creation

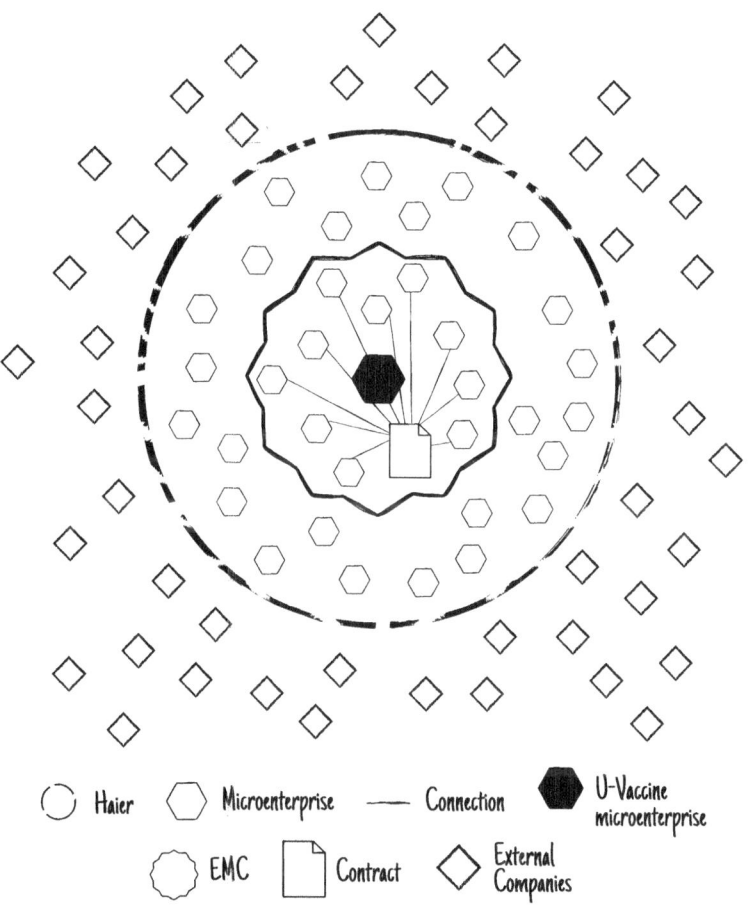

Simple Patterns Repeating

Haier uses the relatively simple to create the complex, always aligning incentives. Some EMCs join others because of a useful specialisation. The result can be an EMC in an EMC... in an EMC.

At Haier's Third International Rendanheyi Model Forum in Shanghai, W Brian Arthur, a pioneer in the field of complexity theory, took to the stage and shared a mesmerising video of starlings in flight, commenting that complicated behaviour of the whole can be caused by simple individual patterns. The film showed thousands of birds doing the same thing: staying as close as possible to those around them while in flight. Each bird's movement results in a complex, dramatic and beautiful pattern in the swirling flock. Arthur argued that the same principles apply to economics: Individual actors react to economic situations created by others. The situation changes, causing others to alter their strategies. This brings us a world in which individuals, banks, corporations, and investors are constantly adapting to the situation around them. Adaptive strategies and actions are constantly being tested for survival potential.

Complexity economics sees economy as ecology: individual behaviour influences and affects others in the system. In another parallel with nature, the extinction of one species could lead to a crisis for others. To survive, individual actors need to keep evolving their strategies. A company that does this more quickly and efficiently than others will have a competitive edge.

The Haier bidding process is conducted on an individual basis by a microenterprise, or groups of microenterprises. To the outside world, this may seem chaotic, but to those aware of the guiding principles it makes perfect sense. No need to worry about every little detail, or who is responsible for what, because the principles provide sufficient guidance.

Repeating Patterns

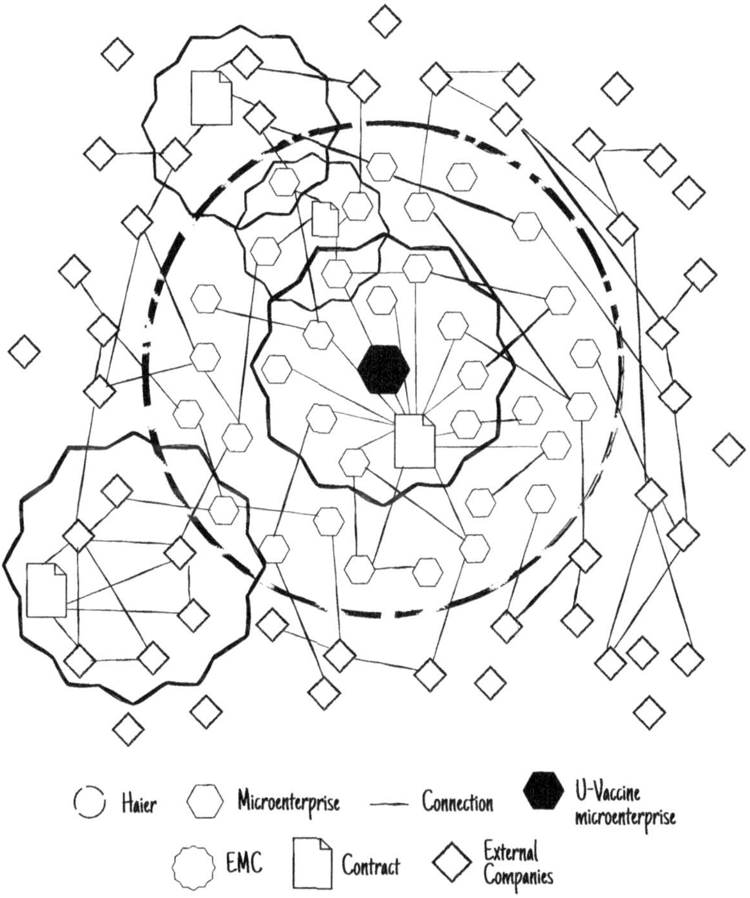

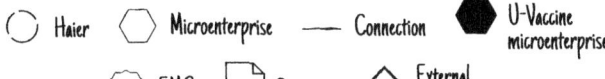

Survival Through Solutions

Gong sees Haier's model of critical importance for his success. "As a regular employee during the pandemic, I could have stayed home, enjoyed a holiday, and had nothing to worry about," he said. "But I am an entrepreneur, and I knew that to survive we had to find new solutions for our users, so we all worked hard —and now are benefitting."

The success did not go unnoticed by the Chinese government. Haier was asked to build mobile vaccination centres to reach remote villages. With the Covid-19 pandemic still wreaking global havoc, it's easy to see how much of a responsibility this was. Such a project requires collaboration with others outside the Haier boundaries. By using the same model, solutions will be developed to respond to government needs.

An Alternative to 'The Other' Universe

Hierarchical organisations are not for everyone, and neither is the Haier model. It's merely an alternative. Even if this solution isn't for you, there is a lot to learn from the way Haier enables resources to flow through a complex organisation. On closer inspection, it seems that the complexity is not as extreme as it first appeared. A simple pattern repeated many times allows microenterprises and EMCs to respond in a swift and dynamic way to sudden changes in the world around them. Even if that change is a global pandemic.

SPACE

'We must elevate the system so that it has "external adaptation with internal perseverance". We must do so on the foundation of human value maximisation so that people are granted autonomy while being internally anchored and externally fluid. When such a balance is accomplished, the model can self-adapt in a fast-changing environment and stay relevant to the times. Organisations and individuals can then achieve a state in which they never forget their original mission and attain eternal enlightenment; they possess ever-living fire.'

Zhang Ruimin, 2022*

*From essay: An Ever-living Fire (Full essay in Appendix 4)

> REBEL LOG: Well, well, after all this time, return to more familiar realms is looming. But our Rebel work here is not yet done. We intend to bring home more than postcards. We'll load the luggage with wisdom, and copious notes, then set the controls for the heart of ... er, hold on. Alexa, get me Google Maps...
>
> **Rebel One, out.**

Rendanheyi in Other Cultures, Organisations, and Beyond

You've accompanied us on Haier's journey, learning how it has dealt with change, how practices have been developed on its road to becoming one of the most entrepreneurial companies in the world.

One of the key elements is the much-praised Rendanheyi management model — but it is not a model that can be replicated. And should any CEO or transformational manager think that simply copying the model is enough, disappointment awaits.

It could be argued that many things make Haier unique, but we beg to differ. The stand-out feature is its culture. That's the big difference. Individuals help the company evolve, and Haier returns the favour. The focus is on innovation and enabling people to seize opportunities.

The Rendanheyi model was developed to help employees organise. By mixing management theories, seasoning the brew with some Eastern philosophy, garnishing it with personal experiences and letting it marinate for a few years, fresh solutions emerged.

CTRL + C, CTRL + V?

Organisational cultures are often hard to grasp and almost always impossible to copy. Thousands have tried to emulate Spotify, Google, and Apple, and many have failed, and learned that lesson the hard way.

It isn't a case of Ctrl + C and Ctrl + V. Culture is intangible. It's a pattern of basic assumptions that help to cope with all challenges and situations, from how people greet one another to what is needed to achieve a goal.

How those solutions emerge is influenced by employees, their experiences, their interactions, and their workplace practices. Finding workable solutions is part of the overall Haier culture. They are taught and transmitted, directly or indirectly. The company culture guides perception, thoughts, and feelings [27].

If companies wanted to implement Haier's model, changes to the organisational culture would be a necessity. As Zhang puts it: "Without culture, a model would be without soul; without a model, the culture would be nothing but a castle in the sky." But it's impossible to transplant the culture.

Haier is Haier.

Can You Get to the Haier Level...?

A more relevant question might be: "Can the Rendanheyi model be applied to other companies?" The answer is yes... but. As model and culture are so intertwined, it's impossible to make an exact replica.

Mergers and acquisitions are an important place for Chinese companies to implement their internationalisation strategy. Haier has completed four important overseas M&As in recent years to complete the global layout of its industry.

In October 2011, it acquired Japan's Sanyo Electric, cracking open the South East Asian market and realising its first profit in 2014. In September 2012, Haier acquired Fisher & Paykel, a New Zealand home appliance brand, and quickly increased its value and market share. An increase of nearly 50 percent has set a new model for China-New Zealand business cooperation. In June 2016, Haier acquired General Electric's home appliance business (GEA) at a price of $5.4bn, completing the largest overseas M&A in China's home appliance industry.

In January 2019, Haier and the Italian Fumagalli family jointly announced the acquisition of international electrical appliance manufacturer Candy, which officially became a wholly owned subsidiary of the Haier Group. But Haier's overseas mergers and acquisitions included not only the export of products and technologies, but also of their management model.

To retain the excellent operating resources of the acquired company, Haier successfully exported its model to the United States, Japan, New Zealand, Russia, and Italy. Rather than trying to replicate other models, Haier has taken a different approach.

Haier uses the "salad analogy" to explain its integrated management process. Zhang: "On Haier's plate there are a variety of different 'vegetables', each of which represents a culture or way of life, but the 'salad dressing' is unified — that's Rendanheyi. For Japan's Sanyo, the Rendanheyi model has changed the service direction, from leader-first to user-first. For Fisher & Paykel, we retained the 'craftsmanship spirit', but used the Rendanheyi model to transfer decision-making power, human rights, and distribution of power.

"For GEA, an American benchmarking company with a history of more than 120 years, we respected and retained its 'culture of contracts' — but we used the Rendanheyi model to implement entrepreneurial microenterprises."

Contextual awareness is everywhere to be found. Microenterprises come in all forms. Some are progressive and showcase the model, others are organised more traditionally. The culture within that latter group does not yet have the requisite ingredients — skills, experience, or knowledge.

Progressive and innovative practices might work perfectly in one place but fail in another — and Haier finds that ambiguity perfectly acceptable.

• • •

Gifts from Far-Off Places

"China did not have its own management models," Zhang told us, "we imported them. Now we should export our models to internationalise them." The company had already experimented by creating microenterprises in other regions; it was time for a bigger challenge: transforming foreign companies.

In 2012, Haier bought Sanyo, the Japanese white goods business that had become a household name — but suffered eight years of losses. It calls to mind the "stunned fish", but things were different this time around. It was the start of another Haier-led transformation.

The former Sanyo staff were used to a strict workplace hierarchy; employees were hired to obey, not to take the initiative. When Haier came along, employees were encouraged to take ownership of their work, understand it in a different way, and heed user-needs.

Such fundamental changes do not come easily, and a shift of focus wasn't enough. Sanyo's existing model — especially the salary management system — conflicted with Haier's. Staff compensation was based on seniority, rather than the customer-centric model. Instead of forcing its views on its new acquisition, Haier introduced them step-by-step [28].

Sanyo employees were used to 12 months' salary and a four-month bonus. Haier adapted this to its own philosophy by aligning the automatic bonus with performance. For outstanding work, employees could receive more still. And performance, unsurprisingly, was judged according to customer satisfaction.

Slowly but surely, perceptions and mindsets began to shift. "The most important element of Sanyo is team spirit," said Zhang. "We didn't change that, only the direction — from following your boss to following users." [29]

Could the Japanese workers adapt? They could, and did. As one put it: "Before, we thought the company should take care of us; now, we take care of the company." [28]

The story of the Japanese Aqua microenterprise is illuminating. It is no longer in the business of selling washing machines but has established diverse laundry scenarios in partnership with thousands of cross-industry players. These include top name retailers allowing customers to do their laundry and shopping at the same place and the same time.

The microenterprise members, listening attentively to consumers, identified a need to wash large items (such as curtains and quilts) which are too heavy for standard home appliances. An investment of $500m addressed this opportunity and resulted in the development of commercial grade washing and drying facilities. Aqua continuously upgrades these machines and has introduced online functionality that allows customers to search for nearby stores, check their status, and make appointments.[30]

Sanyo grew accustomed to Haier's customer-orientation. It learned to transform the corporate culture into a more innovative and entrepreneurial one. The process took years. "It is difficult, but important, to integrate cultures," Zhang Ruimin explained. "Many (changes) are not embraced by employees because they don't match their company's business models and there's no correlation or interaction."[6]

This was the first success in introducing the Rendanheyi model to other countries, but more would follow. Haier subsequently purchased Fisher & Paykel Appliances, which operated globally from New Zealand. There, Haier could apply the lessons learned from the acquisition of Sanyo and apply a suitable strategy. "We didn't want them to follow what we were doing in China. They had to figure it out for themselves," said Zhang.

While the results were still emerging, a new opportunity arose. The company had to respond swiftly to tackle an old nemesis.

• • •

An American Icon Acquired

Back in 2015, General Electric decided to sell its appliances business. After a year of negotiation with Electrolux, a $3.3bn offer was blocked by US anti-trust authorities. This was an opportunity for Haier to gain purchase on US soil. Within weeks, the century-old GEA business had been bagged — by a company that most of the American employees had never heard of — for a staggering $5.4bn.

Why did GE sell to Haier? Because there's no decent margin in making appliances when the competition can do it for a lower price. GE had more lucrative business to do.

This makes sense, if only through the eyes of GE. Yes, it sold its appliance business because apart from anything else, it could no longer make a decent profit on its products. Using the devil's advocate mindset, that may be because it failed to see the opportunities. But Haier did not buy GE to compete on cost. It saw the opportunity to make bigger margins in different ways. Legacy firms (like GE) that had essentially been doing the same thing for decades did not develop product differentiation. They neglected technological change, and this threatened their core business. Digital technologies have the potential to bring differentiation to almost every traditional industry.

Technology-driven companies have convinced their customers to enter long-term relationships, instead of interacting in a transactional way. This has allowed them to accumulate value over time. Haier is essentially following this lead. The company is transitioning one-off sales of kitchen appliances into recurring service offerings through GEA's own technology platforms. These recurring revenue offerings are less vulnerable to short-term disturbances and can cover the weaknesses of a legacy hardware business. By integrating the hardware and software sides of the business (as Apple did with its iPhone, Wearable and App Store lines) Haier might even be on the path of combining high growth with high margin. This is something not all firms are able to do.

Haier had created other factories in the US, but without much success. Acquiring GEA and leveraging its strong brand was just the opportunity Haier had been looking for. On top of that, there seemed to be a personal angle. One can hear the pride in Zhang Ruimin's voice when he reminds everyone that in the early '90s, General Electric had vowed to eliminate Haier.

The tables had been well and truly turned.

Up for Adoption

"It was like having a parent who didn't really love us," says GE Appliances CEO Kevin Nolan. "The one hope was that Haier had bought us because they wanted us, and we were curious to find out what that would mean." The iconic American firm that dated from 1907 was an established brand. Almost every citizen grew up with GEA products in the household. Since 1951, its headquarters had been based in Louisville, Kentucky, and it was there that Haier intended to introduce America to Rendanheyi.

Many GEA workers found the acquisition hard to digest. It didn't seem to be heading for a happy ending. But the eventual results speak for themselves. Since the Haier take-over, GEA has increased its market share every quarter. Even during the Covid-19 pandemic, there was growth across all categories.

Introducing the Model

Kevin Nolan: "In the first year, Haier told us: 'We're going to let you run the business the way you want'." Nolan, who started with GE in '97 and was CTO at the time of the acquisition, couldn't believe it. "You don't spend five billion dollars and not get involved," he said.

He felt the need to better understand Haier's thinking, and spent a good part of that first year in Qingdao. "On the surface, it's a hard company to understand," he admits. "I remember sitting in a meeting, and we talked about the CTO role. Things took an unusual turn. I was given the role — and the next moment, I was being introduced to another CTO, and then another! How do you have three? I thought: 'This doesn't make any sense!' But now I know that it does."

Fear of Change: It Must be Fought

Like others before them, Kevin Nolan and his colleagues struggled to understand Haier. It took them more than a year to begin piecing things together, with much lost in translation. Tom Quick, vice-president of Human Resources at GEA, shared a typical example. "Haier kept referring to '690'," he said, "We would just look at each other and think, 'What are they talking about?' We eventually figured out that 690 was the nomenclature of Haier's stock, and they were simply referring to themselves."

More confusion was to follow, and Nolan realised that the successful adaptation of the Haier model would require some serious study — and he intended to get his knowledge from the source. "The first year was critical for me," he recalled. "You can learn the company philosophy, but that doesn't mean you can copy it. Some things would never work in the US, so I looked for the most valuable parts of the system. Instead of copying, we looked where Haier was going."

Once he was sufficiently confident to start implementing elements of the Haier model, Nolan returned to the States. Home was still "home"; since the takeover, almost the entire GEA management team had remained intact. "That's the beauty of this model," he says. "It's not about replacing people; it's about enabling them."

Nevertheless, the GEA folks were nervous. There was still speculation about Haier's motivation and intentions. "Many of our people got nervous in the early stages," said Quick. "There were rumours about the salary system, and how Haier was going to lay-off a whole bunch of staff when the one-year acquisition date had passed.

"People would come to me and say, 'Well, Tom, why aren't you putting something out, a communication?' And I thought to myself: 'I'm not going to buy into all these crazy rumours. After the first year, things will settle down'." And settle down they did. It became apparent that Haier trusted the US team to run the business in its own way.

The Chinese giant applied the approach it had successfully used with Fisher & Paykel. It wasn't going to tell anyone what to do; it simply offered GEA executives the opportunity to learn, and to apply knowledge at their own speed. Haier kept its word: when it became clear that GEA leaders could still make the important calls, concern was replaced with curiosity. The same pattern occurred externally, recalls Quick. "The community saw that we didn't retrench. We continued to give to United Way and the philanthropic groups. We still had a strong community volunteer organisation. Even the mayor of Louisville will tell you: GEA never missed a beat here."

GEA was able to continue the things that were important to its culture. In the first year after the acquisition, there were no significant attempts to implement the Rendanheyi model. "Only a handful of us had any interaction with Haier on the subject," says Quick. During the transitional phase, the Haier representative responsible for the acquisition, one Mr Liang, went to assist in Louisville. "He invited us to a meeting and explained the concept. We had to sit for an hour and were only allowed to ask questions once he was done talking."

This was the first time Haier had demanded that the GEA executives shut up and listen. It could be argued that this coercion contradicted Haier's non-intrusive philosophy, but in practice things were more nuanced. "Some companies want to turn acquisitions into clones of themselves," said Quick. "That's not been the case with us. Haier was like, 'Okay, we've acquired you. You are where you are in your journey. We've got some things that — if you adopt them — can help you. You know your culture better than we do. Take the best of this and blend it to be as successful as you can'.

"You know what's interesting? If this meeting had happened in 2016, nobody would have been happy. But now we had 13 months of experience under our belt. We knew Mr Liang, and he knew us. And even more importantly, Haier signalled: 'Hey, don't worry, we trust you and think you run a good business.' That made a huge difference." Liang succeeded in transmitting the basic concepts of Rendanheyi: being customer-focused, striving to set leading goals, and unlocking the potential of employees. The meeting, the growing trust in the relationship, and the appointment of Kevin Nolan as CEO meant Rendanheyi could gradually be implemented on foreign shores.

When GEA was still a part of GE, it was serving the market — but its real customer was corporate headquarters. Keep HQ happy, or funding would be cut and there would be reorganisation. Now, operating alone, GEA could focus on customers. Directly copying the Haier solutions wouldn't work; they had to be adapted to the US culture while remaining true to the original philosophy.

But where to start?
"One of the first things Kevin and I did," says Quick, "was hold roundtable sessions with the executives, just the two of us and 15 to 20 of them around a table, talking about the basic concepts." Quick and Nolan tried a similar approach as Liang. They set out to educate, actively engaging people and encouraging them to ask questions. The approach helped to reveal what GEA needed, which Rendanheyi elements would work, and which needed to be adapted. Workers were getting on-board with the idea. Things started to change.

• • •

Some Powerful Questions
The GEA mindset started to change, leaving behind the old ways and moving towards entrepreneurship. Liang knew that asking the right questions at the right time could speed-up the process. "You're not number one. Why not?" and "What's your plan to become number one?" Tom Quick recognised something new. "Very simple questions," he says, "but nobody had asked them before." GEA staff started thinking and behaving differently, making better choices — and believing that they could become part of a winning team.

"The interesting thing was that our employees started to see us competing. They saw our market share growing. They started to feel like, 'Wow, we can do something. We can be better. We can be stronger.' There was this recognition that to be Number One in North America was going to take an awful lot. But now people had started to believe."

Haier had learned a lot from its earlier acquisition of Fisher & Paykel, and GEA could learn from that experience as well. Fisher & Paykel had renamed the Rendanheyi model People Plus Goal, which was easier to understand and sounded more familiar to Kiwi ears.

• • •

> **Fisher & Paykel**
>
> *After taking charge of Fisher & Paykel in early 2020, CEO Daniel Witten-Hannah sent an email to all employees. "You've got our backing to do things a bit differently, to follow your instinct, and to chase opportunities that will see us outperform our competition," he wrote.* [31] *Witten-Hannah knew that a successful implementation of Rendanheyi at Fisher & Paykel required the breakdown of bureaucratic systems. And to achieve further decentralisation, the top leadership team needed to know how to delegate. To kick-start the transformation, Witten-Hannah focused first on management, inspiring the mobilisation of employees' initiative as an entry point and using Rendanheyi to transform Fisher & Paykel.*
>
> *This large company with a legacy stretching back many years, had a lot of work to do at the beginning. In the old days, employees would listen to instructions and work for their managers. Now, senior management delegated decision-making power to the microenterprises. They could skip the approval process. By simplifying things, they hoped that each microenterprise would become motivated to create value for users. And through the implementation and signing of bidding agreements, they hoped to stimulate microenterprises to set their goals and be responsible for the results.*
>
> *They decided on a modest start: they would pilot the Rendanheyi model in the Australian division. Nearly 40 percent of Fisher & Paykel's revenue at the time came from the neighbouring continent, so it was an important market. If it could be made to work there, there would be more confidence that the model could be replicated across the whole company.*
>
> *The transformation began just as the outbreak of coronavirus forced businesses around the world into a sudden crisis. Traditional business models were in for a trying time. But Fisher & Paykel used Rendanheyi*

to avoid any lay-offs during the pandemic — and managed to increase profits. The first-year results were promising: annual revenue increased by 36 percent, while profit grew by 137 percent. [31]

So, what exactly did they do? In short, the Australian Fisher & Paykel team adjusted. In terms of system and process, the business rhythm was revised. The planning cycle was changed from monthly to weekly in the early stages of the pandemic so demand and supply could be adjusted according to market changes. The company encouraged information-sharing. Visualisation and transparency helped employees to clarify their responsibilities and priorities for shared goals.

The top leadership team, meanwhile, started to hold daily half-hour meetings to discuss the priority of tasks and clarify the parallel collaboration of cross-functional teams. For the allocation of decision-making power, the New Zealand HQ decentralised and passed the process to the microenterprises.

That was the most obvious change. Zhao Huaqiang, the leader of the experience-oriented EMC in Australia, said: "In the past, employees were waiting, demanding, relying on HQ. Now we are aware of the changes in customer market demand.

"Fisher & Paykel headquarters and the Haier Group's platforms took the initiative to provide us with support. All microenterprises now meet every week, or even every day, to discuss such things as planning, R&D, marketing and production. We meet to achieve a richer sharing of information in the various EMCs. It's clear that a collaborative relationship has begun to take shape." [31]

Jason Healey, head of retail sales of Haier Brand Australia, said that Haier's rapid growth was the result of co-operation, "not just (of) the sales team, but all the departments involved".

One of Fisher & Paykel's winning strategies was to make everyone in the team move quickly, with clear goals, information-sharing, and decision-making. Jeremy Sargent said Q2 growth in the white goods sector — fridges, washing machines and kitchen appliances — along with the growth of both brands showed the importance of swift responses. Microenterprises were empowered to seize market opportunities.

When it comes to his personal feelings of Haier's insistence on the Rendanheyi model, Sargent added: "Before I joined Fisher & Paykel, I did

> not understand the model, but I think it serves to connect the entrepreneur with the goal. The cross-departmental co-operation realised under this model, especially that of the autonomous employees in the microenterprises, is something I have never seen in my 35 years of working." [31]
>
> There are still challenges to solve and the road of transformation is long. Fisher and Paykel still faces the challenge of formulating a new compensation mechanism, according to local conditions, to realise profit-sharing in microenterprises and EMCs.

• • •

Back to Louisville, Kentucky...

"We knew we were different to Fisher & Paykel," says Quick, "and that the language was not going to work for us. Let Fisher & Paykel do what it needs to in its culture. We'll do what we think will be successful at GE Appliances."

GEA chose its own terminology for Rendanheyi. "We called it end-to-end." Changing the language to fit the culture changed the way people spoke and felt about the model. At the same time, it helped to remove any lingering reservations about being acquired by a Chinese company. But as employees became familiar with the term, it became used as well. "Nowadays, when we say things like RDHY or Rendanheyi, we don't get those blank stares."

Nolan again: "We knew that certain things that Haier does in China wouldn't work here. But instead of saying, 'That just won't work', we said 'That part might not work — what will?' That really helped us with one of the biggest challenges." When he took over as chief executive, GEA was still organised in a hierarchical way. "If you look at Haier's model, you still have functions, but those functions are platforms," he said, "distribution, for example, or HR. So, we changed that right away. We still have a manufacturing 'leader', but he's no longer a functional leader, he's a platform leader."

This approach changed the power structure. Once, the manufacturing leader had called the shots; now, there were other ways to achieve goals. "Some people felt as if they had lost all their power," says Nolan. "We decided to turn product-line leaders into microenterprise leaders — which made it seem as if they had all the power." That wasn't the case, but Nolan had to convince his employees. "The whole concept that power is with the user came across. The power is with the customer. We're here to serve that customer, organising ourselves as efficiently as possible to meet those needs and make sure everything we're doing is right."

Kevin Nolan soon found he needed to reinvent his own role. He started by delegating wherever possible, empowering others to make decisions. "I became more of a coach: someone you can talk to instead of someone who tells you what to do. In practice, something interesting happens. I spent more time with the smaller microenterprises that were trying to gain traction than I did with the larger ones with an established model."

Peter Pepe, vice-president of the Clothes Care Business, expanded on this: "We adopted not the exact structure of microenterprises, but the concept," he says, "where workers really feel, and act, as owners of the business." Across GEA, the swing to the microenterprise structure was gaining momentum. These US microenterprises often had over 2,000 members, more even than those in China, but they functioned in virtually the same way.

This, believes Nolan, is crucial. "What's typical of conglomerates is that they focus on feeding the 'strong child'. The weak ones, they just sell off or starve. And you know where that gets you? Nowhere.

"When larger microenterprises need something, we meet, but not very frequently, whereas I meet with the small microenterprises quite a bit. That is where we're trying to gain traction; and the bigger ones, they basically have an established model and do not need my help."

Smaller microenterprises have started to emerge, says Pepe. "For products that aren't the same, but adjacently tied to the bigger microenterprise, we'll create new microenterprises. If we wanted to start selling a new product, we'd set up a new one for that."

Using the foundations of the microenterprise structure allowed GEA to adopt other elements. Decision-making moved down, enabling those closest to the end-user to have input. Incentive mechanisms were connected to performance.

• • •

A New Mechanism Falls into Place
"When Haier took over, there were rumours that pay was going to drop by 20 percent," says Pepe. The fears were sparked by the Chinese salary model, where employees receive a low basic salary in combination with a secondary amount based on performance.

This wasn't adopted at GEA. "What everyone was making, from a compensation standpoint, stayed the same. There was no going backwards." The system wouldn't have exported well to the US, from legal or cultural perspectives, but it was tweaked to fit by redesigning the bonus structure.

"Before, each function was designed to be the best in its own area," says Pepe. "You're the best manufacturing plant operation, or the best finance person, or the best technology organisation. You worked for the product line, or you worked within the product line. But now the goal is betterment of the whole product line, the microenterprise, our consumers, and the marketplace. It's a very subtle focus shift, but it's a big deal for us."

GEA adopted the new bonus structure in 2017, says Quick. "Even if you're a finance person dedicated to the laundry business, your bonus — at least half of it — is derived from the success of that business. That person's peer could be, say, a finance person supporting the cooking business. Well, 50 percent of that person's bonus is derived from the success of the cooking business."

Prior to the acquisition, bonuses were only available to executives. Now all employees received bonuses, which was, compared to competitors, a giant leap forward.

• • •

Smiley Faces, Pink Pigs or Teddy Bears...?

To successfully implement Haier's model requires more than the adoption of big ideas. It's about considering the smaller elements and seeing how well they fit local needs. Changing smiley faces for teddy bears, for example.

At Haier factories, teams start the day next to a whiteboard bearing the names of team members. Each worker selects an emoji to describe their current mood and places it next to their name. Often it will be a smiley face: the bigger the smile, the happier the employee. This helps colleagues to communicate stress or feelings of being overwhelmed by work or home issues. It allows the team to be aware and act: reschedule tasks, for instance, or send someone home. It's a simple and effective practice to increase psychological safety and support.

GEA tried to implement the smiley faces, but it didn't work as planned. In US culture, emojis are used for WhatsApp messages, not workplace whiteboards. GEA employees came up with alternatives: pink pigs and teddy bears. However small and odd this change may have been for outsiders, the effect on behaviour was exactly what had been hoped for. Employees were taking ownership of a problem and coming up with alternative solutions while keeping an eye on the principle at hand. It helped them to understand that they do have an influence — it allowed the true potential of the Rendanheyi model to surface.

• • •

> ### Splashdown in Russia
> One of the best examples of that sort of ownership came about when Haier opened a factory in a Russian industrial park.
>
> Development was costly and time-consuming, which is not surprising: winter temperatures in Naberezhnye Chelny often fall to minus 20, making it impossible to pour concrete. Construction usually takes place for only six months of the year, and with those constraints erecting a factory would take at least three years. Another factor causing concern was the wildly fluctuating value of the Russian rouble.
>
> But one microenterprise leader wasn't letting any of this get in his way. Haier's goal was to open the Russian factory in 13 months. The microenterprise leader showed his confidence by gathering a million roubles in follow-up funding from his team, who invested in the project themselves. With everyone motivated to reach the goal, it was time to get creative. Heating was installed and concrete poured in small sections to allow it to properly cure.
>
> The factory opened a month ahead of deadline.
>
> Haier was thrilled. It had struggled to convince overseas employees to invest their own money; the development in Russia took things to the next stage. This reinforced Haier's belief that employees who invest will fight harder to reach their goals.

• • •

Back in Louisville, there was still some resistance from those who didn't yet know Haier. "When something is different, a lot of people discount things," Kevin Nolan notes. "And I get it, we're basically throwing the corporate playbook out the window. But is that bad?" According to many of the people we have interviewed, not playing by the book is a strength. It works for Haier, making it nimble and able to react swiftly.

For GEA, the Covid crisis brought this strength to the fore. The company is increasingly focused on hands-on problem-solving. "We had issues with so many people being out due to Covid, and we had to run these factories. What were we going to do? We felt the opportunity in the market and then we just asked people to sign up on a Friday, and on the Monday those people — including executives and myself — were working on the factory floor. That would have never happened previously."

"We're now able to look at a situation and adapt to it, instead of looking at a playbook. There's a huge industry out there built around your corporate playbook, by consultancies and others who want to advise you how to run things. I'd say we're listening to the market more than the consultants — and that's working great for us."

Although GEA had started to heed the market, it did benefit from the experience gained at the source. It has managed to implement some of the fundamentals of the Rendanheyi model and is glad of it. It didn't get rid of all management layers. Its microenterprise structure isn't as refined as that of Haier. And not every employee can make big decisions. So, is GEA "mature" in the model? "No," admits Nolan, "and I think that's what's promising. You don't have to move as fast as Haier. In the industries we're in, even scratching the surface showed great power in our ability to differentiate ourselves from our competitors."

Getting to a point where the company could start to benefit hasn't been easy. A lot has been learned — and, in retrospect, there are things that could have been done differently. "Our early communications could have been better," Nolan and his colleagues confess. Their efforts seemed to trigger questioning aimed at the source — and focus on the questions rather than the model. "The Chinese-sounding name didn't help us. We should have focused on using terms people were familiar with, like entrepreneurship. No one in America is against that."

What GEA realised is that while the concepts of the model are universal, the language is not. It struggled to find the words to best fit its context, and — as so often — it all came down to simplicity. But even something simple can be tricky to communicate.

Another major learning moment came when GEA saw that implementing the new ways without the microenterprise structure in place wouldn't work. GEA couldn't get its employees to "take ownership", and there was a lack of flexibility. By introducing the microenterprise structure, those problems disappeared.

• • •

One Final Lesson...
Even though GEA is still transforming, there was one lesson learned along the way that had nothing to do with the model's implementation. It was something much more personal.

We discovered this by asking our interviewees a simple question: "Could you ever go back to working in a traditional company?" The answer has been a consistent, unanimous, "No."

Some of the benefits of alternative ways of working:

Paul Surowiec, vice-president of Cooking: "It's given me a sense of energy and excitement. I wouldn't want to go back to a stiff-shirt company. It's just not for me anymore, and that says something because I've done that for over 30 years."

Tom Quick, vice-president of Human Resources: "I think that the journey we're on — trying to be recognised as number one in concert with the RDHY philosophy — gives me the freedom and autonomy to try to make this HR organisation the best it can be. I don't want to go into a cookie-cutter environment again."

Kevin Nolan, CEO: "I try to manage my people to 'own' their decisions. I like that kind of ownership. I think the employees here feel that, and it's exciting. I wouldn't want to give up the feeling that everyone can make a difference. Freedom of ideas and expression is more important than money."

• • •

Dreaming Big Can Pay-Off

While it might be too early to decide if the experiment has been a success, early indications are positive. The flexibility of the Rendanheyi model is promising and seems to yield positive results. By using it as a source of inspiration, companies have reached their true potential. With case studies on exporting the model to other countries and industries, Haier's way of working is getting noticed around the world.

Even companies not owned by Haier have been inspired to start implementing certain elements of its philosophy. Zhang's dream to help create and export a management model in which entrepreneurship and autonomy are central is becoming a reality.

• • •

REBEL LOG: This is mighty interesting; the model is still used in the Haier empire, and there is at least some cultural overlap. But will it work elsewhere? With Zhang's positive attitude and a willing workforce, we are starting to believe that anything is possible.

Rebel One, out.

Adoption of the Model Outside the Haier Universe

More and more companies that have no affiliation with the Chinese giant have been "coming out" and sharing the news that they too are adopting principles and philosophies pioneered by Haier.

Multiple companies have been transformed and now lean towards Rendanheyi-inspired models — and some have received a Haier Zero-Distance Award. Sometimes the changes have been implemented while maintaining close contact with Haier and its Model Institute. In other cases, the transformation has taken place without direct involvement from Haier.

Fujitsu Europe

One of these companies is Fujitsu Western Europe. Bruno Sirletti and his colleague João Domingos told us how their transition began.

Fujitsu had always been a risk-averse company, but it was now becoming apparent that it was too slow. "At one point we had a customer that wanted to work with us," said Domingos. "The assignment was pretty clear, but still it took us almost six months before we had one of our consultants ready to set up the services. Around that time, I read in the paper there was a new company that had grown into a unicorn within half a year.

"They had created a company and built it up to be worth a billion dollars in the same time we needed to get one consultant working with one customer that called us. It was then that I realised we needed to change if we were going to stay around for the next couple of decades."

Fujitsu took a different approach to GEA when adopting the model. "We took about a hundred people outside the organisation and enabled them to develop the new business," said Sirletti. "These people were organised into small microenterprises and participants were not selected on hard skills alone. We looked for people who also had entrepreneurial or leadership skills."

The microenterprises were then freed from the existing bureaucratic structures inside the company. They appointed microenterprise leaders and granted them the freedom to self-organise. They could decide which markets they wanted to target and could hire employees or consultants. Employees could approve deals directly while meeting with customers, all without having to go through the bureaucratic processes. It gave them that much-needed agility.

Within the microenterprises, employees receive a fixed salary and a variable part based on performance of the microenterprise. If the microenterprise were to become profitable and surpass its targets, everyone in the microenterprise receives a bonus. "They win together, and they lose together, so all members get the same bonus," said Sirletti.

Encouraged by the autonomy they had received and the potential of receiving a bonus, the microenterprises started a hunt for customers in new markets. They tried to sell things Fujitsu had never sold before, such as AI systems and blockchain technology.

Unfortunately, most of the microenterprise members lacked skills and experience in those areas, so the microenterprise members needed to collaborate to explore, sell, and deliver these new services and products. More importantly, they needed to find which customers to pursue.

Domingos: "Before we started the experiment, I met with the heads of all departments and tried to convince them. I needed to show I was serious, and they needed to support the idea as well. I said: 'Look, this microenterprise experiment is what I want to do, if you do not agree speak up now or forever hold your peace. Because once we have started this journey, there's no going back'."

The heads of the departments needed to adapt to the new reality, and so did Domingos: "Some microenterprises did things that I would not necessarily do. I needed to let microenterprises be free to succeed, or to fail … I could only share a different perspective, but other than that I needed to shut up. As leader, this is hard. It takes courage to shut up."

Sirletti and Domingos believed they needed to lead by example hoping to inspire others to follow. "We gathered some momentum," Domingos explained. "First, we needed to motivate people to join our experiment, and now colleagues are seeing this and asking how they can join, or how they can recreate the experiment in their own departments."

What Fujitsu learned, along its relatively short journey, was profound. "The microenterprise leaders had different backgrounds. Some were managers, others we hired from small external companies, and a third group were internal candidates without management experience. To our surprise, the last two groups performed best."

According to Sirletti, the existing managers were biased because of their previous experiences and struggled to leave those views behind, and so were unable to fully embrace the new approach. Those were the people whose job was only to manage staff and they were too much used to following processes. "The introduction of the microenterprises forced people to make decisions instead of following processes," notes Domingos. "Middle managers struggled with that and found it difficult to take ownership of their decisions. The others found it much easier to take that responsibility. They were less afraid to fail."

Daring to fail is important. Without this, people are not prepared to take the necessary risks to find new solutions. Fujitsu educated employees to be ready for this new way of working and made sure they had the skills needed to become entrepreneurs. On top of that Fujitsu created a support layer that could help the microenterprises with any problems they ran into.

Domingos says that support layer really helped to rapidly increase the number of microenterprises. "They're dedicated to get rid of anything that blocks the microenterprises by providing education, coaching or in some cases solving problems."

More than a year in, Domingos is optimistic. "Not all microenterprises were successful, but overall, most were. One even tripled its revenue. Pipelines are fuller, and we've gotten some deals we probably wouldn't have had otherwise. More importantly, our employee engagement improved, even during the pandemic, from 64 to 73 percent, and customers were happier than ever before."

Even though these results are promising, Sirletti and Domingos can't be certain that the rest of Fujistu will follow. "I'm a regional leader and there are decisions I cannot take," says Domingos. "I can only plant a seed hoping that a tree will start growing at some point."

• • •

Z-Awards

Each year the Business Ecosystem Alliance (BEA), initiated and supported by the Haier Group, awards "Zero Distance Awards" (Z-Awards) during Haier's annual Global Rendanheyi Forum. Award-winners are recognised for their efforts to directly connect business with end-users so value is created as seamlessly as possible — ideally reducing the distance to zero. This philosophy is central to Haier's management model for the IoT era.

In Japan in the 1980s, the quality/efficiency revolution revolved around producing products with zero defects. But, with Haier championing zero distance, the focus shifted from product to customer. Superior experiences, the argument runs, bring higher commercial value. In September 2020, the BEA launched the Z-Awards to recognise organisations putting end-users at the heart of their operating systems.

At the inaugural ceremony, BEA and Haier rewarded 10 organisations from around the world for their enrichment of the zero-distance concept. Domingos and Sirletti received awards for pioneering the Rendanheyi model in a foreign corporation: "decisive action to create and drive a customer-obsessed mindset". "That's a source of great pride," said Domingos. "External recognition is always a boost for confidence and a sign that our organisation is moving in the right direction. We have been pushing for a customer-obsessed mindset. Zero distance means we're putting the customer at the heart of things, and we're more agile and more responsive to customer requests and needs."[32]

GEA was another winner. "It means that our transformation is working," said Nolan. "It was only four years ago when we read for the first time about Rendanheyi and its zero-distance principle. In 2020, we confirmed the power of zero as a business driver that's enabling a successful performance. We've taken the concept to a new level, applying it to every angle of our work."[32]

Jaipur Rugs and Severstal

Another company inspired by Haier to translate the Rendanheyi philosophy is India's Jaipur Rugs. Jaipur Rugs was founded by Nand Kishore Chaudhary in 1978 with just two looms and nine workers. Today, it has a network of 40,000 artisans spread across 600 Indian villages and is one of the country's largest manufacturers of hand-knotted rugs. CK Prahalad included Jaipur Rugs as a success story in his bestseller The Fortune at the Bottom of the Pyramid, citing it as an example of a social business which helps in tackling world poverty.

Jaipur Rugs won a 2020 Z-Award for embodying zero distance: artisans were in direct contact with customers in the Western world. BEA and Haier recognised the culmination of a 42-year journey that had transformed the lives of 40,000 weavers.

In recent years, Chaudhary, inspired by Rendanheyi, got in contact with Ruimin and the Haier Model Institute. After some knowledge-sharing, the founders of Jaipur Rugs followed the microenterprise model and started its own transformational initiative, dubbed "Each Artisan an Entrepreneur", advocating self-management and connecting the weavers with underserved customers. Zero defects, zero wastage, on-time, every-time delivery. "This makes the supply chain more agile and creates an emotional bond between weavers and consumers," said Chaudhary.[32]

Through Rendanheyi, Jaipur Rugs aims to reduce the distance still further. "We are fully committed to bring it into our entire business," he said. "We are constantly learning and implementing it throughout the organisation. We plan to integrate technology, develop the world's best artisan proposition, expand our retail presence and collaborate with more likeminded partners." One other winner that year was Severstal, a company that wanted to learn directly from Haier. The Russian steel and mining company, headquartered in Cherepovets, has 50,000 employees, and produced 11.3m tonnes of steel in 2020—resulting in revenues of $6.87bn.

Severstal won the award for introducing the zero-distance concept to reinvent the conservative steel industry. In the second half of 2019, a group of Russian Severstal employees travelled to Qingdao to learn about the Rendanheyi model at first-hand. Not much later, the company began introducing the model.

• • •

Shangdong Tianbao Group

Closer to the Asian roots of Rendanheyi lies the transformation of the Shangdong Tianbao Group. Founded in 1996 by Zhang Chuanfa, the group is also located in Qingdao. The company, with some 200 employees, trades mainly in iron and steel products. Tianbao is the link between raw-material producers such as steel and iron mills and SMEs that create the products. It must satisfy both sides of this relationship.

But the interests of the raw material suppliers and the many small vendors are misaligned. The production process is flawed: volumes are high, the quality of products often low. Innovation is negligible, with slow response to the needs of manufacturers. These smaller organisations have little say, or bargaining power, in how the raw material is delivered. By championing simple transactions, the relationship between supply and user sides will improve.

Chuanfa believed that the "ecosystem thinking" of the Rendanheyi model can potentially solve this. He was right. With the help of experts from Haier's Model Institute (HMI), he has built an interconnected system between Tianbao, suppliers, and manufacturers. Tianbao created its own digital platform, Kuaigang Cloud, directly connecting the upstream with the downstream.

It was a success. Within six months, 100 suppliers and 10,000 vendors from warehousing, manufacturing, logistics, finance, and delivery sectors were connected to the Kuaigang Cloud.[31] The platform was specifically designed to empower vendors. The purchasing of small amounts of raw material would run into problems because of the scale of the order. In the new situation, the Kuaigang Cloud takes over the process. It collects vendor demands and makes the purchasing request directly to the steel mills. The platform even takes care of financial transactions to speed-up the order. Six months after the introduction of the Kuaigang Cloud, Tianbao saw its annual sales nearly triple in the first two quarters of 2021.

Tianbao started to encourage employees to come up with better ways to organise themselves and work more efficiently. Next steps included the introduction of bidding mechanisms, EMC contracts, and market-driven reward mechanisms. Employees become Haier-style entrepreneurs, motivated to chase external market opportunities. Chuanfa encouraged employees to visit Qingdao and the institute to have in-depth conversations with Haier's entrepreneurs.

Tianbao has shown that to implement Rendanheyi, businesses should choose to adopt only the parts that will work for each specific situation. In the case of Tianbao, that was ecosystem thinking, the starting point to implement a more comprehensive Rendanheyi philosophy. Other companies have started by restructuring the organisation (as in Fujitsu's case) or the reward mechanisms (as at Sanyo).

MAQE

Thai software company MAQE is another Asian example that transformed with close contact from Haier's Model Institute. Based in Bangkok, with about 80 employees, the transformation started with a focus on Rendanheyi-inspired contract mechanisms tailored to specific cultural and business needs. Three kinds of contracts related to employment, internal entrepreneurship, and external partnerships.

Employment contracts moved towards a VAM-inspired reward policy consisting of two components: a base salary and bonuses for entrepreneurship and risk-taking. As at Haier, if an employee at MAQE fails at his or her entrepreneurial initiative, they can fall back on the base salary and try again.

To boost entrepreneurship, MAQE introduced a contractual mechanism to let employees introduce ideas for new products or services, and start their own microenterprises. This involves a special contract that outlines all things related to the incubation stage and ownership of the microenterprise. Each receives support and guidance from founding members to bring concepts to market.

When microenterprises graduate from MAQE's incubation programme, they are spun-off as separate entities. The contracts outline how the ownership of this new entity will be divided between employees and MAQE. Generally, the employees receive a major stake in the new entity, and MAQE receives a minor stake based on investment during the incubation phase. Expectations for all of this — who gets what, and when — is detailed in the contract that is signed before incubation.

Also implemented were EMC-inspired contracts that allow microenterprises to partner with one another (or with any external partner). These partnerships are designed to allow groups of entities to work together and address unmet customer needs. The contracts are results-orientated, to solve a particular un-met need and achieve a specific quantitative result based on forecasts. The partnership contracts give details of who the contributors to a specific project are, why they work together, what they are aiming to achieve, and, crucially, how they will split the proceeds.

•••

Not all companies that transform towards Rendanheyi-like models are in close contact with Haier during their transformation. Many move toward the model without contact with the inventor — including the Amazon-owned Zappos.

Zappos

Zappos, founded in 1999, is an American online retailer specialising in shoes, with about 2,000 employees. The late founder, Tony Hsieh, started to transform his company towards "Holacracy" in 2015 to steer the company towards a more decentralised structure. Holacracy is a method of decentralised management and organisation which distributes authority and decision-making through a holarchy of self-organising teams. At the time, Hsieh was inspired by the idea of turning a company into a city-like environment — without central planning. Why? Inspired by the book Scale by Geoffrey West, he argued that cities are resilient and flexible, and every time one doubles in size, productivity per resident rises by 15 percent. Traditional companies usually see per capita productivity fall as they grow.

Hsieh chose Holacracy as the tool to access that kind of resilience and productivity. But why? His reasoning at the time: "Aside from it arguably being the most publicly well-known, it is one of the only pre-built, out-of-the-box options that any organisation, regardless of size, sector, or industry, can implement. It immediately provided us with a set of rules and processes that everyone could see, with a lot of the nuances and checks-and-balances already figured out for us." [33]

Implementing Holacracy as a pre-built, off-the-shelf model is the path they chose. In 2015, they did away with managers, and restructured into 400 holacratic circles — overnight. This dogmatic approach was not always easy to apply, admits Christa Foley, senior director of brand vision and culture. "Holacracy has been a big exercise in getting comfortable with experimentation and trying and reiterating, then backing up and going forward again." [33]

And the change was mandatory for all: that is how Zappos changed overnight. In March 2015, Hsieh gave an ultimatum to employees: commit to the new model as a genuine participant, or leave the company and receive a generous buyout offer. About 18 percent of the workforce took the offer.

Holacracy provided Zappos with a tool to break free of traditional organisation and introduced a shared vocabulary, a terminology to help people understand what it means to be self-organised and self-managed. Yet, after practicing Holacracy for about three years, the company went further and started to introduce a model dubbed market-based dynamics (MBD) in March 2017. Zappos executive John Bunch said that pure Holacracy created big challenges in its business metrics and employee focus was again directed to the customer. [34]

"Our circles were still arranged hierarchically, where budgeting or head count was allocated from the top down," Hsieh explained. "Instead of circles arranged hierarchically, we're transitioning so that each circle is its own small business or start-up." [33] As part of the solution, each circle had to manage its own budget and determine the services it would provide. These can be within the company, or involve outside clients. The e-retailer started to introduce a Haier-style internal marketplace where teams are run like small, independent businesses — including managing their own P&L.

Rachel Murch, who implemented MBD at Zappos, said teams operate like micro-businesses within an enterprise. "If Zappos is the enterprise, there are teams that live within it. They got the opportunity to manage and deliver products or services, if they lived within the three sides of what we call the Triangle of Accountability." [35]

Zappos turned to MBD and let its circles operate like autonomous microenterprises with a strong customer-focus. Zappos' units operate like companies, with far-reaching decision-making rights and responsibility for their own P&Ls. The Triangle of Accountability is a framework set up by leadership in which all market dynamics between the microenterprises take place. If microenterprises stay within this framework, they enjoy autonomy. The framework is based on guidelines that dictate respect for the company's core values, deliver the highest customer satisfaction possible, and have healthy team-level financials.

"You had to differentiate based on culture and core values," says Murch. "You had to deliver the very best service. That had to be a differentiator, and you had to basically pay the bills. Break-even in our model meant using a P&L structure. Every team had their own P&L, and we kind of blew up the traditional budgeting system. In a traditional organisation, there is a top-down budget. [35]

"You're also incentivised, in a traditional organisation, to spend as much money as you can, so that you can get more money the next year, or at least the same amount. And that's not how we live our day-to-day lives. In my personal bank account, I'm not trying to spend all the money by the end of the year so that I can start afresh the next. That's just not something we do. Why not apply that thinking, and make budgets basically bank accounts? [35]

"Every team had a bank account, and every team had an opportunity to be a customer, and a service provider and an investor. We had service agreements between teams. If I'm in the development team, I'm providing services to the merchandising team to let them put their goods on the website. There's a service agreement between those teams. That's where you're getting your money. We call that customer-generated budgeting (CGB). And all of that was tracked using a homegrown system. It gave teams the opportunity to reinvest in themselves to grow their team. [35]

"If they wanted to charge more internally, or externally, they could sell their services externally. They could reinvest the way they wanted to. We also started experimenting with things like team-based compensation and being able to pay your team what you feel is necessary. Obviously, you still had to pay the bills…" [35]

Also implemented was an internal contracting mechanism between microenterprises and external partners. This was also based on customer-generated budgeting. "Every team had to put together a menu of what services it provides, and what the cost is for those services. That's where we started as a baseline. And this is what we do. [35]

"We kind of took it to another level and put it into the CFO (circle financial overview) tool, so everybody could find what services exist. And then based on that price, you'd enter into a service agreement with whatever teams need your services. You're then a customer of other teams, or you want their services. It creates this service-provider to customer relationship. At the beginning, we had a kind of block-funding, but it didn't take long for it to become more of a network — a network with a bidding system, basically." [35]

According to the principle of CGB, each microenterprise puts together a list of services, including costs. Anybody can find what's needed and set up a service agreement to become a customer. The digital CFO tool manages all the transactions, including invoicing, in a transparent manner. Expenses and costs can be seen by others, and include the percentage of time spent, as well as overheads, benefits, taxes, and profits. The CGB mechanism levels the playing field, compelling all microenterprises to provide services or products and get revenues from at least one customer.

Microenterprises had to pay the company 50 percent of additional revenue. They could keep the other half to invest however they chose. This led to some teams going truly entrepreneurial, in various directions. "A lot of teams were able to experiment with different things," says Murch. "Look at the last few years, when Zappos took over a theatre on the strip in Las Vegas. There's Zappos Theatre. There are some interesting businesses: the audio-visual team, for example, provided services to external clients and grew. There are many great examples. And one of my favourites is Zappos' Adaptive Team that started in the early days of the market-based dynamics initiative. That came from a phone call from a customer expressing a need. [35]

"One phone call turned into this amazing business to help people who have adaptive needs, things that they're challenged with, and the Zappos adaptive platform provides functional clothing for them." [35]

Zappos insists it didn't force anyone into an entrepreneurial role. "There's a place for everyone. Especially if you're on a team, you don't have to be the entrepreneur. We did introduce a programme to help people experience an entrepreneurial mindset." [35]

Later in the process, the company began experimenting with team-based compensation mechanisms to boost entrepreneurship. Murch said: "We hadn't quite reached a point where they were able to give bonuses to team members and truly give compensation, you know, whatever made sense for them. We did have some small teams experimenting with that, but it hadn't got through to the organisation yet. I think that's really where we wanted to go." [35]

> **Bol.com**
>
> *Holacracy has not only represented the initial stepping-stone in Zappos' evolution towards self-organisation, it has also been crucial in some other transformations too. Bol.com, founded in 1999, is a Dutch online retailer offering music, film, electronics and toys. Zappos is American and Bol is Dutch, but similarities between the companies are so strong that they could be twins. Both are e-commerce players, both were founded in 1999, both are owned by larger retail organisations — Zappos by Amazon, Bol by Ahold/Delhaize. Both generate annual revenues of around $3bn, both have about 2,000 staff, and both started to radically transform their organisational structures around 2015.*
>
> *And both started their transformation by first implementing Holacracy. Like Zappos, Bol was not completely satisfied with what Holacracy brought. And, just like Zappos, Bol eventually implemented Rendanheyi-inspired elements. At Bol, it was not the CEO who started the change. It was Harm Jans, now director of People & Organisation Development, who laid the foundation known as the Spark Initiative. Jans was then a team leader in logistics. At the time, Bol faced the challenge of coping with rapid growth. It hired experienced people from established companies and retailers. The new people brought knowledge and experience in logistics and operations, along with traditional ideas about how to run companies.*
>
> *Organisation became more hierarchical and bureaucratic. People became less engaged. But the original Bol staff knew, from their start-up days, they did their best work in small, autonomous, cross-functional teams with challenging goals — and enough room for fun. "We were desperate to explore flatter operating models for the whole organisation, which distribute decision-making power effectively and place accountability at*

the lowest level," said Jans. [36]

When he started considering how to implement Holacracy at Bol, he knew he could not be too dogmatic, and would have to tailor it to specific environments. If he wanted this to work, he had to be pragmatic. "People at Bol have a rolled-up-sleeves, down-to-earth mentality. They were not going to buy into Holacracy if they first had to read a 40-page constitution with all the rules, structure, and processes of the operating system." [36]

The company simplified the constitution, and condensed it to a single page that covered the core principles. The word Holacracy wasn't used; it was all about Spark. The model adopted the basic principles behind circles and sub-circles, plus the role of the lead link, and elected roles such as facilitator and secretary. The role of the ratifier was abandoned, with the concept of cross-linking to keep things straightforward. "We do not follow all the rules of the governance processes and meetings that are in the Holacracy constitution," says Jans. "We allow teams to combine governance and tactics into the Spark meetings. We tend to be somewhat more flexible in the creation or removal of circles." [36]

Jans started small when implementing the change. He created a bottom-up movement. People could adopt Spark when they were motivated to do so — and at their own pace. Jans started the first experiment with two teams in his logistics department. Everyone involved became a Spark ambassador. Other teams joined, asking for help in adopting Spark.

Soon, the Spark Model became the default way of working in logistics. Jans' movement spread to other departments, such as customer service and commerce. Now in a new role, Jans still leads the movement, inspiring people to join, and change the way they work. Around 1,300 people now follow the Spark Model in 170 circles. "We have not yet gone all-in on Spark," says Jans, "but we're slowly reaching the tipping point where everybody is working more in circles instead of their functional departments. Departments like finance and HR are starting to adopt Spark. Our model is open and anybody who wants to can start using it." [36]

Zappos has distanced itself from the dogmatic aspects of Holacracy that employees found challenging early on. Now, they have moved beyond pure Holacracy and created their own models. Just like Zappos, Bol is now launching pilots in the direction of Rendanheyi-inspired internal

> *marketplace dynamics.* "We recently started experimenting with giving store teams budgets and the freedom to spend. We see that circles take accountability for spending in an appropriate manner, delivering value to Bol.com. We may scale that practice to other circles." [36]

• • •

Bosch Power Tools

Bosch Power Tools (Bosch PT) is another company that embraced a Rendanheyi-inspired model without close contact with Haier. Bosch PT is a division of the German engineering and technology giant Robert Bosch GmbH, which has 400,000 employees and products that are a part of everyday life.

Over the past five years, there have been many developments in the Power Tools division, where some 20,000 employees make drills, chainsaws, belt sanders, and the like. In 2015, things had started to sour. The division was still successful, but the team could see the need for major changes in the work environment.

Jochen Goeser, project leader of Bosch's Agile Transformation project, says the shift in the organisation and business environment amounted to three major trends. "Digitalisation changed our customer focus. Earlier on, when we talked about making customers happy, we referenced the retailers who sold our products. But that changed.

"The people who use our tools are our customers. We came to have much more direct interaction with them. Think of the famous five-star rating on Amazon; these ratings started to determine our sales. We were not set-up for this. The challenge was to become more concentrated on the user.

"We saw another trend emerge regarding powerful growth outside our home markets. Asia, Africa, and Latin America became very interesting. With this globalisation of our business, we needed to step-up our game to take full advantage of the opportunities.

"We asked ourselves, 'How can we create a more motivating work environment? What do our people really want? How can we attract new talents and skills? How can we become more appealing to people who don't have Bosch at the top of their employer wish list?' Because of the changes we were encountering, we needed more digital marketing and Internet of Things skills. We needed to compete with big tech companies for talent.

"The digitalisation, globalisation and collaboration needs prompted three important questions: 'Are we close enough to our customers? Are we sufficiently innovative? Are we fast and flexible?'"

The answers lit the touchpaper of a remarkable journey.

Bosch PT introduced a Rendanheyi-style, decentralised organisation by transitioning functional, siloed departments into cross-functional teams — a move away from separate marketing, manufacturing, and engineering departments.

The teams, like microenterprises, took responsibility for their own business, and were granted the autonomy to unleash entrepreneurship and creativity. The original six business units became 54 business teams — but not every associate of Bosch PT works within them.

Some 60-70 percent of employees are involved in these entrepreneurial units, while the remainder work in "expertise teams". These provide specific skills to the business teams, much like Haier's supporting microenterprises. But Bosch PT decided not to implement internal contracting mechanisms between the various businesses and their supporting teams.

Each move to a cross-functional team entailed an important decision: How should the teams be divided? There are several possible approaches. Teams could be responsible for a specific geographical area (as at Haier). They could take responsibility for one or more clients. They could also be made responsible for a particular service, as at Fujitsu Europe.

The best way to organise microenterprises varies, according to organisation, type of business, market sector, geography, and other factors. When breaking away from silos, two more crucial questions must be considered: What division of teams will place customers at the heart of the business, and which method will allow the most autonomy for teams?

Bosch PT decided to use Rendanheyi as inspiration for team division. They identified nine sections: fixing, cutting, removing, cleaning, lawncare, autonomous lawncare, tree care, plant care, and new business. All business teams focus on one area. People with engineering and manufacturing skills work in permanent teams to provide applications that meet customer needs. According to Goeser, "This new organisational design helps us focus more on our customers. Plus, it allows teams to be far more entrepreneurial and autonomous."

As we saw at Haier, it is important for autonomous teams to know exactly where they stand. Without transparency, entrepreneurship can't be fully unleashed. All teams at Bosch PT assumed full responsibility for their performance. They needed to be objective to become truly entrepreneurial. They scrutinised profit-and-loss accounts and customer feedback. Expertise teams rely on feedback from their internal clients: the business teams.

More transparency is created through a renewed business rhythm. Twice a week, representatives of all teams come together for 30-minute meetings. "As teams have end-to-end responsibility, we ask them what their bottlenecks are," explains Goeser. "Why can't you resolve them yourselves? Where do you need help from the other teams? That's it. We try to minimise complexity and detail."

In the transformation, Bosch PT's senior leaders played a vital role. "It was really important to create a feedback culture from top to bottom and from bottom to top," says Goeser. "Our senior management, for example, uses a monthly TV-show format to update everyone on how the division is doing, and let them know what is going on. They have a lot of feedback sessions, with associates included. They meet on a weekly basis with a smaller group to encourage meaningful feedback."

Goeser says employee satisfaction is high: "Our review scores on Glassdoor and similar websites have improved too. If you ask anyone: 'Do you want to go back to where we were six years ago?', the answer is a resounding 'no'. I think that's a very good indication of where we are.

"Our people are now much closer to the users, and they have more market 'nous'. Teams ask themselves: 'Is there still a compelling need for this new product?' There's much more testing in our product development process these days.

"We also kill (unpromising) projects early, rather than keep going for two or three years and then realise that they don't make sense. There's much more iterative testing — because we are so much closer to the user."

DIY Rendanheyi

REBEL LOG: Transplantation: can Rendanheyi be brought to bloom in foreign soil...? The answer is a solid "Yes". And "No" — if you do it wrong. As in every avenue of life, there are rules to follow. At Haier, and the firms it engages with, we're seeing healthy buds at the tip of every branch where change is fully embraced.

Rebel One, out.

According to the architect, inventor, and futurist Richard Buckminster Fuller, "You never change things by fighting the existing reality. To change something, build a new model that makes the existing model obsolete." [37]

We've seen that sentiment put into action by Zhang Ruimin. His vision gave Haier a unique management model. And while no other company has completely implemented Rendanheyi 3.0 thus far, the model has attracted attention. There are many promising signs; fundamental ideas can take root in different cultural and organisational contexts; think GEA, Fujitsu Europe, and Bosch PT.

Many who have studied Rendanheyi and introduced it into their own companies report positive results. Rendanheyi 3.0 might be too big a step for some organisations, but the power of the model is that one doesn't have to go all-in. It can be implemented piecemeal by adopting the parts most likely to help.

Unleashing potential by encouraging employees to become entrepreneurs has proved to be key. By creating self-managing microenterprises as close as possible to the customer — and connecting them via internal contracts to form temporary micro-communities that create specific user scenarios — that entrepreneurial energy was harnessed. The small units, enjoying free-market relations with the outside business world, flourished. So did the company; Haier became stronger than ever.

The model stimulates individual growth and rewards it fairly. It focuses on knowing what customers need and want. Whether this is achieved by creating a refrigerator that can warn us about rotting tomatoes, a delivery service that goes anywhere, or a brand-new hospital, really doesn't matter. The model works across industries, in various locations, for many people.

What if you want to embark on your own Rendanheyi journey? A few pioneers have cracked the code of organisational transformation: companies in Haier's inner circle and those far from the Haier galaxy. The ones we have met and written about on our travels are a drop in the ocean; examples abound. But there are many who still feel stuck in traditional organisations, knowing that radical change is needed — and believing they can't do a thing about it.

While it may seem that nearly every company is setting-up an agile transformation project nowadays, the projects undertaken by GEA, Fujitsu Europe and Bosch PT go way beyond hype, buzzwords, and superficial fixes. They are transitioning from bureaucracy to entrepreneurship. What can these pioneers teach an organisation about to embark on its own journey towards a Rendanheyi-inspired workplace?

We have identified five key steps.

1. Get Inspired

First, get some inspiration and knowledge about the ways in which workplace pioneers organise their business. Become familiar with concepts of microenterprises and micro-communities. Be serious about this. Kevin Nolan of GEA spent a year learning about Rendanheyi in Qingdao before even starting to consider implementing the model at his own company.

Get to understand what other pioneering companies are doing. Identify online resources and communities; check out our Corporate Rebels blog at www.corporate-rebels.com/ or go to www.rendanheyi.com/ to get in direct contact with Haier's Model Institute. Visit online learning platforms such as our Corporate Rebels Academy at www.corporate-rebels.academy/ to locate e-courses on pioneering organisations and practices. Much can be gleaned from the world's pioneers, risk-takers, and experts.

Remember that successful organisational transformation does not come easily. Is it best to drive the transformational journey yourself, or bring external partners on board? Over the years, we at Corporate Rebels have been working closely with Fujitsu Europe, Severstal, Jaipur Rugs, and Bosch PT. Some companies heed external input only at the early stages, while others hire external partners to progress the entire effort. A few need no help at all.

At Zappos and Bol, a copy-and-paste, off-the-shelf solution — in their case Holacracy — worked. But the model will have to be adapted to an organisational culture at some stage. As Bol did from the outset. It's no wonder that the stellar companies mentioned here did not downgrade into over-hyped frameworks. They adapted the lessons learned from pioneering models to meet the needs of their own culture — while remaining true to the original philosophy.

"We looked into how other companies were managing," says Bosch PT's Goeser, "and it became clear that we should not simply be replicating their methods. It doesn't work. That's why I discourage people from copying the example of Bosch Power Tools."

You know your culture better than outsiders. Take the most suitable parts of the pioneering models and blend them with the demands of your own culture — and your customers' needs — for optimal success.

2. Set Guiding Principles

At the outset, identify a set of guiding principles to provide direction. The introduction of Market-Based Dynamics at Zappos called for respect of the company's core values, delivery of the highest level of customer satisfaction, and healthy team-level financials.

Most often it is the leadership, or a dedicated transformation team, that defines the guiding principles. At Bosch PT, a team defined the elements of the transformation project. As Goeser explained: "The underlying assumption is that you go in with strong principles. This gives you direction. Are we on the right path — even though we don't know where we may end up?"

At Bosch PT, five principles were established: strong purpose, permanent, cross-functional teams, flat hierarchies, new understanding of leadership, and open communication. The application of each was then determined by the employees. There was freedom on how to apply the principles — but the vision was clear.

The concepts of Rendanheyi are now universal, but the term is not. When developing guiding principles, care must be taken to create terminology that fits the model. Domestic adaptations include GEA's "End-to-End", Fisher & Paykel's "People+Goal", Jaipur's "Each Artisan an Entrepreneur", and Zappos' "Market-Based Dynamics". Wording that fits the culture will make people feel more comfortable and accepting.

3. Invite Others

Organisational transformations are not the exclusive domain of board members, nor are they fancy prestige projects for executives. The proposed look of the new organisation — and the path it chooses to get there — should be high on everyone's agenda. Invitations should go out as early as possible. With motivated people from various parts of the organisation securely on board, you can co-create, deciding how best to bring the leadership vision to reality.

Before GEA embarked on its transformation, Kevin Nolan and the other executives held countless sessions with employees to explain the vision and basic concepts of the End-to-End model. People could ask questions, become fully engaged, and join the process.

At Bosch PT, the dedicated transformation team was connected to the leadership team. The goal was to facilitate wider discussion and support business units that were experimenting with new ways of working. "It is not only leaders that are interested in what the organisation looks like," points out Goeser. "Every associate is keen on knowing 'What is my new team? Who are my new teammates? Who is my new boss?'

"All these questions impact our day-to-day work and are important. That's why we wanted to get as many people as possible involved."

Bosch PT called on volunteers to set-up transition teams for each of the six business units. They were going to define the look of the new Bosch. And while the rough vision of the new organisation was laid down by top leadership, its design and execution were in the hands of the teams.

The locals didn't define work packages, set milestones, or create elaborate PowerPoint demonstrations. They were all about action. "This was a big — but positive — shock for many. We didn't force a top-down transformation, but allowed each of the business units to experiment and iterate. You cannot start such a transformation, call it 'agile' and then do it the old school way. We decided to focus on action."

4. Start Small

Any vision of transforming a company top-down overnight is a mirage. There is only one way to climb a mountain, and that's one step at a time. Fisher & Paykel pioneered its People+Goal model solely in its

Australian division. Bol's transformation was carried out by just two teams in the logistics department. Fujitsu Europe started out with just 100 people. Domingos and Sirletti allowed their people to be pioneers, without fear of failure. They needed everyone in the organisation to feel safe in this learning phase. Teams could come up with their own solutions; coaching and knowledge-sharing ensured collective advancement.

Bosch PT kicked off their transformation in a single business unit. "We gave them the opportunity, the guidelines, the freedom to experiment and iterate," Goeser recalls. "And based on what they came up with, we could draw lessons for the next units. We didn't have to wait for everyone to be ready at the same time, we could focus on the doing and the learning. Plus, this way they could focus on the needs of their specific unit."

The Home and Garden business was the first unit to make the move; a few months later, another joined. They learned from one another, but didn't use a copy-and-paste approach. Each transition team felt the need to create its own solutions. The businesses were discrete, and differed.

5. Scale
Although starting small is smart, the change initiative must be scaled throughout the organisation. Others in the company should jump on the bandwagon sooner rather than later — but the wider group must know that the bandwagon is there. You need to create a buzz around the transformation.

At Bol, soon after the two pioneering teams started their bottom-up transformation they began to produce videos, blog posts, and presentations. Soon 50 teams were on-board. A year later, that figure had doubled. The benefit of scaling in this way is that companies can learn and adapt more quickly.

At Bosch PT more business units gradually joined the movement as lessons were learned and shared. This fostered an attitude of knowledge exchange — without anyone being forced to implement the same way of working.

There are no hard, fast, and simple solutions. Organisational transformation calls for staying power, time, and continuity. It can be a long-winded affair, but that's how it is for large-scale organisational transformation. At Bosch PT, it took five years for all 20,000 employees to reinvent their way of working.

Epilogue

Haier has come a long way since its less-than-promising debut. Today, it's a company with decades of experience and phenomenal growth — and yet as nimble as any start-up. Haier is one of the most entrepreneurial and innovative companies in the world.

In November 2021, after leading the company for 27 years, Zhang Ruimin stepped down as CEO and chairman of the board. However, he did not exit the firm but has taken on the role of honorary chairman. This extraordinary pioneer is succeeded by Zhou Yunjie as CEO, and Liang Haishan as president. Both are long-serving Haier entrepreneurs and have been with the firm since graduating from university in 1988. What does the arrival of a new CEO and a new president mean for the innovative management philosophy of the Chinese white goods giant? Only time will tell. But there is confidence in the future, and expectations are high.

Even as this book comes to an end, it would be naïve to think that the journey has been completed. Haier will never stop evolving and searching for optimal solutions to its problems. Corporate Rebels will keep a close eye on developments and report back.

No matter how innovative and pioneering Rendanheyi 3.0 seems today, within a few decades it will be outdated. And that's OK. We understand that "there is no such thing as a successful company, only one that successfully moves with the times."

Acknowledgements

Most companies that have recorded their histories cannot resist the urge to control every detail of the research process. They want to control each published word. CEO Zhang Ruimin and Haier's Model Institute (HMI) were different. They gave us ample space to develop our own plan, conduct our own research, and report our findings in our own words.

We're proud of the book that's now in front of you, but we realise that none of this would have been possible without the help of others.

In the first place, we would like to thank Bram van der Lecq for his collaboration on this challenging book project. Our joint research, and the shared experiences on trips to China, were a joy. His way with words is always pleasing.

As important, we want to give thanks to Haier for funding this research project, and Zhang Ruimin personally for giving us the opportunity to learn how the company functions. We also thank Guan Junhui, Wang Yan, and Shi Lutong, who did a wonderful job in helping us conduct our research. Without their organisational skills, the interview trips would have not been so fruitful and full of insights, and we wouldn't have discovered as much as we did.

We deeply appreciate the efforts of the skilled translators that helped us along the way. Without their work we would have been lost in translation. Special thanks go to Xiaochuan Cao & Wenkai Ji, whose efforts were of especially great value.

We are grateful for what we learned from more than a dozen top academics and high-profile management gurus we met at Haier during the various stages of our research. There must be special mention of Brian Arthur, Rosabeth Moss-Kanter, Stowe Boyd, James Moore, Oliver Hart, Gary Hamel, and Michele Zanini.

We appreciate professors Michael Lee and Wesley Koo for their collaboration on INSEAD teaching of the Smart Cooking EMC.

We'd also like to thank Simone Cicero, Bill Fischer, Stina Heikkila, and Stuart Crainer for acting as sparring partners during the research stages of this book. It was insightful, and good fun at the same time.

Our thanks go out to all the people from Haier we met and interviewed. Some of those interviews didn't make it into the book, but the conversations brought clarity, greatly improved our understanding, and enhanced the quality of the finished product.

Over to the other side of the planet, and GEA. Big thanks to Kevin Nolan, Tom Quick, Peter Pepe, and Paul Surowiec. You welcomed us with open arms, and spoke from your hearts.

We benefitted from the shared experiences of people working at outside organisations as Rendanheyi spreads like wildfire. Thanks, in particular to João Domingos and Bruno Sirletti from Fujitsu Europe, Jochen Goeser from Bosch Power Tools, and Nand Kishore Chaudhary from Jaipur Rugs.

We learned a great deal while collaborating with our trusted editors, John Mann and Hal Williams. The way you make any story sing and a pleasure to read is astonishing — and has had enormous positive impact here. Thank you for that.

We are also most grateful to Marie-Louise van der Weijst, Javier Juvera, and Keno Cordero, who have made our book look pretty. You came up with some wonderful illustrations that simplify the complex.

A special thanks to all our colleagues at Corporate Rebels, who showed interest in the project, were very supportive when it was needed, and always patient if we had to share our story.

Last, but certainly not least, we want to thank the fellow rebels who read our blogs, respond, and ask important questions. Knowing there are people out there who want workplace change as much as we do is always motivating.

Keep up the good work!

Appendices

Appendix 1. Translation of Zhang Ruimin's Essay from February 10, 1994.

Appendix 2. Translation of Zhang Ruimin's Essay from November 25, 2014.

Appendix 3. Translation of Zhang Ruimin's Essay from January 1, 2018

Appendix 4. Translation of Zhang Ruimin's Essay from January 4, 2022

Appendix 5. Formulating Goals

Appendix 6. The OEC Method

Appendix 7. The Budgeting Process

Appendix 8. Rendanheyi Scorecard

Appendix 1.
Translation of Zhang Ruimin's Essay from February 10, 1994

Haier is the Sea

Haier should be like the sea. Only the sea has the breadth to accommodate hundreds of large rivers and small streams. It takes cascading muddy waters and purifies them in its vast blueness. Thanks to the sea, the Yangtze River rolls on, the turbid Yellow River clears, and the many streams trickle down. Despite the twists and turns, these rivers race to join the sea at the convergence of the inexhaustible blue ocean to become part of its unmatched splendour.

Once joining the family of the sea, the individual streams group together with remarkable affinity to form waves that persistently and steadfastly charge to a common target at the sea's call, undeterred by the possibility of failing into foam. The sea owes its wonderous power of crushing any obstacle to this formidable force.

Humanity praises the sea for its silent but relentless contributions, year after year, that show its selfless heart. Because it "multiplies all, yet claims no possessions; it benefits all, while expecting no return". It demands no payback, and this becomes its source of eternal being. This existence, in turn, provides the necessary environment for all things in the sea to survive and thrive.

Haier should be like the sea. With great ambitions, Haier should open itself, attracting resourceful talent from every corner and self-purifying, so that every person in Haier's ecosystem can improve and excel. Haier employees should be competent, rather than redundant or mediocre, because the success of Haier depends on the support and contribution of all types of talent.

Only by rallying all of Haier's employees together can the company unleash power like the sea. This process depends on a corporate spirit of "creating resources and building a global reputation," which we have been advocating all along. When we work together as one, despite personal differences, when we work towards contribution regardless of education, and when we turn the unthinkable and impossible into reality and success through our shared efforts, Haier's billowing waves will be able to crush all obstacles and careen forward!

Haier should be like the sea, giving back to society and humanity where we can. When our love for society and humanity is "forever sincere," society will love us in return forever. In doing so, Haier will gain sea-like longevity, and Haier employees will reap handsome rewards as they generate top returns for the enterprise and make meaningful contributions to society. Haier employees will become part and parcel of society as a whole.

Haier is the sea.

Appendix 2.
Translation of Zhang Ruimin's Essay from November 25, 2014

A Dust Particle and the Three-Thousand-Fold Sutra Scroll
Every major boom and instance of humanity's progress has been on the back of a technological breakthrough, while every leap in human civilisation has been the result of the emancipation of minds. As the Internet brings about the exponential growth of technology, we are once again on the cusp of a revolutionary trend. Just when we are in danger of becoming cogs in the big machine of industrialisation, the train of the times switches to a new track. Ideas of the Internet age such as "zero distance", "decentralisation", and "distributed networks" have led us into a vibrant yet challenging time of individualism, where anyone can become an entrepreneur.

After three decades of innovation and growth, Haier has gone from a small collective factory on the brink of closure to the world's No. 1 white goods brand today, with hundreds of millions of users worldwide and more than 100,000 Haier products entering markets around the world every day. The advancement of industrial civilisation has allowed Haier to become what it is today, enabling Haier to advance along the evolutionary path in just 30 years — a journey that took a century for most enterprises in developed countries. We have caught up with our former role models, and we are now running out of guides to follow. In the face of new challenges, our only remaining ammunition is our undiminished commitment to entrepreneurship and innovation.

Emperor Taizong of Tang once asked his ministers, which is more difficult, starting or running a country? The answer he had in mind was that it is difficult to start a country and even more difficult to run it. In the context of Haier's corporate culture, the answer to this question is that there will never be a correct answer if starting a business and running a business are seen as two separate acts. The only solution is to stay entrepreneurial and to never be on the defensive.

The enemy of entrepreneurship is complacency and inertia arising from the experience of one's former success. According to the Tao Te Ching, "To conquer others is to prove one's force; to conquer oneself is to prove one's strength." Haier's cultural DNA has only one code, self-questioning. This is as true for businesses as it is for individuals. In the Internet era, everyone is his own CEO, and everyone should become an entrepreneur.

In Chinese, an "entrepreneur" and a "business owner" may be easily confused, but what they involve and imply are worlds apart. Business owners focus on the business, while entrepreneurs focus on the users. Business owners take on the mission of creating the perfect products and services, while entrepreneurs set out to deliver the best user experience. Size and profit are the business owners' proxies for success, while user resources and loyalty are entrepreneurs' true north. Business owners wield the sceptre of power through management and control, while entrepreneurs work up magic through self-organisation. It takes thousands of people to make one successful business leader, but each innovative individual can become an entrepreneur. As the Buddhist saying goes, "Break open a dust particle and release the three-thousand-fold sutra scroll."

On Haier's entrepreneurial platform, employees can assume the identity of an entrepreneur.

Thirty years can be as light as a dust particle and disappear with a flick of the fingers, or the years can become heavy baggage that is difficult to leave. The difference is whether you are an organisation that produces products or a platform that produces entrepreneurs. Haier has chosen to transform itself from a closed bureaucratic organisation to an open entrepreneurial platform, from a walled garden to a self-evolving ecosystem of diverse species.

In the eyes of aspiring entrepreneurs, Haier's platform is the perfect launch pad.

At the start of Haier's own entrepreneurial journey, we provided Haier branded products; then, Haier branded services became our mission. Today, we open up Haier's resources, and we provide the Haier branded entrepreneurial platform to the many entrepreneurs within the company.

On the surface, Haier provides public access to the API of its U+ Smart Life, and every entrepreneur can use this to advance a product.

On a deeper level, Haier opens its supply chain resources, and every supplier and user can participate in the entire cycle of value creation for user experience at Haier.

In essence, Haier provides the soil of institutional innovation to society, develops the rules of the game with equal opportunities and fair distribution, and calls on all stakeholders to contribute and share in win-win results.

Since 2005, Haier has been experimenting through trial and error with the win-win model of Rendanheyi. For that, we were willing to move away from the single-minded pursuit of performance results. In our quest without a clear beacon, we accept skepticism and criticism, but we do not give up lightly. What keeps us going is not just success, but the search for the spirit of the times.

In 1994, 10 years into Haier's entrepreneurial journey, I wrote a short essay entitled Haier is the Sea. Today, I would like to compare Haier to a cloud. Even the most expansive sea has boundaries, but even the smallest cloud can connect a million endpoints.

Open, open, and stay open. Today, more than 100 entrepreneurs and microenterprises have been incubated on Haier's cloud-like entrepreneurial platform. Some of these have left Haier to start their own businesses, and others are external entrepreneurs who have been attracted to Haier's platform. They have earned our respect, and I owe them my gratitude because Haier's transformation to become an entrepreneurial platform is, in and of itself, an entrepreneurship in action. Haier as a platform does not carry any baggage from our 30-year history; rather, it is a newborn, a rising sun. Every entrepreneur on the Haier platform thrives from the platform and contributes back to its success.

Hail to the entrepreneurs, and hail to this great age for entrepreneurs!

Appendix 3.
Translation of Zhang Ruimin's Essay from January 1, 2018

A New Year Just Adds a Number; a New Me Means New Prospects
The calendar adds only a number with each new year. This way of timekeeping seems to promise each of us more time, but time is ever shrinking.

A new year also brings great expectations for the future. I think what people long for is a new start, not another year to come. The ancient Chinese sexagenary cycle made up of stems and branches is more in line with this method of philosophical questioning. When heaven, earth, people, and the four seasons are in harmony, the cycle repeats itself without a beginning or an end. The ancients revered heaven and earth and the four seasons with restraint and rationality, but they always tried to master the laws of time through their diligence and wisdom. In doing so, they transformed the world to be in conformity with such laws.

The same is true for organisations. Vertical linearity in traditional management theory runs deep in Western organisations, which are motivated by their purpose of maximising shareholder value and the principal-agent incentive scheme to pursue growth until no more is possible. Eventually, they must face the inevitable fate of decay after their prime. Industrial Darwinism and the entrepreneurial spirit of "creative destruction" have contributed to the fact that the average lifespan of Fortune 500 companies is becoming shorter and shorter. The atomistic cultural genes of Western civilisation became increasingly entrenched, along with the miracle of manufacturing through three industrial revolutions. This was the trend until the arrival of the Internet and its next significant economic innovation, the Internet of Things, when the once-powerful cultural genes became an asylum of intellectual and organisational rigidities. Classical physics, based on Newtonian mechanics, allowed us to see one segment of the space-time continuum of the vast universe, yet it left a larger white space to quantum physics. In the quantum era, the system theory in the Eastern cultures will again become the light for illuminating the night sky of science and philosophy. That light has never ceased to shine.

The organisation was once built on the steel and concrete of bureaucracy. Now, bureaucracy is destined to collapse.

The organisation is a community of human values and missions, and relevancy is its main theme.

A closed corporate empire will either collapse or become a self-organisation far from equilibrium. The momentum of this inevitable change is as forceful as rivers rolling to join the sea. The enterprise, as a product of the industrial revolution, has become obsolete. Gone, too, is the once unbreakable hierarchical pyramid and the control enforced by the vertical, linear structure. Just like the Arabian caravans on the ancient Silk Road, enterprises will eventually disappear into the dust and smoke of history.

Humanity is the master of the earth, but no one person — neither you, nor me — can dominate the world. Only an organised people can become the most powerful entity on this planet. The enterprise will face its inevitable demise, and a self-organisation will live on. A company that lasts must be self-organised to fit the dissipative structure theory. A brand may be transitory, while an ecosystem can be sustainable, and a sustainable ecosystem must be a win-win community where all stakeholders can create and share value together.

On the Internet of Everything, you, I, and every product are nodes on the network. Once you become a node, you are the centre. Yet, a product that becomes a networked appliance connected to the Internet of Things has lost its inherent utility and becomes a carrier of services or solutions. On the network, adding any one node will further amplify the network effect, while deleting any one node will not affect the operation of the network.

No enterprise can escape, yet enterprises may find the transition from product value to an ecosystem value of win-win co-creation a difficult one. The barrier between the two sets of value creation networks and value transmission networks is neither the Chu River nor the Han Border. It is more difficult to transcend than any physical or institutional barrier because the devil sets the barrier of complacency in the mind. It is a mirror image of our past laurels, the mist of 200 years of linear management dictated by atomism, and only the Rendanheyi model based on the user multiplier theory can remove this barrier.

Rendanheyi is the world's first management model adapted for the community economy of the IoT era. Rendanheyi has chosen Haier more than Haier pioneered Rendanheyi. Rendanheyi needs three conditions to come alive: first, the commitment to the core value that "human value comes first"; second, the commitment to the value of co-creation and win-win value delivery systems; and third, the commitment to the culture of self-questioning, entrepreneurship, and innovation. Therefore, Rendanheyi and Haier are the gift and choice of the times. Haier and Rendanheyi together show the awakening and celebration of humanity.

It is still unclear how the IoT era will be remembered, but it is certain that enterprises in the IoT era must become an ecosystem, the organisation in the IoT era must become a self-organisation, and management in the IoT era must become Rendanheyi. At the same time, the ecosystem, self-organisation, or the Rendanheyi model must be living organisms of continuous evolution. As the Greek philosopher Heraclitus pointed out, all things started with "a live fire that burns and dies by certain laws". His analogy was shared by the ancient Chinese philosopher Zhuangzi, who spoke of passing down the fire. The enterprise will eventually go up in flames, while the ecosystem will become an eternal living fire. The microenterprises converge and disperse, whereas in an ecosystem the entrepreneurial spirit will be passed on like a torch.

In the traditional era, I wrote Haier is the Sea. Tolerance fosters greatness!

In the Internet era, I wrote Haier is the Cloud that connects all.

In the IoT era, I want Haier to be a fire that warms every user's life and sparks every entrepreneur's passion — a fire that will be passed on, and that will live on.

The discovery of fire allowed our ancestors to embark on an extraordinary journey. The Haier model should be like a fire, leading enterprises around the world to blaze a new trail in the IoT era.

The Sun is new every day. A new year just adds a number; a new me welcomes new prospects.

Happy New Year to Haier's global community of entrepreneurs. We wish you progress in each new day!

Appendix 4.
Translation of Zhang Ruimin's Essay from January 4, 2022

An Ever-living Fire

Upon deep introspection, one can see an on-going theme which runs through the entrepreneurial journey of Haier over the past 30 or so years: maximising human value. This has been the prevailing force behind Haier's strategic transition. It has driven the organisation's expansion into different countries, and sustained its momentum during the various phases in its development. And the notion of maximising human value has animated Haier's commitment to making each individual their own CEO, an autonomous person whose performance and potential is maximised by their membership of the organisation.

According to the ancient Greek philosopher Heraclitus, "Fire forms the basic material principle of an orderly universe." The word "fire" here connotes energy, which moves independently, but also moves everything else along with it. For me, this interpretation of the power and nature of fire relates directly to the concept in contemporary quantum management theory of the "quantum self". The quantum self is both an independent self and an altruistic self. If each individual can become a ball of energy — in organisational terms, a self-driven entrepreneur — what emerges will be akin to Heraclitus' prediction of "an ever-living fire". This is the philosophical context in which Haier has evolved to become the entrepreneurial ecosystem it is today, an ecosystem driven by energy, momentum, self-realisation, and mutual benefit.

The Chinese philosopher Lao-Tze was an Eastern contemporary of Heraclitus in the Axial Age (which ran from the eighth to the third century BCE). Lao-Tze sought eternity in the idea that "the Tao follows what is natural", whereas Heraclitus pursued it in "an ever-living fire". The two notions of eternity reflect both the similarities and nuances of the ancient wisdom of the East and of the West. The concept of eternity in "the Tao follows what is natural" laid a framework for the Eastern philosophical worldview of "holistic association and dynamic equilibrium", while "an ever-living fire" engendered the contemporary quantum worldview of "dynamic relationships as the basis of all existence".

My belief is that these two interpretations of eternity are in alignment. In practice, their application at Haier has led to the creation of the ecosystem brand.

The Rendanheyi model is the cornerstone of Haier's approach to management and organisation. It is rooted in the profound wisdom of ancient philosophers and the fertile soil of modern ideas. Its context is our current era of momentous change: "The Master, standing by a stream, said, 'It passes on just like this, not ceasing day or night.' In this context we must elevate the system so that it has "external adaptation with internal perseverance". We must do so on the foundation of human value maximisation so that people are granted autonomy while being internally anchored and externally fluid. When such a balance is accomplished, the model can self-adapt in a fast-changing environment and stay relevant to the times. Organisations and individuals can then achieve a state in which they never forget their original mission and attain eternal enlightenment; they possess ever-living fire.

Appendix 5.
Formulating Goals

To help microenterprises and platforms in their efforts to formulate goals, Haier has identified five conditions:

1. Each goal needs to come, directly or indirectly, from customers. The creator of the goal must do market research and understand the problem they're trying to solve.

2. The end-product should add unexpected and exceptional value for users. Haier holds itself to the highest standards and measures itself against its competition by asking: Are we number one? If not, how can we become number one? If we are, how can we extend our lead? In practice, this translates to trying to exceed user expectations. Don't just create a fridge, create one that keeps track of the food in it — and sends an alarm when your tomatoes are beginning to rot.

3. The goal should align all entrepreneurs involved and focus them on creating value. Haier reasons that the happier customers are with the product, and the way it soothes any "pain" they're experiencing, the more willing they will be to pay. Then both sides benefit, users from the product that takes away their problem, and the entrepreneurs because they can sell more products at higher prices.

4. Setting unrealistic goals can lead to demotivation. At Haier, goals are fixed, which means that if the context changes, for better or worse, the target stays the same. It may seem logical to change the goal, but Haier has learned that such safety mechanisms tend to make entrepreneurs less creative and less persistent. A

common practice is to set goals in relation to growth in market share. This lowers the risk for entrepreneurs, because if a market is declining and sales are dropping, it could still be possible to outperform the competition and increase the market share.

5. The goal is part of a larger system to harmonise entrepreneurs and resources. Haier knows that without the alignment of all of those involved, reaching the goals becomes harder. Goals need to be directly linked to value created. You won't find targets such as "Produce 1,000 washing machines and receive $10,000 if you succeed". That way, the producing microenterprise would not care if their washing machines end up with the customer or not; they would get paid anyway. The goal should be formulated along these lines: "Help us produce and sell washing machines by taking care of the production, and earn a share of the total profit we make in selling those washing machines." All microenterprises are motivated to see others succeed as well, and will try to help, even if it is not officially their job.

The Bidding Process

When a goal and, even more importantly, a potential reward are interesting enough, it's time for the bidding to begin. The process for an individual bidding on a goal on the marketplace is the same as that for microenterprise bids. It even allows individuals that are already part of a separate microenterprise to bid on a new goal, provided they come up with a plan on how to make it work.

From an entrepreneur's perspective, the bidding process has three different stages.

Analysis

Proposal

Bidding Process

Decision

Analysis

An entrepreneur will use available information and their own research to decide if the goal is realistic. Is the reward suitable? Is the goal realistic and fair? And do they want to work for that microenterprise? This analysis gives them the power to decide.

Proposal

The second stage is where the bidding begins. The winner is not always the one with the highest bid. Each entrepreneur creates a detailed business plan, describing how they will carry out their part of the work. Bidders define their own targets, and sometimes even make suggestions for the reward. This self-setting helps them better understand the way the company works, and that understanding leads to improved performance, sales, and profits. It also increases motivation, trust, commitment, and job satisfaction [37].

However straightforward the creation of a business may sound, in practice things are much more complicated. Requirements for a successful proposal can differ greatly, and usually depend on what the initiating microenterprise lacks in terms of special skills, knowledge, or money. It is not uncommon for entrepreneurs to bring their knowledge and expertise, and co-invest — using their own money. It works in a similar way at many start-ups around the globe.

Co-investment can be arranged in different ways. Bidders can agree to simply co-invest, or place 30 percent of their salaries into a risk-capital pool, which will turn into stock if the new microenterprise succeeds and grows to become an independent company. The reasoning is sometimes purely financial, i.e., the microenterprise needed money. But there's a secondary motive. Entrepreneurs who invest their own money form an even stronger bond with the initiating microenterprise. Similar mechanisms can be found in Silicon Valley, where highly skilled professionals join a young company at a low salary — but with a share option. If the company becomes successful, they'll get rich. It aligns their incentives with those of the company.

Decision

The goal creators decide on the winning bid. Whether those creators are a microenterprise, a platform, or the board of Haier is irrelevant. They formulated the goal, and they pick the winner. That decision is based mainly on the strength of the proposal, but the in-house performance ranking system is another powerful tool that helps them judge the capabilities of the bidders. In many cases, microenterprises and individual entrepreneurs end up with multiple goals, sometimes in entirely different parts of the organisation, that can be combined as if working on separate projects.

A range of skills is required for the successful completion of a project, and entrepreneurs are encouraged to find goals that match their talents.

Appendix 6.
The OEC Method

Overall/Everyone/Everyday/Everything Control and Clear: according to Haier, this mouthful translates and abbreviates to OEC. Just how it manages to shoehorn six words into a three-letter acronym remains unclear, but we do know that the execution model helps entrepreneurs to become achievers. And getting things done can be rather lucrative.

At the core of OEC is the goal to improve everything that is done, every day. The model isn't just for people working on the factory floor; it applies to everyone. The aim is to formalise a plan for the day, create a summary of the work done, evaluate the plan, and consider how outcomes could be improved — by at least one per cent each day.

This drive for continual improvement shows how the company is pushing itself. It's not an optional extra or a dream to be pursued: it's a daily commitment and part of the culture. Entrepreneurs break down the larger goal for which they won the bid, into quarterly, monthly, weekly, and daily targets. Sub-targets make the end goal more tangible and achievable. Entrepreneurs are free to decide exactly how to break down a goal, but they must bear in mind the main criteria:

- They must be objective, specific, quantifiable, and realistic
- They must provide clarity about individual responsibility
- They must encompass all aspects of the business.

Each entrepreneur knows their responsibility, what they need to achieve, and when. If the goal is to sell a million refrigerators in a specific segment of the market over the coming year, their first quarterly target could be to install the production line and have 100,000 fridges ready to go to the stores. By breaking that target down to an even smaller scale, each entrepreneur will get more clarity on the priorities.

This clarity is essential for the daily summary, a core element of the OEC method. As the name suggests, it is a daily summary in which five elements are considered:

1. **The Result Summary:** At the end of each day, entrepreneurs record the work done for every task they were due to accomplish. If they didn't complete those tasks, they identify the gaps between target and achievement. In Haier-speak this is referred to as "spotting the gap".

2. **Cause Summary:** The writer tries to identify and make a summary of the causes of each problem, as well as formulating potential solutions.

   The first two sections are completed each day by every employee. To better understand how that would look for jobs in which productivity might be difficult to quantify, we asked Wang Yan to help us with our research. "We log everything," she explained. "So, for today we have a lot of meetings. I've booked those meeting rooms via our internal system, and — because I must enter a code to unlock the door — it gets noted in my summary that I was here, having a meeting. Others that join the meeting can scan a QR-code and get added. For each meeting, I'll write a short summary. My summary will probably consist of four short reports of the interviews you're conducting, and I'll share some insights with my colleagues."

OEC DAILY SUMMARIES

1. Result _____

2. Cause _____

3. System _____

4. Strategy _____

5. Philosophy _____

This almost unnoticed data-gathering creates, in a paradoxical way, a certain level of trust and transparency. The need for that is high; if your income depends on your colleagues' success, you want to make sure they're not slacking. Haier employees must have faith in the daily summaries they provide. The parts that are autogenerated can't be altered — and because they are publicly available, trust and transparency get a lateral boost.

3. **System Summary**, the third section, focuses on identifying system-wide problems. Root causes of individual problems are ferreted-out to determine the cause of the gaps. Salespeople in remote villages who are struggling to reach their targets may realise that they are not entirely to blame, and that other forces are influencing the situation — for example, maybe the marketing department focuses on richer cities. By identifying the true cause of a problem, it becomes solvable.

4. **Strategy Summary** The goal is to learn if the daily objectives are still leading to the desired result. The OEC model is for everyone, so microenterprise leaders and board members reflect on strategy and consider whether the objectives are feasible. Should they refuse to co-operate, the model is doomed. This has happened at many places that tried to adopt the OEC model.

5. **Philosophy Summary** is the fifth and final section — and according to Haier the most important. The goal is to find ways to develop the individual, to help entrepreneurs reflect on themselves, and overcome problems: personal growth and skills development.

The summaries help entrepreneurs reflect on their work and enable them to identify and solve problems that might otherwise have gone unnoticed. By clearly formulating the targets for the day, it becomes easier to see when entrepreneurs are in trouble or falling behind, allowing them to ask for help, or others to offer it.

Appendix 7.
The Budgeting Process

Haier leverages financial information in the planning and budgeting processes. It moved away from fixed annual budgets and towards planning for success, leaving behind traditional financial statements that were backward-looking.

The problems with these retrospective financial statements, so commonly used in organisations around the globe, can lead to some bizarre situations. Departments that still have some budget left at the end of year deliberately spend the surplus on non-essentials. Why? To ensure that the budget won't be cut in the following year.

The reasoning is odd: why would you punish an entire department for saving money? Why not allow it to add its savings to the upcoming budget?

At Haier, the budget is formulated based on how much money is needed to turn a plan into success. It has nothing to do with previous years. Instead, budgeting and planning have a central place in day-to-day activities, they are not a means to keep track of income and expenses. To make it work, all microenterprises and entrepreneurs are involved in the process, which is constructed in clearly defined stages.

The first is what Haier refers to as the Pre-plan Stage. It forms a roadmap: concrete goals are described to create clarity. Haier wouldn't be Haier if it didn't challenge its entrepreneurs. It encourages them to formulate leading goals by comparing many different data sets and analysing market and user needs until a goal — preferably one that allows Haier to outstrip the competition — has been identified. The plan describes the future goal in detail; it needs to be measurable and clear, with no room for ambiguity. Then the task is to work backwards to identify what steps should be taken, and when.

If your goal is to sell 10,000 new fridges within eight months, you need to know where you should be seven, five and three months from now. This is usually clarified by using the letter T. The day the goal should be reached is T. The day before T is T-1. If you want to reach your eight-month goal, you consider intermediate goals for T-50, T-100, T-200, and so on. The plan defines goals and necessary resources. It does not describe how goals need to be reached; entrepreneurs can find their own solutions. Formulating goals starts with the users, or more precisely, sales. Manufacturing and production follow user needs. By breaking the goals down into smaller steps, and combining them with the OEC execution practice, it becomes possible for entrepreneurs to gauge their progress.

The other element of Haier's budgeting process is called Prepayment. In essence it is a way to show how much entrepreneurs could earn if they reached (or surpassed) their targets. It's something that has already been made clear during the bidding process, and integrated when the roadmap has been finalised. Knowing potential earnings stimulates planning and budgeting processes. Entrepreneurs can estimate how profitable they'll be. And since rewards are often tied to a percentage of the profits, those employees will identify customers and commit themselves to some of the sub-goals.

The third segment is to lock in the planning. Creating long-term plans is somewhat counterintuitive for an organisation that strives to be dynamic. Deviating from the goal and not getting the full reward is unthinkable.

To be flexible enough to adjust to changes, Haier has invented the 1-6-1 system. Chen Jiao from Financial Services: "The 1-6-1 is basically a weekly working plan. You have a goal; you break it into pieces and check at the end of each day whether you achieved it. The 1-6-1 means one week in the past, six weeks in the future; the final 1 refers to the week ahead."

Planning for Success

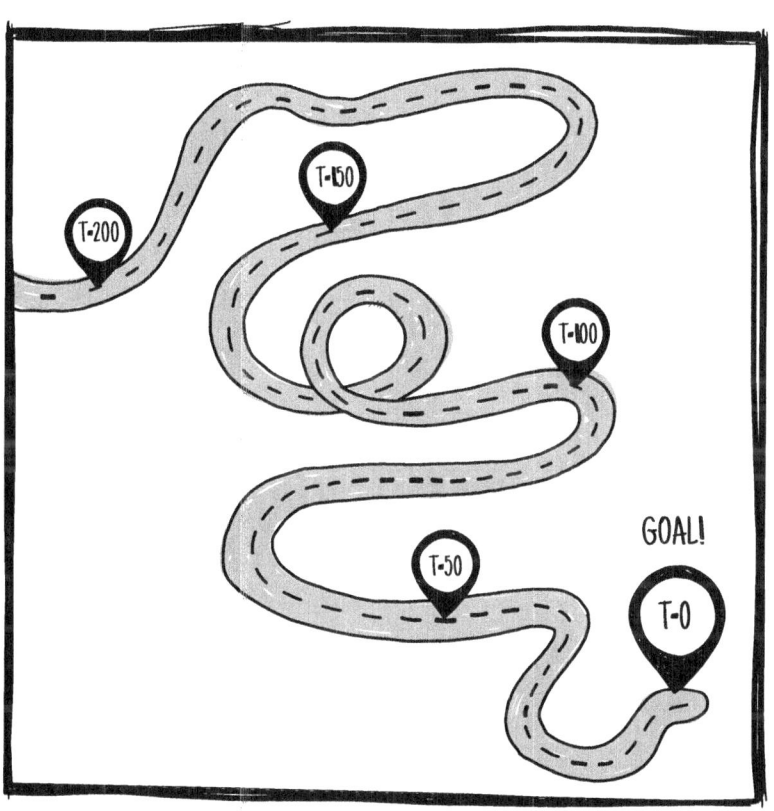

The microenterprises compare their performance with the goals and identify any problems using the OEC method. They'll define where they need to be six weeks hence to remain on track of quarterly targets and the larger goal, make projections and set tasks.

When "this week" is locked-in with clearly formulated objectives and tasks, entrepreneurs know what lies ahead. With access to relevant data and the observations of the OEC, they'll be equipped to make changes whenever required.

Appendix 8.
Rendanheyi Scorecard

To measure progress and guide EMCs, Haier has developed a way to gauge their maturity. The tool identifies two different dimensions: a "co-evolving", and "value circulating" dimension. This helps EMC-leaders understand how to create brands with lifelong users, strong revenues, and flourishing collaboration. The ultimate focus of the scorecard is on exponential growth by creating high demand or "Megahit", a single scenario that everybody wants to buy.

The Co-evolving Dimension
This dimension measures how self-adaptive the individual, team, and business are. The dimension consists of three different stages, with each stage being identified by a different "self":

Self-driven: this stage is "giving away the 'three rights' to microenterprises". These rights are to hire, set employee compensation, and make unilateral decisions. This stage starts when a bid on a leading target is successful, and the EMC can start to be self-driven by its members.

Self-organised: this stage begins when an EMC contract is successfully signed. The EMC opens its boundaries to anyone that can add value, allowing it to attract quality external resources to best fulfil the needs of users. The EMC becomes a self-organised system, meaning that the EMCs are in direct contact with their users, and depend on their needs to develop new scenarios. All microenterprises in the EMC reorganise when a change in context occurs, or user needs call for it.

Self-gap-closing: during this stage the core elements of the EMC have come together, and a driving mechanism allows it to create more value for the user by closing the gap between the leading goal and the actual performance of

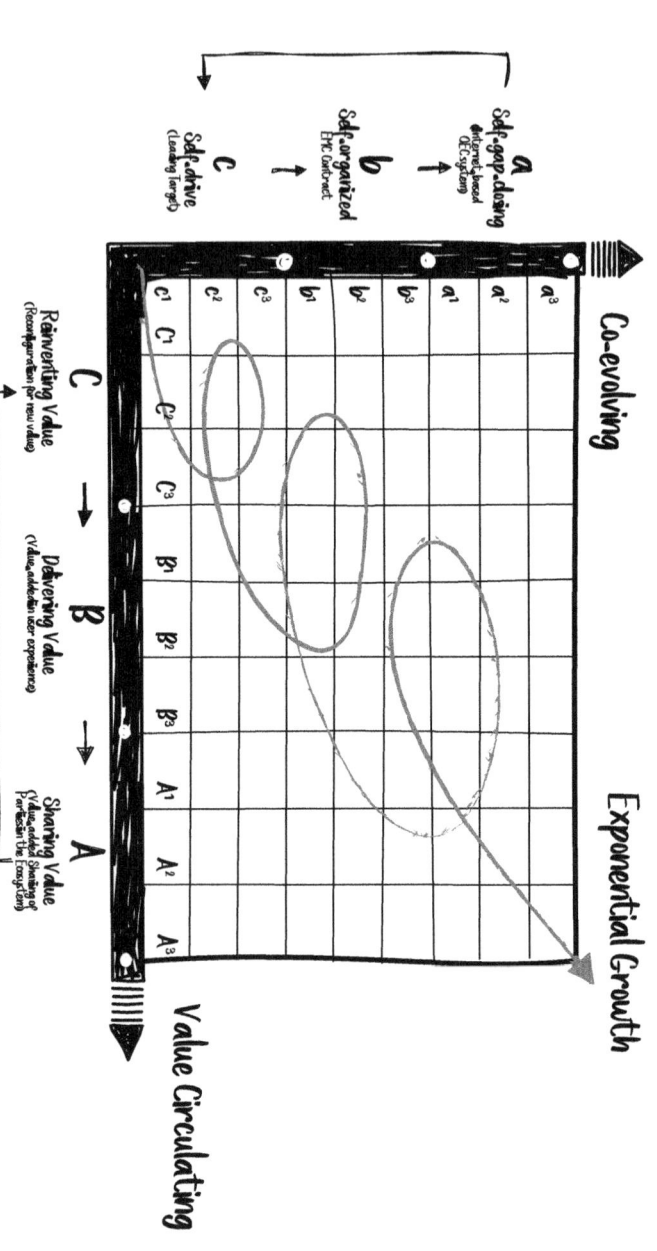

the EMC. The more it creates, the more it can share throughout its network. On top of being self-organised, the outcome should be profitable for all parties. Once an EMC has successfully reached this stage, it has completed its journey from a bureaucracy to an ecosystem.

The Value Circulating Dimension

This dimension measures how well the individual, team and business has created a lifelong customer. This dimension also consists of three different stages.

Reinventing Value: in this stage EMCs focus on connecting Megahit appliances to a network, allowing products to communicate with one another, increasing their value as scenarios with the likelihood that users will buy them. The stage involves the same value sharing mechanism that is used within the microenterprises: the paid-by-customers system. It uses the value-added mechanism, or VAM, to distribute salaries in a more dynamic way. The better they do their job, and the more thresholds are reached, the higher the rewards.

Delivering Value: in this stage all products are connected to a cloud, becoming part of a larger network and connect to devices outside the network to deliver value to its customers. The stage brings profit-sharing to the EMC. From there, the focus is on expansion. This stage focuses on allowing individual microenterprises to receive higher shares of profit if they add extra value.

Sharing Value: this stage is reached when the EMC starts acquiring lifelong users, those who do not want to leave the brand and continue to use the EMC services. If that's successful, the transition from product brand to an ecosystem brand has been completed. This final stage focuses on increasing marginal revenue created throughout the ecosystem, making sure that everybody profits along the way. Any EMC that completes all the stages has moved away from product revenue and replaced it with ecosystem revenue. They are no longer dependent on the success of a single product, and have created a resilient business ecosystem.

Bibliography

1. Drucker Institute (2020) About Peter Drucker
2. Gallup Inc (2017) State of the American Workplace Report
3. McKinsey (2018) Unlocking success in digital transformations
4. Haier (2019) Annual Report of Haier 03 Smart Home Co., Ltd
5. BrandZ (2020) Top 100 Most Valuable Brands Report
6. C. Yangfeng (2018) The Haier Model: Reinventing a Multinational Giant in the Network Era, LID Publishing
7. S. Cicero & B. Fischer (2020) A Framework for A Practice of Ecosystem Enabling Organization
8. M. Porter (1998) Competitive Advantage: Creating and Sustaining Superior Performance, Simon & Schutser
9. S. Boyd (2019) On Emergent Leadership, Medium
10. D.Ancona, E.Backman, K.Isaacs, (2019) Nimble Leadership, Harvard Business Review
11. G. Hamel, M. Zanini (2018) The End of Bureaucracy, Harvard Business Review
12. G. Hamel, M. Zanini (2020) Humanocracy: Creating Organizations as Amazing as the People Inside Them, Harvard Business Press
13. P. Bernstein (1978) Guidelines for the Design of Economic Feedback Systems
14. S. Nandram, N. Koster (2014) Organisational innovation and integrated care: lessons from Buurtzorg, Journal of Integrated Care
15. Yahoo!Finance (2020) Haier Smart Home Reopens Domestic Factories and Resumes Production at Full Speed
16. Lehman, Lee & Xu (2021) Validity of Valuation Adjustment Mechanism ("VAM") Agreement
17. Oxford University Faculty of Law (2020) Contractual Innovation in China's Capital Markets
18. D. Graeber (2018) Bullshit Jobs: A Theory, Penguin UK
19. Corporate Rebels (2017) Rebellious Practices: The Power of Open-Book Management
20. M. Mars, J. Bronstein, R. Lusch (2012 The value of a metaphor: Organisations and ecosystems, Organizational Dynamics
21. PRNewswire (2020) Haier's Shenyang Interconnected Refrigerator Factory Joins the World Economic Forum's Global Lighthouse Network as Haier Second End-to-End Lighthouse Facility
22. Haier (2016) Gary Hamel Took a Positive View on Haier's Management Transformation During His Second Visit
23. D. Tapscott, A. Williams (2008) Wikinomics: how mass collaboration changes everything, Portfolio
24. G. Hileman (2018) Chatham House Primer: Blockchain
25. Reuters (2018) The unfolding of China's Changsheng vaccine scandal
26. BMC Public Health November (2019) Vaccine confidence in China after the Changsheng vaccine incident: a cross-sectional study
27. E. Schein (1983) The role of the founder in creating organisational culture, Organisational Dynamics
28. C. Sánchez-Runde, Y. Lee, S. Reiche (2020) Haier in Japan: An Ongoing Transformational Journey, IESE Business School University of Navarra
29. R. Moss Kanter, N. Hua Dai (2018) Haier: Incubating Entrepreneurs in a Chinese Giant, Harvard Business School
30. P. Ghosh (2022) Beyond the Three Decades of Economic Drought in Japan: Strategic Relevance of Rendanheyi Model?
31. Haier (2021) Internal document
32. Business Ecosystem Alliance (2021) Zero Distance Award Winners Survey
33. Jennie Bell (2019) Exclusive: Zappos is Looking Beyond E-Commerce to Ensure It Lasts for 1,000 Years, Footwear News
34. Aimee Groth (2020) Zappos has quietly backed away from holacracy, Quartz at Work
35. Boundaryless (2021) #10 – EEO Conversations – Rachel Murch
36. A. de Man, P. Koene, M. Ars (2019) How to survive the organizational revolution, BIS Publishers
37. L. Sieden, (2011) A Fuller View - Buckminster Fuller's Vision of Hope and Abundance for all, Divine Arts Media
38. M. Gagné, E.. Deci (2005) Self-determination theory and work motivation, Journal of Organisational Behaviour

About the Authors

Joost Minnaar

Corporate Rebels co-founder Joost Minnaar left his corporate job in Barcelona, where he lived after completing his master's in Nanoscience and Nanotechnology at the University of Barcelona. He travels the world researching progressive organisations (including Haier), blogs about the discoveries he makes, advises leadership teams on organisational design, and is a part-time Doctoral Candidate at the Amsterdam Business Research Institute (VU University, Amsterdam). Together with Pim de Morree he co-authored Corporate Rebels: Make Work More Fun, which has been translated into ten languages. Alongside the rest of the Corporate Rebels team, he supports the growth of a global movement to make work more fun.

Pim de Morree

Pim de Morree co-founded Corporate Rebels after saying goodbye to a corporate job. That was just three years after finishing his studies in Industrial Engineering and Management Science and Innovation Management at the Eindhoven University of Technology. Besides travelling the world and researching, he writes for the Corporate Rebels blog, advises companies, and gives keynote presentations to inspire organisations to radically change the way they work. Together with Joost Minnaar he co-authored Corporate Rebels: Make Work More Fun, which has been translated into ten languages. Alongside the rest of the Corporate Rebels team, he supports the growth of a global movement to make work more fun.

Bram Van Der Lecq

After completing his bachelor's degree in Human Resource Management, Bram van der Lecq started working for a big Dutch corporate. Within a year he left, worried that he would become just like his colleagues. Bureaucratic, slow and — perhaps most important — forgetting they were human beings. Bram went on to study Culture, Organisation and Management (VU University, Amsterdam). For his master's thesis, he focused on alternative ways of organising to improve malfunctioning organisations. The paths of Bram and Corporate Rebels crossed and things took off. When the opportunity arose to write a book about Haier, a partnership was formed, allowing Bram to become a lead author for the first time. Besides his work for Corporate Rebels, Bram is involved with several other projects that, just like Corporate Rebels, set out to rehumanise the way organisations work.

Printed in Great Britain
by Amazon

45130472R00148